NEPAL

First Edition
1990

TABLE OF CONTENTS

FEATURES

TRAVEL INFORMATION

LIST OF MAPS

Please note: in some cases the spelling of the place names on the maps is not the same as in the text, because the spelling on the maps is according to UN guidelines, whereas the usual English spelling is used in the text.

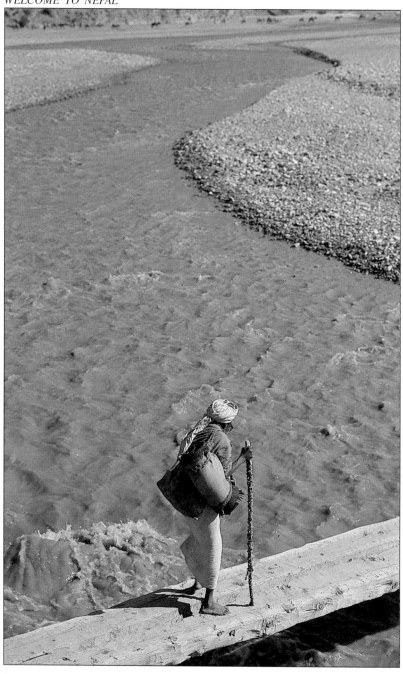

Namaste
Welcome to Nepal

It is Nepal's unique landscape, its cultural diversity, but above all its unforgettable people which make it such a fascinating country. It is among the ten poorest nations in the world but the Nepalese enjoy their lives, and nowhere else will you see so many smiling people as in Nepal. Hinduism and Buddhism are united here in an almost inseparable unit, and provide a unique diversity of festivals and rituals. The puja in a monastery, the little sacrifice on a household altar, the countless thangkas in the souvenir shops of Kathmandu – a trip to Nepal is always a confrontation with its religions.

The *Nelles Guide Nepal* introduces the visitor to the Hindu Kingdom – to both its beauties and its problems – in authoritative articles and essays. It guides you through the cities of the Kathmandu Valley as well as the remote valleys of West or East Nepal, and gives an insight into religious life or ecological problems.

The *Nelles Guide to Nepal* begins with a geographical overview and familiarizes you with its geography. The Legend and Reality of Nepal presents an overview of its history, and in a detailed article the various ethnic groups are described. A special article is devoted to gods and religion, in order to help orient you among the multiplicity of cults and godly figures.

In the travel section the royal cities Kathmandu, Patan and Bhaktapur are described in just as fine detail as the Kathmandu Valley itself. In further articles the most important trekking routes and hiking paths are introduced; precise maps of all areas facilitate your orientation. In the information boxes you will find all the essential information and addresses.

In the third section of the *Nelles Guide Nepal* there are features to familiarize you with the specialties of Nepalese cuisine and the education system, an introduction to the traditional health system, or inform you about the most significant festivals and celebrations. Symbols and Gurkhas, monasteries and the eight thousand meter peaks are only a few further themes.

Preceding pages: A Newar with his traditional head-covering, the topi. The decorated Ganesh statue at the Hanuman Dokha palace. Left: A pilgrim crosses the Kali Gandaki on the path to Muktinath.

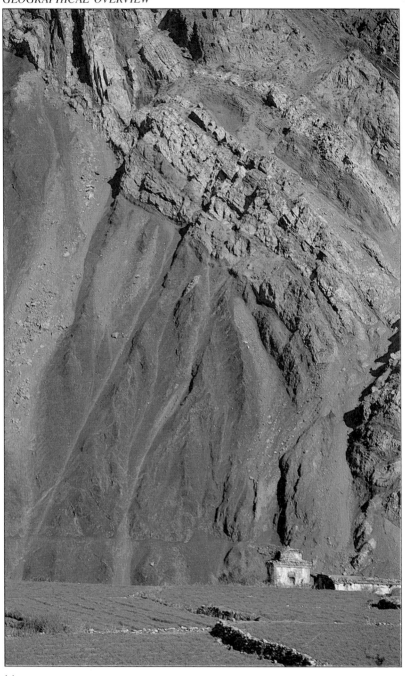

GEOGRAPHICAL OVERVIEW

On entering Nepal, the traveller finds himself in a region of incomparable orographic, botanical, zoological and ethnic diversity. The geo-historical origins of the imposing Himalayan range alone – which comprises a considerable portion of the country – makes fascinating reading. Through our understanding of plate tectonics – from which the theory of the continental drift is derived – we know that the Indian continental plate separated from the old southern continent of Gondwanaland and moved toward the north, where it crashed into and slid under the old Eurasian plate. In the process, the southerly Sea of Tethys narrowed.

In the course of time, as the Himalayas arched ever-higher, rivers, whose sources are found on the Tibetan plateau, carved deep into the young mountains. This created the impressive traverse valleys which serve to this day to make the range penetrable to traffic and trade at several locations. With the incessant pressure of the Indian continental plate on the Eurasian, the growth in height of the Himalayas continues at a rate of one millimeter per year. The question of which is greater – mountain-building or erosion – is a matter of dispute among researchers. But even as the peaks and ridges grow higher, the enormous erosion of slope material is visible everywhere.

Nepal comprises an area of about 147,000 square kilometers. It stretches over 800 km from the northwest to the southeast, and is an average of 200 km wide. From the Ganges plain to the main

Preceding pages: The all-seeing eyes of the Buddha of Svayambhunath. The sleeping Vishnu in Budhanilakantha. Left: The landscape in the upper Kali Gandaki Valley.

range of the Himalayas, Nepal ranges in altitude from 60 meters above sea-level in south-eastern Terai up to 8,848 meters at the summit of Sagarmatha (Mt. Everest). More than a quarter of the land area is higher than 3,000 meters, and the country is broken up by mountain ridges, plains, valleys and basins to such a degree that travel is extremely difficult.

It is impressive to find – in one single country – almost every form of landscape and vegetation, from subtropical jungle to mountain tundra and desert within a horizontal distance of only 200 kilometers. By its geographical latitude between 20 degrees and 26 degrees 15" north, Nepal is comparable with Libya, but because of its alignment from northwest to southeast, its southeastern tip is 450 km further south than its northwestern extremity.

Terai and Siwaliks

The geography of the country has led to the development of very clearly distinguished landscapes and natural regions. Drawn along the Indian border, Terai is a lowland with an altitude of between 60 and 280 meters above sea level. It is covered with a thick, dry jungle, and was long called Nepal's "fever- hell" because of the malaria which is endemic to such areas. However, since this danger has been brought under control for the most part, Terai has developed not only into a settlement and immigration area for people from both the mountains and India, it has also become the kingdom's bread-basket. It now yields some 77 percent of the rice, 80 percent of the oil-seed, 94 percent of the sugar beet, and 94 percent of the tobacco harvests. Because of the deforestation in more recent years, Terai now possesses only 10 percent of Nepalese forest assets, however, it now has 42 percent of the agricultural lands.

Also situated in Terai is the main industrialized area outside of the Kath-

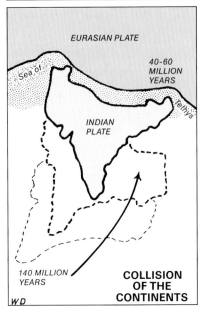

EURASIAN PLATE

Sea of

40-60
MILLION
YEARS

Tethys

INDIAN
PLATE

140 MILLION
YEARS

**COLLISION
OF THE
CONTINENTS**

WD

mandu Valley. The border cities and their populations are: Biratnagar (94,000), Birganj (44,000), Nepalganj (34,000), and Bhairahawa (32,000) – which has more recently been named Siddharthanagar. In addition, Janakpur (35,000) which is known for its temple, is the goal of many religious pilgrims. These cities make the most use of the nearby, little controlled border, and located just across it, the terminus of the Indian railroad network. The small industrial cities of Dharan (43,000), Hetauda (35,000), and Butwal (23,000) are located at the feet of the northern chain of hills known as the Churia Mountains or Siwaliks. The cities of Terai, which were at one time oriented exclusively towards either India or the Kathmandu Valley, are now connected with each other as a result of an East-West highway, the construction of which is almost completed. Where only a few years ago one had to use the Indian railway and road networks to travel into eastern or western Terai, the same is now possible on the Nepalese road network.

Alongside the old sugar, cigarette and match factories, new cement factories, metal works, and other industries are being established.

At the Siwaliks, which reach heights of around 1,500 meters, one enters the foreland of the Himalayas. The land here is composed of a very mixture of soft and hard rocks, gravel and sand, highly susceptible to erosion. The area can not be used for agriculture, and is therefore barely inhabited. These forest-covered ranges are broken up by the gravelly beds of larger and smaller Himalayan rivers. They have now become a destination for loggers, and are losing more and more of their protective function – without yielding equivalent usable farmland. As a result of this general deforestation, the seasonal flooding in Terai is becoming ever-more catastrophic. Those parts of the Terai which are enclosed by the Siwalik hills and the Ganges Plain, and which form shallow basins, are referred to as Terai's interior. To this area belongs, for example, the eastern Rapti Valley, which also contains the Chitwan National Park. Here one finds protected jungle with wild game, as well as systematically planned settlement zones. The Dang Valley and the valleys of Sindhuli and Udaipur in the East are also in inner Terai.

The flora and fauna include an abundance of varieties, some of which are endangered species. In southern Nepal up to an altitude of 1,000 meters the plant communities are dominated by shorea trees and limbas along with bamboos, canes and reed species and gallery forests with umbrella acacias.

Besides birds and butterflies, there are also large mammals such as elephants, the Indian rhinoceros, Bengali tigers, wild cattle, and various kinds of deer and apes. Many of these are being deprived of their natural homes as a result of the continuing expansion of human colonization and will have to be protected in national parks and wildlife reservations.

CROSS-SECTION

The Mahabharat Chain and the Highlands

The Mahabarat chain is the pre-Himalayan mountain range which runs north of the Siwaliks over the entire length of the country. Its peaks range in height between 2,000 and 3,000 meters. With them we enter into an old Nepalese settlement area, which is protected from the south by fever-swamps, and from the north by the main range of the Himalayas. It was therefore excellently suited as a retreat area. In fact, enemy armies have hardly ever invaded Nepal, because peaceful coexistence in both the south and the north has always been the rule. The mountain chain consists of crystalline minerals facing conditions of constant weathering and erosion. The river gorges are steep and narrow, offering little space for human settlement. Therefore, people have established themselves on the flanks of the valleys, where they cut down the forests and dug out terraces for their agriculture. Flying over the Mahabharat range, the density of human habitation is clear from the degree of deforestation and terracing. But, also obvious is the physical threat of the landscape from soil erosion and landslides.

The highland stretching from the north of the Mahabharat range to the actual high range of the Himalayas is called the *pahar* in Nepali. Its English name, "hills" is somewhat of an understatement. This is the living area of the Nepalese where we find the valleys of Kathmandu and Pokhara with significant urban settlements. The extensively deforested slopes and valley pastures contain many district governmental seats, villages and scattered towns. Here the various ethnic groups of Nepal live together. Over many centuries farming the land enabled them to be self-sufficient, until the population pressure on the land became too great, with soil erosion and the departure of some people as the inevitable result. In the 1960s, this area still provided almost two-thirds of the national population with economic survival. The highlands, which

17

stretch from the eastern to western borders, are between 50 and 100 kilometers in width. They are, in fact, the continuation of the main range of the Himalayas, which run in a north-south direction and in places reach heights of 4500 meters. The rivers follow the chain until they are forced by the Mahabharat range into a west-easterly direction and they manage to break through the mountains.

This zone, which was originally covered with thick deciduous forests of chilaune, mock chestnut, rhododendron, oak and alder became, in the course of time, a preferred logging area, and finally a land of small private and tenant farmers. To protect the deforested grounds, in certain areas the inclines are terraced into true staircases, which testify to the almost super- human efforts of many generations.

The crops cultivated here include rice up to about 2,000 meters, millet up to 2,350 meters, corn – the main crop of the highlands – up to 2,500 meters, and wheat to 2,800 meters. Around the mostly very attractive farmsteads one finds fruit-trees, and growing in their gardens are leafy and root vegetables. Because of the extensive destruction of the mountain forests in many areas, the collection of fuel wood, the most important energy source, is becoming increasingly difficult. The increase in soil erosion and landslides, which often carry entire villages into the depths, shows that the young, unstable mountains cannot withstand the further increasing population pressures much longer, and catastrophe draws ever nearer. Nevertheless, every year the cultivated areas expand ever further. The land has been decreasing in productivity for years, and the inhabitants lead a poor existence. 60 percent of them live below the poverty line as measured by Nepalese standards. 47 of the 55 highland districts are unable to feed themselves and must buy their food from outside – mostly from the Terai.

Only a few roads suitable for motor traffic penetrate the area, so the greater part of goods transport is done on the backs of carriers or on pack animals.

Erosion of the forests has severely confined wildlife's living space however in the remaining groves and glades there are still supposed to be snow leopards, wild boars, muntjak or barking deer, the blue sheep and the red panda.

Himalaya Main Range

The main range of the Himalayas rises rather abruptly out of the highlands. Above the snow line, which is on average around 5,200 meters in altitude, the peaks are covered with permanent snowfields. The glaciers, which are resupplemented with snow during the monsoons, feed the larger rivers. Eight of the ten highest peaks in the world are in this region, including Sagarmartha (Mt. Everest) at 8848 meters. The high mountains have only a few habitable places, and these are only sparsely populated. The Sherpas are the most well-known folk here. Their summer settlements range up to 4,500 meters and even higher, where their natural pastures are. More recently, they have offered their seasonal services to mountain climbing expeditions. There are reports of settlements as high as 4,900 meters in some places. Naturally, the altitude of the settlements depends on the growing altitude of their crops; potatoes grow at over 4200 meters, barley at 4,500. The tree-line is generally around 4,200 meters, however all of these figures depend upon the exposure of the cliffs and other micro-climatic conditions. Among the most important tree species here are maple and birch, firs and stone-pines, before scrub and brush take over.

The Himalayas play a significant role as a climatic boundary. They separate the monsoon-wet lands to their south from the dry continental climate of the Tibetan plateau. Paleo-climatic research has

Legend:
- ≤ 500 mm
- > 500 < 2000 mm
- ≥ 2000 mm

PRECIPITATION

shown that before the raising of the Himalayas the climate of Old Tibet was substantially wetter. This explains the fact that several Nepalese rivers have sources in Tibet, before they break through the main range. The traverse valleys of Kali Gandaki, the Arun, and as well the Buri Gandaki and the Karnali are some very impressive examples. The average annual precipitation in the Pokhara valley is more than 3,800 mm, whereas Jomosom – only 70 kilometers to the northwest – receives less than 250 mm. This shows the dramatic shielding effect of the Annapurna range – with peaks higher than 7,000 meters – which lies between the two areas.

The north-Himalayan dry zone includes a part of Nepal's national territory because in the West the northern border lies 50 to 60 km north of where the main range expires. In this area, referred to as the Himalayan Interior, we find the high-lying, sparsely populated area of Nepal, where the agriculture is limited to watered oases and sheep breeding on wild

pastures is of particular importance. These are found in the districts of Mustang, Dolpo, Jumla and Humla – to the extent that they are protected by the Main Range of the Himalayas. From the north this area is surrounded by the old Tibetan border range, which is not even 7,000 meters high and which is uninhabited and can only be crossed by a few trading paths which are little-used today. The wild pastures continue into Tibet and are traditionally used by both peoples.

The primary vegetation of the high mountains – juniper, rhododendrons and birches – is reduced here to grasses and rushes, and low, often thorny species. The animal world includes mountain goats, yaks, foxes, wolves and rabbits.

The kingdom of Nepal, now the home of 19,000,000 people of various cultures, is a place with a wealth of life-forms and species; a landscape unequalled in its variety and beauty. But it faces difficult problems: The fragility of the natural world places extraordinary demands on future development planning.

19

LEGEND

AND REALITY

The cradle of Nepal's artistic and cultural evolution is the present-day Kathmandu Valley. Its history is closely connected with the Newar ethnic group, which also gave the country its name. The Newar were the original occupants of the valley. They gradually mixed with other ethnic groups and finally, partly as a result of the introduction of the caste system in the fifth century A.D., developed an independent and unparalleled culture.

The country bears the stamp of the teachings of a variety of religious orientations and their orthodox rules. Important among these are Hinduism and Buddhism, as well as numerous sects and their cults within the spectrum of the larger religions; for example Shaktiism, Tantric Buddhism and the specifically Nepalese Shiva-Linga cult.

This variety of religious influences, combined with the somewhat unique folk-beliefs has provided with a profusion of motifs painters, sculptors, architects, gold-, silver-, and coppersmiths, woodcutters and stonecutters.

Nepal is the only Hindu kingdom in the modern world. In addition to substantial influences from Tibet, it has been shaped above all by the socio-political, religious and cultural influence of India. However, in spite of all this, Nepal has managed to retain its own identity. Over centuries, from this exceedingly complex ethnic inheritance, a state of many peoples has steadily developed which, when viewed from outside, appears relatively homogeneous.

In 1768, King Prithvi Narayan Shah brought the various disjointed principalities and kingdoms together into one country. At that time the so-called Gurkha Authority was instituted, whose ascendancy has endured since then up to the present day.

Through the centuries various events have, of course, altered the fate of the country, but the Nepalese rhythm of life has changed little.

The Origin of the Valley

Conditioned by factors such as the weather, agriculture and especially by religious beliefs, legends and myths have held up especially well, in a land ruled by natural forces and gods. A myth tells of the origin of the Kathmandu Valley. According to this myth the valley was originally a lake without an outlet, in the middle of which a lotus flower grew upwards. On this blossom appeared the original Buddha – the so-called Adi-Buddha – as Svayambhu, or " he who exists through himself."

Then the Bodhisattvsa Manjushri came from China, and, as a sacrificial offering, split open the ridge at the south of the lake. The water flowed out of this opening and the valley could then be populared. A visible sign of of this sword-stroke today is the Chobar Gorge, through which the holy Bagmati River, the primary stream of the valley flows. It then flows on to North India, where it empties into the Ganges.

According to tradition, Manjushri stayed in the valley until the first settlement of farmers from the surrounding area was established. This stretched from the Hill of Svayambhu to the area of what is today the Pashupatinath Temple.

Manjushri's escort Dharmakara was the first king of this city, which was named after the Bodhisattva Manjupattana. To this day, the highest being – the original or Adi-Buddha – is worshipped by Buddhist believers on the Hill of Svayambhu.

Left: The Newars have perfected the art of wood-carving in the Kathmandu Valley.

21

Early Rulers

The Adi Buddha first revealed himself in Svayambunath.

It is frequently difficult for historians to determine the value of such legends. There is a great deal of source material available concerning the ruling houses in the Kathmandu Valley. First of all in Sanskrit or Newari, and then later in Nepalese, the histories were written down by Pandits or Brahmans or Buddhist Vajracharyas. In these cases it is no simple task to differentiate between legend and reality.

The Licchavi ruling house (fifth through ninth century A.D.) is the first that can be historically authenticated. Its existence is verified in an inscription dating from 464 A.D. on a sculpture of Garuda in the temple area of Changu Narayan

One can only speculate about the preceeding time. It is not certain whether the Gopala (cowherders) or the Kirata ought to be considered as the first ruling house in the Kathmandu Valley. According to uncertain sources the Kiratas probably ruled over the valley for almost a millenium before they were displaced by the Licchavis. During the Kiratas' rule, Gautama Buddha, as the son of a prince, is supposed to have lived in Lumbini in the south of present-day Nepal around the sixth century B.C.

Ashoka – the Indian Maurya ruler – is also linked with the Kiratas. It is not proven whether (as reported in legends) he really came to the Kathmandu Valley around 250 B.C. in order to to erect four stupas in Patan.

On the basis of the inscriptions on one of the stone columns in Lumbini named after him, we know only that Ashoka sought out these places as a devout Buddhist, in order to worship Buddha at what is believed to be Buddha's birthplace.

To be sure, in both of the great Indian epics – the *Mahabarata* and the *Ramayana* – ,the Kirata are mentioned. It is assumed that they advanced into the Kath-

Traditional prayer wheels in Nepal with the sacred mantra: Om mani padme hum.

mandu Valley out of the northeastern mountainous region somewhere between 1500 and 1000 B.C. The Rai and Limbu, who live today in the east of Nepal, are believed to be connected with them. Finally, the Kirata probably took up residence in Gokarna.

The Licchavi Dynasty

The Licchavis, who are supposed to have governed the Kathmandu Valley for some five centuries (464-897 A.D.), originated with greatest probability in the north of India. They may well have been threatened by the expansion of their neighbors, and therefore retreated – moving into the Kathmandu Valley, which was conveniently situated for commerce. Because the valley has alwys been a thoroughfare between Tibet, China and Indias' cultural areas of influence, the population there was con-

stantly under new cultural influences. As a result, their art and handicrafts developed a thoroughly unique character.

This cultural exchange encouraged the powerful Tibetan King Songtsen Gampo to have a trade route extended over the Himalayas through the Kathmandu Valley and on to India; he also took a Licchavi princess as his wife. She then brought along, as a gift, some Buddhist cult-illustrations. Still today, the Nepalese Princess Brikuti is revered as much in Tibet as in Nepal as the so-called "Green Tara," and is thought to have contributed to the extension of Buddhism in Tibet.

Another spouse of the Tibetan King Songtsen Gampo was the Chinese princess Wen-Cheng, who is revered today as the "White Tara." Through this double marriage, the positions of Tibet and Nepal as independent thoroughfare countries between India and China were established. Since then the trade routes have been considered the best connection over the Himalayas, and are later thought

23

to have played a role in the cultural blooming of Nepal.

The Chinese pilgrim Hsüan-Tsang described the everyday life of the Licchavi period, as well as giving an impressive account of the artistic talents of the Newar in the use of metal, stone, wood and paint. A number of temples establishments which are still very significant today were already in existence at that time. Among them are the Shiva sanctuary of Pashupatinath and the temple of Changu Narayan dedicated to Vishnu, as well as the stupas of Svayambunath and Bodnath.

During the Licchavi period the rulers showed tolerance toward the various religious practices of the valley population, even though – as a result of their origins – they had a particular leaning in the direction of Hinduism. Buddhism was widely disseminated. While the people spoke a variety of dialects, above all Newari, Sanskrit was the language of the royal courts, which also represented the center of cultural activities. But scientists, theologians, astrologers and men of medicine also made their appearances there.

Today this period is renowned not only from an art-historical point of view as the "Golden Age". At that time – significantly – the Indian Calendar was replaced by the Nepalese system, which is still in use today.

Thakuri Period

There is a shortage of documentation in connection with what is generally referred to as the Thakuri period (ca. 879-1200 A.D. – some see the beginning of the Thakuri era already from 602 A.D.). "Thakuri", a word from Sanskrit, means "distinguished ruler" and was used as a name of honor. According to written sources, during this period the valley was ruled by various houses of Indian princes – mostly Rajputan – and just as the political conditions were confused, many writ-

ings in Sanskrit and in the Newari language testify to a similarly animated religious and cultural atmosphere.

Since the eighth century the secret or Tantric Vajrayana Buddhism had been promulgated in Tibet by the Indian master Padmasambhava; it now made its entrance into Nepal. It had an especially attractive character due to its magical practices and secret teachings – which were connected primarily with elements of pre-Buddhist and pre-Hindu folk-religions, shamanism and the various cults of fertility.

The so-called "matrikas," maternal forms, are revered in Nepal. They are put on the same level as the primeval powers that influence all processes of becoming; one must please or assuage them with sacrificial offerings. Incalculable numbers of natural forces – mostly associated with demons and gods – can be banned through the use of certain magical incantations – the so-called *mantras*. An ever-increasing importance was attributed to the cult rituals.

The representations of eroticism that one comes across in the artistic creation of sculptures and temple ornamentation have their origins often in the imagery of Tantrism. Tibetan and Indian monks came to the Kathmandu Valley in order to take up the new religious teachings, or to carry them further into the other religious centers of India, Tibet and China. It is frequently said that in the Kathmandu Valley, questions of caste and differences in notions concerning religious beliefs have only rarely led to war or violent conflicts. One often hears talk of the great tolerance of the various ethnic groups in Nepal, with their multiplicity of religions – however, the person who is really familiar with the source material knows that it has not always been this way. For example, it is known that around 800 A.D. the Indian scholar and yogi Shankaracharya ordered Buddhist writings burned in many places in Nepal, and

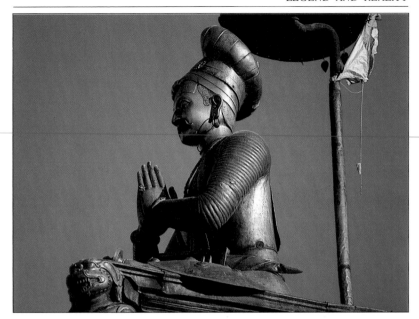

The statue of Bhupatindra Malla in Bhaktapur, all aglow.

so contributed to the progress of Hinduism in Nepal. Even more frequently one hears that Buddhist monks had been forced to marry Buddhist nuns.

Obviously tolerance is out of the question in these cases. At that time numerous monks sought refuge in Tibet, only making their return to Nepal after the tide of authoritarian violence had ebbed – carrying with them a new set of religious ideas, namely Tantric Buddhism.

The Malla Dynasty

The power of the Thakuri dynasty ended in the year 1182, and – without going further into the details of the change in powers – the Mallas proclaimed themselves the rulers of the Kathmandu Valley around 1200 A.D. They would decide the history of the country for over 500 years – until 1768. In its literal translation from the Sanskrit,

the name Malla means "wrestler." Once again, according to a legend, the first Malla prince of the Kathmandu Valley is said to have received tidings of the birth of his son during a wrestling match, at which time he procured this surname.

Already in the time of Gautama Buddha – in the sixth century B.C. – this name appears in connection with a royal lineage, and during the Licchavi reign (5th-9th century) Malla princes were already living in western Nepal.

It is probable that after the invasion of the Moslem Moguls – at the beginning of the 13th century – many of the relatives of this lineage fled from India to Nepal, in order to build a new existence there.

However, later on Nepal was not to remain spared from the invaders either. For a short time in 1349, the Moguls under the rule of Shams-ud-din Ilyas took over the Kathmandu Valley, and there destroyed temples and monasteries, particularly the Pashupatinath sanctuary. Soon afterwards the Moguls withdrew.

The Malla epoch is divided into two

periods – from 1200 to 1482 and from this time up to 1768, the year of the conquest of Prithvi Narayan Shah. Both periods were of great importance for the social, religious and cultural development of the valley. There is now a tendency to consider these periods of history as the age of blossoming – or golden age – of the Kathmandu Valley. During the second part of this period, the three royal cities – Patan, Bhaktapur and Kathmandu – gradually developed their present incomparable splendor. At any rate there were also some darker times for the population of the valley, which people prefer to overlook. For example, in 1255 an earthquake left the valley in ruins. One third of the population fell victim, including the King Abhayamalla. Somewhat later, beginning in 1288, the various princes of Jumla (in present-day western Nepal), who are counted among the Khas, plundered the valley over and over again. In the middle of the 14th century, the unity of the valley was shattered, as local families of nobility proclaimed themselves independent

This modern painting by Jagdish Chitrakar shows Bhaktapur of old.

and took over the rule in such localities as Pharping, Patan and even some neighboring valleys, among them Nuvakot and Banepa.

With the reign of Jayasthiti Malla, who ruled from 1382 until 1395, some transformations were instituted. The inhabitants of the valley were classified into different castes following the Indian system of orthodox Hinduism. The entire structure of the country was changed, a change which held up to the 18th century. The previous, – to an extent – chaotic conditions were undone through a rigorous process of "Hinduization," with unprecedented results. Jayasthiti Malla transformed an, as it were, open society, which was always ready to assimilate newly arrived groups, into one which was closed in on itself. With this measure he wanted to eradicate the looser forms of the Vajrayana and Tantric cults. However, he also attempted to preserve the exist-

A farmer from the Bhaktapur area brings in his harvest.

ence and further development of the old order, which was threatened by the Moguls in India.

In 1482, a successor of Jaya Malla allocated the cities of Bhaktapur, Patan and Kathmandu to his sons as autonomous dominions. At that time the Mallas probably stood under the nominal rule of the Moguls.

This influence showed itself, for instance, in the clothing and hair-styles of the Mallas and in the fact that court harems were maintained. Under their artistic influence many more miniatures were painted. Mural painting received a variety of ornamentation with rather superficial results. In spite of all this, the Kathmandu Valley was able to keep its Hindu inheritance intact through all these years because of its relatively protected geographical situation.

A great period of artistic blossoming was stimulated by the rivalry between the city-kings. The three capitals were enlarged and ornamented. During this period, stone-cutters, woodcarvers, and thangka- painters (*thangkas* are religious cult paintings) from the Newar ethnic group created extraordinary artworks. A variety of cults were in existence, for example the Kumari cult. Even though the northern (Buddhist) and the southern (Islamic) influences were quite significant, the art of the Malla period still possessed a strong individual creativity and power of expression.

Critics today characterize the later Malla era as a period of extravagance at the cost of the Nepalese people. The life of luxury under the Moguls exhausted the state treasuries of the three monarchs who, during this period, even compared themselves to god-kings. High tax revenues became necessary in order to finance the pomp and splendor of the palaces. The personal quarrelling among the three parallel dynasties – and their vying with each other over power and magnificence – on the one hand ate up

27

their treasuries, but also encouraged an enormous amount of artistic activity. Never had there been so much pure gold, silver and precious stones worked as in this epoch. State-subsidized art came to symbolize status and power, as was also true later during the Rana period. However, under the Mallas the artists do not seem to have profited much from their efforts. With few exceptions, their names and schools have been forgotten. In Kathmandu under Jayaprakash Malla relations with foreign rulers deteriorated so badly that the king was even forced to sell jewels and temple treasures – including those of Pashupatinath – in order to afford to recruit troops for his military.

A guard of honor at the Hanuman Dhoka during the Dasain festival.

Shah Rulership

This situation was changed by Prithvi Narayan Shah, who took over the valley in 1768. It took him 25 years before he succeeded in the conquest of the three royal cities from the mountain city of Kirtipur. Angered by the bitter resistance put up by the inhabitants of Kirtipur, he ordered the noses of their men cut off as a warning. The army unit of the British East Indian company, which Kathmandu called for help in its defense, was unable to impede the overtaking of the valley. Instead, they were put to flight. Prithvi's ancestors probably originated in Rajasthan, and in the fifteenth century took refuge in the village of Gorkha, which lies west of Kathmandu. There, one after another, they united the various surrounding principalities and small kingdoms of the local ethnic groups. The legislative structure which they founded played an important part in the later unification of the country under Prithri Narayan Shah.

The Shah rulers did not destroy the traditional crafts, but nor did they give them much support. Their attention was directed toward the development of a new nation – the unification of the west-

The portrait of King Birendra on a processional float.

ern and eastern sections of present-day Nepal.

The relationship of the Shah with Tibet as well as with China and the British is thought to have been of significance to the further development of artistic handcrafts and pictorial art connected with the later Rana period. Over and over again, war-like confrontations over trade resources erupted with Tibet, which was at the time under the subjugation of the Chinese Manchu dynasty.

After the establishment of peace pacts with the Tibetans – and with that the Chinese, direct contacts developed with Peking, which gave the Shah a certain surety against the increasing activity of the British in India, who had been there since the end of the 18th century. The Shah maintained a very cautious relationship with the British, not only because he feared having to share various trade privileges with them, but also because he had a rather low opinion of people who didn't worship their gods.

Border difficulties led finally to war between the Nepalese and the British. In 1816 a peace treaty was signed which above all stipulated that from then on the British could recruit the Gorkha soldiers into the British army, and that in Kathmandu a British embassy should be established. Despite the reservations of the Shah, the British won ever more influence as a result of their various trade advantages.

In addition, the Royal Family became weakened through intrigue. Cultural life during this turbulent political period was seriously neglected. In spite of this, the legacy of traditional and religious art survived, but it shifted to a folklore level. In matters concerning religion, the Shah permitted only the teachings of Hinduism and Buddhism. Muslims and Christians, whose presence and religious activities had experienced no limitations whatsoever under the Mallas, were now banished from the land.

29

Rana Oligarchy

In 1846, a commander of the Shah army, Jang Bahadur Kunwar (later Rana) brought the intrigue in the court of the Shahs to a bloody conclusion, and built up a family oligarchy that would last for more than a century. With tight administration and new legislation, the Rana premiers hoped to secure their collection of tax revenues and maintain law and order. Moreover the family also managed to usurp the entire strength of the economy, while the royal family of the Shah was degraded to a shadow existence. After Jang Bahadur Rana made himself the Maharaja of Kaski (Pokhara area) and Lamjung, he was of equal birth to the King and so was able to take such measures. This title was particularly important for the arrangement of marriages. To the present day the Shahs and Ranas are allied in this manner. For example, today's ruling King Birendra Dev Bikram Shah is married to the Rana Princess Lakhmi Devi.

In order to obtain coverage to the rear (China and Tibet) and to prevent an uprising of the opposition which was exiled in India, the Ranas cultivated a close relationship with the British and even visited Great Britian – in contrast to the Shahs. In 1857 Jang Bahadur sent the English 8,000 Gorkha soldiers to put down the Sepoy uprising in India. Closely interwoven trading relationships developed with India, which had experienced drastic industrialization and urbanization since the British occupation. Nepal exported more than it imported, and the earnings flowed to the Ranas. From 1854-1856 J.B.Rana won total victory over Tibet, which as a result had to agree to an annual payment of tributes, the establishment of a trade mission, and the elimination of tolls on goods.

Nepal's first industrialization came under the Rana ruler Chandra Shamser (1901-1929). He had a diesel electricity plant built and erected a cable railway for the transport of loads. He also abolished slavery in 1924. Tradition, art and culture were threatened under the Ramas insofar as that they scarcely cared about it. There were also few people contracting artistic work. Following the British example, the Ranas, including the Nepalese aristocracy, developed an ever-increasing taste for western culture and consumer goods, which served as a representation of their power. Their ostentatious whitewashed palaces, built in pseudo-baroque style, are also still to be found in Kathmandu.

Only the Rana families and their favorites enjoyed the benefit of schools and higher education. Their despotism went so far that normal households had to keep their windows which stood across from a Rana house closed. It was exactly this sort of behavior that smoothed the way for opposition to the Rana regime which received additional nourishment from the independence movement in India. It was not surprising that in 1936 the followers of the Shah royal family and the opposition removed to India, in order to put together an anti-Rana movement there.

From this there later developed the Nepali Congress Party. After India won back its independence from the British it was only a question of time before the Ranas gave up. In 1951, after King Tribhuvan fled to India, the Ranas had to agree to a coalition government which – with Indian mediation – was arranged between representatives of the royal family, followers of the Nepali Congress Party and Rana members.

But all is not well in the kingdom. In February 1990 violent demonstrations broke out protesting corruption in government. The opposition scored several victories suggesting that the world's only Hindu Kingdom might be on its way to constitutional democracy.

Right: A Garuda statue in Bhaktapur.

THE POPULATION OF NEPAL

The Himalayan Range acts as a tremendous natural barrier between South and Central Asia, but its passes have provided, for thousands of years, a place for encounters between the "Mongolian" groups of Tibeto-Burmese speakers, who adhere to Tibetan Buddhism and numerous "natural religions"; and the "caucasian" groups with Indo-Aryan languages and Hinduism as their religion.

Different worlds met here in military expeditions, migrations and trading relationships. These led to such a great variety of cultural and social, economic and political forms, that there is no single "Nepalese" culture as a single unit.

The area populated by the peoples of Nepal climbs, from south to north, from about 150 meters altitude to around 5,000 meters in the direction of Tibet. The Mongoloid groups live primarily in the northern sections; Indo-Nepalese mostly in the southern half of the country. Since agriculture is insufficient to support life in the high mountains, the Mongoloid groups have for centuries been livestock breeders (yaks, goats and sheep) and traders. They have traded, above all, Tibetan salt and wool over the Himalayan passes for Nepalese grain, and as a result developed long-term contact with Tibetan culture. In the last decades, however, this trade has decreased sharply, because of political confrontations in Tibet and competition from Indian goods.

The Indo-Nepalese in flat, bountiful Terai had been producing – in step with the fight against malaria – agricultural surplusses, which they brought to market in the closer and more easily accessible

Left: A woman from the Kathmandu Valley in Dakshin Kali with her sacrificial offering.

Indian markets. In the Eighties, though, the needs of the locals themselves for their own agricultural products have increased, leading to a substantial decline in the export of these goods.

Mongoloid and Indo-Nepalese groups have contact with each other principally in the third main region of Nepal, the central mountains, which in English is referred to – not exactly fittingly – as the "hill region". Here, on carefully terraced fields between 500 and 2,000 meters altitude, rice and other grains are cultivated. The barely sufficient output is increased by seasonal migration and the hired services of the Gorkha troops. Around 60 % of the total population of Nepal lives in the hill region and till about 30% of the total land area, whereas in Terai – with only 30 % of the population – almost 70% of the land is arable.

When trying to assign individual ethnic groups to particular geographical regions (and no area of Nepal is the exclusive territory of one ethnic group) one must recognize substantial variations within single territories. Single ethnic groups, for example the *Tamang*, exhibit considerable variations in their ecological adaptations. They plant rice on fields reaching down to 700 meters in altitude; pasture their livestock up to 4,500 meters; and cultivate potatoes, wheat, buckwheat, millet and corn up to over 2,000 meters altitude.

Terai and Hill Region

The main ethnic groups represented in the Terai include the *Tharu*, the *Darai*, the *Kumhal*, the *Danuwar* and the *Majhi*, as well as the Hindu population with its roots in India. These groups primarily speak Nepalese and north-Indian dialects. They live from agriculture, mostly as tenant farmers on private estates, which they were unable to register for in time, thus losing their land. In addition, the *Majhi* are employed as drivers, the

33

Kumhaal as potters, and the Danuwaar as fishermen.

In the hill region numerous ethnic groups are settled in the neighborhood of the Hindu population. Progressing from west to east one finds the *Magar*, the *Gurung*, the *Tamang*, the *Newar*, the *Sunuwar*, the *Rai* and the *Limbu*. Counted among the smaller groups are the *Thakali*, the *Chantel*, the *Chepang*, the *Raaji*, the *Pahari* (Pahi), the *Thami*, the *Haayu*, and the *Dhimal*. A major part of these groups belong to the Bodic group of the Sino-Tibetan language family; the Dhimal, the Newar, and the Pahari can be placed between the Bodic and Burmese language groups. Several of these groups (Chepang, Raaji, and Kusunda) were previously hunter-gatherers. Only the Newar have brought forth an urbanized culture.

The Northern Region

In the far north live – among others – the *Sherpa*, the *Dolpo-pa*, the *Bara-*

Despite their hard work, often as porters, the Nepalese laugh a lot.

gaonli, the *Manangi* and the *Lopa*. They derive their subsistence as leaders and carriers for mountain climbing expeditions, as high mountain farmers, and as yak and sheep breeders. They are linguistically – as well as culturally – connected to Tibet. In general they are often referred to as *Bhotiyas*. The previously mentioned traders are recruited from these groups in particular. Also to be counted among them are the *Humli-Khyampa*, who earn their living as nomadic traders in the westernmost section of the country.

During the cold winter months several of these groups set off on trading expeditions to the south of the country, where they sell the products of their homelands – herbs and spices – so that they can purchase the products of the south. Certain of the Bhotiyas even travel as far as Bangkok and Hong Kong to carry out their business on a larger scale. Altogether the Nepalese ethnic groups make

POPULATION

up approximately half of the population. Because no single one of these ethnic groups comprise more than 4% of the combined population of Nepal, they are considered to be minorities. In comparison to this, 45% of Nepal's population are so-called Hindus, who, undifferentiated in their various origins, present themselves as a single cultural unit. They owe the security of their key position in the national government to this sense of unity.

There is precious little clarity concerning the origins and migration processes of the various ethnic groups in present-day Nepal. The *Khas* have had a rather unique "career." They came from a region of India (Kumaon) to the far west of Nepal as a relatively lowly-placed group in the Hindu caste system. There they built up their position substantially, with which they were capable of achieving a considerable step upwards within the Nepalese caste hierarchy. A portion of today's *Chetri* are recruited from this ethnic group.

Kiranti and Tamang Peoples

As a rule, the *Kiranti* (predecessors of the Limbu, Rai, Sunawar and other ethnic groups that live today in Nepal) are considered to be the oldest inhabitants of central and eastern Nepal. Numerous myths exist about their origins and role in the process of history. It is certainly questionable whether the Kiranti had in reality stayed part in Benares, part in Lhasa and part in the Kathmandu Valley in "early" times, as is portrayed in their myths.

It is also difficult to verify the myths of other ethnic groups, with their supposed glorious pasts as kings and high dignitaries. Their origins, the time of their arrival in Nepal, and their political development are all difficult to research.

Amid constantly changing circumstances (subjugation to the rulership of various princes, integration into a united Nepalese kingdom, economic changes, etc.) the ethnic borders in Nepal were redrawn and the culture altered. In-

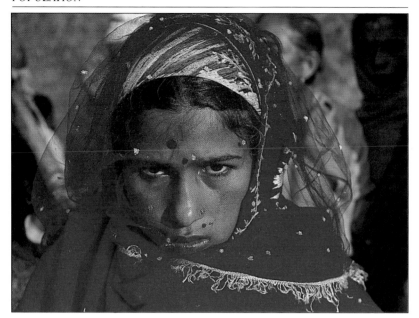

dividual groups and ethnic clans have, as a result, received names only in the last century. For example, the above mentioned Tamang, who were settled to the north and east of the Kathmandu Valley, first received their name from the Nepalese rulers in the middle of the 19th century, as the latter proclaimed the first civil legislation. Thus the Tamang, today generally considered to be of one ethnic group, are composed of exceptionally heterogenous sub-groups, with substantially different languages, cultural lore and social customs.

The generally ascertainable mobility of the Nepalese population is, with greatest probability, to be traced back to economic transformation and the historical processes of adaptation to the customs of the respective power groups.

Ethnic Diversity in the Kathmandu Valley

The colorful mixture of peoples presents itself to the traveler directly on ar-

Brahman woman in festive garb. Right: Father and son playing.

rival in the Kathmandu Valley. In just the last few years, the influx of folk from other parts of the country has increased substantially.

Here one encounters people from every region; the city's architectural character is stamped primarily, however, with the imprint of one particular ethnic group – the first encounter with "Nepal" in the Kathmandu Valley is to a certain degree an encounter with the culture of the *Newar*. This group, which governed the valley for centuries, was, thanks to its fertile soil and strategically important position as a trade center between India and China – able to give the exterior appearance of the cities, and especially the sacred structures, a character fascinatingly rich in forms.

Worthy of note are Hindu as well as Buddhist places, since the Newar have managed to integrate both religions to an exceptional degree; even though the extention of Hinduism sometimes filled the adherents of Buddhism with bitterness in the process.

As the only group in Nepal that were able to develop an urban culture, the Newar have also been successful in agriculture. At harvest time the connection between life in the cities and agriculture is especially visible. At these times every free spot in the plazas and also some streets change function to dry the harvested crops. The Newar – as administrators, farmers and craftsmen – have played a key role in commerce over centuries, which has encouraged the flourishing of craftsmanship.

Today many Newar are still occupied as tradespeople, owners of small tea-shops, middle-sized textile businesses, but also as directors of large import-export outfits. Newar families who had resided in the valley for hundreds of years, were at the instigation of the local rulers to travel to remote and underdeveloped parts of Nepal to develop trade.

Although the presence of the Newar is still strongly felt in the Kathmandu Valley from their art and craftwork, their role in politics has considerably diminished, although they do occupy a portion of the official positions.

Since the Newar kings of the Malla dynasty were overthrown by the Gurkha rulership in the second half of the 18th century, the power and jurisdiction of the primarily high-caste Indo-Nepalese group has decreased. Some among their ranks were recruited to the Shah dynasty, which is in power today. With the consolidation of the latter's power in the course of the so-called "unification" of Nepal (1744-1814), a large number of such high-caste families populated the Kathmandu Valley and there asserted their influence.

The notion of a "national culture", often mentioned nowadays, is associated in the first place with those cultural elements, values and norms that are

manifested particularly in the language. Indo-Aryan, derived from Sanskrit "Nepalese" (earlier called "Khas kura") is today the lingua franca, and is used as the official language. Only half of the population speaks it as their native language; it is the sole language used in education. This does not please the Newar, for example, who value their writings in "Newari" highly, and occasionally rouses them to vehement resistance. The Nepalese-speaking high caste Hindus have achieved key roles in the economic process, thanks in part to their political dominance. They are, before all others, those who occupy the top positions in the political and administrative apparatus, and to them also belong the extensive landed estates. Not only in the nation's capital city, but also in the combined Hill-Region, they assume the key political positions and have at their disposal a large portion of the land.

Only a few members of the original non-Hindu ethnic groups are involved in the central political processes. The traveler will probably have his first contact with these groups when he avails himself of the services of a travel agent or goes on a shopping trip. In both areas the groups from the far north are predominant – particularly the Sherpas, the Thakali and the Manangi. These groups have made profitable use of the fact that they live at the thoroughfare passes between Nepal and Tibet, and that rulers had to rely upon their services for the collection of tolls.

Many families have succeeded in achieving great affluence, and have expanded their business activities in every direction. Especially since the partial closure of the northern border, which occured as a result of China's annexation of Tibet, they have been shifting their residences and businesses to the more southerly regions of Nepal (especially to Terai and the Kathmandu Valley). Here they have been able to use their capital and their flair for business to set themselves up quite successfully. With their trade and travel businesses and factories they

have attained considerable influence, which they share only with the Newar and several Tibetan families. These latter, after their traumatic exodus from Tibet, were at first gathered in refugee centers, where they were given the task of weaving Tibetan carpets, which have now become well-known. Today this business is flourishing, and it has also been entered into by other groups, among them the Sherpas. The Tibetan religious centers have proven to be a great attraction for practicing western Buddhists, who seek out Nepal to study meditation under the instruction of famous lamas. None of the other groups which reside in Nepal have been able to establish such strong bonds with the West as the Tibetans.

The men who entered the Gurkha troops as mercenaries in service to the British are rather widely-travelled. Whether in Italy during the Second World War, South-East Asia during the battles for independance, or more recently in the British-Argentinian conflict on the Falkland Islands, the Nepalese "Gurkhas" have distinguished themselves everywhere with their courage and endurance as hired soldiers. In spite of the dangers, service in the Gurkhas – well-paid by the British – has always been held in high regard. Members of a variety of ethnic groups, particularly the Gurung and the Magar, have been able to eradicate their debts and enlarge their properties with saved wages and pension benefits.

Prospects and Problems

It is not only the well-to-do who seek out the area around the Kathmandu Valley. Carriers, riksha drivers, waiters, hotel workers, servants of various rank and janitors are recruited from the stream of migrants – who come in increasing numbers in search of work in the Kathmandu Valley, because there is less and less land available in the surrounding Hill

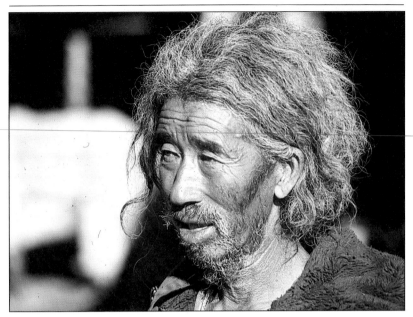

A pilgrim from Mustang. Left: Fast asleep on mother's shoulder.

Region. The population of every ethnic group is confronted with this problem, whether Tamang or Rai, Magar or Chepang. They must take on the most difficult, lowest levels of employment in society, since they usually lack extensive vocational training. Competition is becoming increasingly tough. The level of unemployment has increased to such an extent that, paradoxically, people who stand on higher rungs in the Hindu caste hierarchy are struggling to get work normally relegated to the untouchables – street sweeping, for example.

The city – with its increasing "modernization"; with its chaos of automobiles, tourists, cacaphonous radios, landing aircraft, and with unimagined opportunities – naturally exerts a strong attraction on many young people. Even without economic compulsion they are turning their backs in agrarian existence, which they consider to be both boring and bur-

densome. They leave the lands of their fathers, even rejecting service as teachers in their local schools, in order to hurry to the city and be willingly hired to the most inferior positions. Wealthier farmers now complain of the lack of workers, and are confronted with major problems – the hiring of farm workers costs money. The older heads of households must also accept their loss of authority over the younger generations of males.

The disintegration of family relationships is being generally decried in Nepal. As regards the youth who have emigrated to the city, they are just about exhausted by the hard working conditions, loss of status, and general loss of identity. No matter how colorful and quiet they appear, in fact the Nepalese population faces numerous difficult problems. While the government has already drawn up many ambitious plans for the year 2 000, the population of Nepal looks to an uncertain future of environmental destruction, increasing economic pressures, and the weak leadership of the political elite.

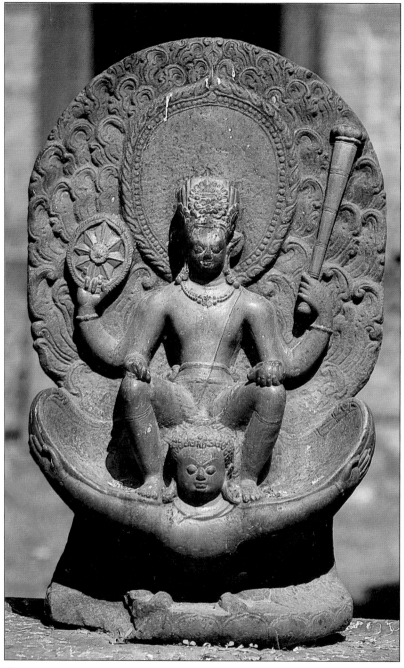

THE RELIGIONS
OF NEPAL

If you were to ask a Nepali whether he is Hindu or Buddhist, he might well simply answer you – with an entirely straight face – "Yes". Did he misunderstand the question – or was it incorrectly put? In the majority of cases, both would be true. A Nepali, especially a Newar, can worship both Buddha and Shiva without falling into a conflict of beliefs. He is reluctant to fall out of favor with any of the gods, and so – just to be on the safe side – he would rather worship all of them. Many pilgrims who seek out a temple during a festival strew their offerings (flowers, grains of rice, powdered cinnabar or coins) at all sorts of shrines and holy sanctuaries. There might even be a fire hydrant deprived of its normal function, just because it has the phallic form of a linga.

Officially, Nepal is the only Hindu kingdom in the world. That being so, Hinduism has been declared the national religion and other religions are viewed as sub-forms of Hinduism. However, the statistical computation of religious membership is difficult, if not impossible. According to the government census of 1971, almost 89.5% of the population are Hindus. Small in comparison, and therefore almost unbelievable, the figures for the other religions are 3.4% Buddhists, 1.9% Moslems, 1.8% Christians, and 3.3% other religions. At the main national holy sanctuary, Pashupatinath temple, hangs a sign, as at many other temples, forbidding entrance to non-Hindus. In principle, however, only foreigners are not admitted. Since Buddha is considered in Hinduism to be a manifestation of

Left: Vishnu and his mount Garuda in Changu Narayan are found on every ten rupee note.

Vishnu, Buddhists are allowed entrance.

Frequently in rituals and religious festivals, especially in myths, the distinction between the gods is consciously blurred. Once a year the *linga* in the then overcrowded Pashupatinath temple is worshipped as Avalokiteshvara, during which the linga is adorned with the crown of the Bodhisattvas.

Shiva and his Company

Hindus worship two major gods – Shiva and Vishnu – together with their accompanying hosts. While Shiva appears as a wild, fear-inspiring god – in classical myths he is often the destroyer of the world – Vishnu has a mild, more world-protective character. The third god in the old Hindu god-triad, named Brahma, scarcely plays a role in the temple cult today.

Shiva (also referred to as *Maheshvar* or *Mahadev*) is worshipped most frequently as a *linga*. This might be a quite plain and unpretentious abstract phallic symbol, but it may also have the four-sided face of the manifestations of the god. A temple to Shiva rarely lacks his riding mount – the bull *Nandi* – or his weapon, the three-pronged *Trishul*.

In the classical myths of India, Shiva appears on the one hand as evil and dangerous, and on the other, kindly and benevolent. In Nepal, however, he is mostly only a peaceful god, to whom one goes seeking support and assistance. Thus, many votive-temples have been erected in his name.

In the Kathmandu Valley it is more likely to meet gods who are dangerous and require appeasement. These reduce even Shiva to a position of subordination, as can be seen in one particular festival which the Newar celebrate in springtime, mainly in Kathmandu.

This festival is held in March or April. The inner court-yards are cleaned of garbage and other debris. In the process a small linga is dug out from under the piles of garbage, which is worshipped in the night. This linga is named *Luku-mahadyo*, which means literally "hidden Mahadev" (= Shiva). According to oral tradition, Shiva had sought protection here because he was threatened by wild goddesses, evil demons or even ignorant Buddhists, depending on who's telling the story.

The degree to which Shiva himself has been superimposed on local gods is seen in the god *Nasadyo*. Newar musicians have a god of protection whose course one dare not hinder. Therefore there are slits in many walls and specialized shrines, through which the god may pass without having to make any detours. Originally, neither the cult nor the manifestation had anything in common with Shiva. But in Indian high tradition, Shiva is also the god of dance (*Nateshvar or Nataraja*). So, it was an easy step to connect the two gods, especially as it would also mean an increase in the musicians' status. The god of protection then

The elephant god Ganesha is especially popular in Nepal.

received the name *Nasadyo*, the Newari version Nateshvar ("god of dance").

Although in Hindu mythology the elephant-headed god *Ganesha* (another name is *Vinyaka*) is thought of as the son of Shiva, he has a character all of his own in Nepal. Pre-Hinduist traits have been connected with this beloved Indian god as well. For example, he receives blood sacrifices and alcohol much more frequently than in India. Ganesha not only watches over each quarter of the city, but also from Bhaktapur, Chaba, Kathmandu and Chobar he watches over the entire Kathmandu Valley.

Coarse, unhewn stones are also used to signify Ganesha, who is otherwise represented by the typical elephant's head. In any case, one can recognize Ganesha in them with enough imagination. Even *Bhairava* (in classical Hinduism a fear-inspiring form of Shiva) is not always represented as a mask or statue, but often

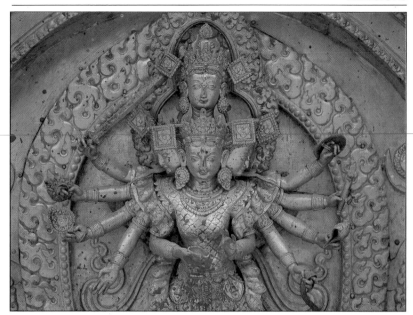

The goddess Taleju enthroned on the "golden gate" in Bhaktapur.

only as a simple stone. In these phenomena there is clear evidence of pre-Hindu divinities, which in the process of Nepal's "hinduization" were promoted, so to speak, by being given prestigious Sanskrit names.

Goddesses

Occasionally, Shiva is accompanied by his female companion in her benevolent aspects. *Parvathi* ("mountain daughter"), *Uma* ("sunrise" or the "rose of dawn") or *Gauri* ("golden") are her most frequent names. She may appear either in isolation, as, for example, the great Gauri-stone in the Bagmati River north of the Pashupatinath Temple, or together with Shiva. The image is then usually named *Umamaheshvara* and portrays the couple in a peaceful embrace.

Shiva's female companion can also appear as wild and threatening. She is then referred to as Shakti, or the embodiment of the feminine-cosmic energy of Shiva. Often one can scarcely make out any connection with Shiva, and the pre-Hindu characteristics of such goddesses are hinted at. In the Kathmandu Valley, their names and manifestations, as well as their temples and shrines, are virtually countless.

One of the more frequent motifs is that of the Mahisha-killing demon *Durga* (often called *Bhagavati* in Nepal). It appears over and over again, especially on gate-arches above the entrances to temples or on elaborately carved wooden roof-beams. On these, Durga is usually portrayed standing on the demon, who has assumed the form of an untameable buffalo. Durga then impales the demon with a long spear. This motif comes almost to life in the *Dasain Festival*, which is dedicated to Durga, among others, and when the heads of hundreds of small water buffaloes are hewn off at the Hanuman Dhoka in an exciting and bloody ceremony.

43

The manifestation of the goddess as *Taleju* is of great significance. This has to do with one of the goddesses of protection of the Malla rulership, who is worshipped in secret rituals and whose Mantra (a magical incantation for protection) is supposed to guarantee the power of the king. In all three royal cities of the Kathmandu Valley, the most magnificent temples are dedicated to Taleju.

In less prominent places, the goddess is represented under various names. Frequently her temple or shrine is located outside the settlement, from where she should protect the inhabitants. As a rule a movable idol for her worship is kept in the city, which is taken out on special festivals and carried about on precisely predetermined paths.

It is clear that in the cults, the mythology, the forms of worship and the iconography are in fact always concerned with one goddess, who appears in a variety of manifestations. Certain groups of goddesses arranged in cosmic diagrams (mandalas) are also basically representations of the one and the same supreme goddess.

So, we frequently find either the Eight Mothers (*Asthamatrika*) or the Nine Durgas (*Navadurga*), who surround a village or a temple. The most common grouping consists of the eight goddesses *Brahmani, Mahesvari, Kaumari, Vaishnavi, Vahari, Indrani, Camunda*, and *Mahalakshmi*. They can also be joined by a ninth manifestation.

Not only can a goddess have several different names, but a goddess may be represented in several different ways under the same name. For example, the goddess *Lakshmi* has no temple of her own, but she is portrayed on many plastic Vishnus as his female companion. Her likeness is also worshipped in many private houses as the completely independent goddess *Shri* who is supposed to care for wealth and well-being. And finally, she appears in Tantric rituals as

Vishnu's Shakti and as *Vaishnavi*, one figure from the Eight Mothers.

The situation is similar with *Sarasvati*, who is worshiped as the goddess of the arts and sciences. She is seen as both Vishnu's female companion and that of the bodhisattva Manjushri. But she also appears in Tantric rituals – which often speak of the Dark or Blue Sarasvati as opposed to the White Sarasvati.

Vishnu, Rama and Krishna

In contrast to Shiva and his linga, *Vishnu*, who is also frequently called *Narayan*, is rarely symbolically or abstractly represented. The plainest form of his presentation besides the black ammonite are his stylized feet (*Vishnupadaka*).

More frequently, Vishnu is represented as a human or animal figure. Thus he appears at times as *Budhanilkantha*, as he reposes on a snake in the primeval waters; at times as *Narasimha* ("half man, half lion"), as he conquers the adversaries of the gods; at times as a boar (*Vahara*); and at times as a dwarf (*Vamana*).

According to mythology, Vishnu appears on the earth in nine manifestations (*Avataras*) altogether. His tenth form of manifestation – the horse Kalki – will only appear at the destruction of the world, at the end of the present Age of Kaliyuga.

Several of the sculptures on which such scenes are portrayed are among the earliest artworks of Nepal. From new revelations it appears, that in the first half of the first millenium A.D. Vishnuism was far more widely disseminated than had been previously assumed.

Vishnu's attributes, the *Conch* – or shells – and his weapon, the discus, (*Cakra*) are not infrequently put up on particular columns in front of temples to Vishnu. They usually surround Vishnu's riding-mount, the mythical bird *Garuda*.

Hanuman, a god in the shape of an

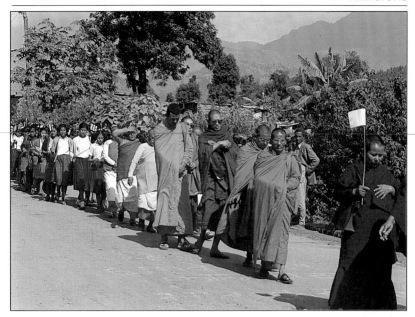

Procession of Buddhist Theravada monks in Pokhara.

ape, also appears in many Vishnuist holy places. He is especially beloved, since he helped a further manifestation of Vishnu, namely the heroic god *Rama*, in many emergencies. Shrines dedicated to Rama are certainly found less frequently in the Kathmandu Valley, most are in Bhaktapur, which calls itself the city of Rama, and in Deopatan.

Patan – a city which bears a strong spiritual and material imprint from Buddhism – is a center for the worship of *Krishna*. Here there are many beautiful temples and shrines to this well-loved god. Krishna is a god with many pastoral and heroic traits. But his widespread popularity is based above all on his romantic love-relationship with Radha. In the worship of Krishna and also of Rama such devotion is of great importance. One prays intimately to them and sings of them with poems and songs which are full of ardor and love for the gods.

The Buddhist World

As is well known, the historical Buddha was born in the middle of the sixth century B.C. in what is today an area of Nepal, more exactly in Lumbini on the southern foothills of the Himalayas. It took more than a thousand years for the first ascertainable relics to be left behind in the Kathmandu Valley. These include early statues of the *Buddha Shakyamuni*, which are named after Buddha's family name.

The original Buddhism is a teaching of salvation, but in Nepal only a little of this content still remains. Here, primarily *Vajrayana Buddhism* is still alive. This is a form of *Mahayana Buddhism* that bears a strong imprint from Tantric rituals.

With this "Great Course" of Buddhism the conception that prevails that anyone can become a *bodhisattva*. Bodhisattvas are beings which have received enlightenment, but have chosen to refuse the reward – namely entrance into Nirvana, so that they might remain to assist others on

45

their paths toward enlightenment. In Nepal the bodhisattvas have become regular gods in their own right, and are worshipped in temples with lavish and partially secret rituals.

The bodhisattvas are also thought of as offspring or emanations of the *Dhyana-Buddha*. They are mystical-transcendental Buddhas who also embody the five basic elements of ether, air, water, fire and earth. Feminine aspects are also associated with them – the *Buddhashaktis*.

One of the most well-known bodhisattvas throughout Nepal is *Padmapani-Avalokiteshvara* (also called *Lokeshvara* or *Lokanatha*, "Emperor of the World"), who is at the same time Tibet's patron saint.

Avalokiteshvara means literally "the god who gazes downward", an expression of the compassion, by which this bodhisattva is primarily characterized. Another Buddhist name, *Karunamaya*, also means "the compassionate". His character shows itself primarily in the sagas of the Macchendranath cult, in

A Hindu ascetic on a pilgrimage to Pashupati, a manifestation of Shiva.

which, after a long period of drought, he brings the much needed rain to the sorely tried people.

In this cult an originally pre-Hindu and pre-Buddhist deity by the name of *Bungadyo* (literally " the god from Bunga", a village that is today named Bungamati), has joined with gods from both pantheons. For Avalokiteshvara is *Macchendranath* for the Hindus , for whom there is a variety of local manifestations. In this way the village of Chobar knows one such god; Kathmandu a White Macchendranath; and Patan a Red Macchendranath and a *Minanatha*, who sometimes appears as a child, sometimes as other forms of Macchendranath's manifestations. In spite of these various names and forms, there is scarcely a god in the great Buddhist pantheon who is so consistently worshipped by the diversity of population groups as the Red Macchendranath in Patan.

Tibetan musicians playing at a Puja in a Nyingma monastery near Mustang.

Another bodhisattva (*Manjushri*), has become closely associated with a Hindu deity, namely the goddess *Sarasvati*. In Vajrayana Buddhism, for example, she is seen as Manjushri's spouse. They are both gods of knowledge and the arts, and it is astounding that in this case, even in spite of their differing sexual indentities, they are treated as equals.

Religious Tolerance

Just as Buddhist deities can become manifestations of Hinduism, as Newaric Buddhism also takes, for example, Shiva and Vishnu as bodhisattvas into its pantheon. In general, however, Hinduism is the more widely embracing religion. The reasons for this lay, in part, in the fact that the kings were closer to the Hindu gods and therefore encouraged this.

For the majority of the Newars, these distinctions are insignificant. They worship almost all of the gods – either Buddhist or Hindu – to the same degree. Thus, in the main sanctuaries of "Buddhist" monasteries a Hindu god may be found just as – on the other hand – Hindus include Buddha in their pantheon as a manifestation of Vishnu. Only the orthodox priests occasionally lay emphasis on their membership of one religion and decline attendance to the festivals and temples of the other religious community.

It is unusual – but typical of Newaric Buddhism – that, strictly speaking, there no longer exists a real order of monks. Instead of this there are two groups of "married monks" *Vajracaryas*, who are Buddhist priests, and *Shakyabhikus*, a grouping which traces its ancestral roots back to Buddha's familial name. Each male member of this caste is a monk for only four days during his initiation. Afterward, however, he remains an active member of his cloister community for the rest of his life, even when he has long since been married. Both in beliefs and in religious viewpoints, there is much toler-

47

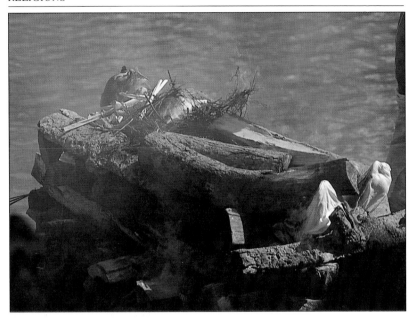

ance. It is a matter of family tradition which god should be worshipped for protection. And it is up to the individual to choose which god he declares as his or her personal god. For the most part it is also left to the individual whether he or she goes to the temple daily, or sings religious songs at night, or whether he pursues and obtains religious distinctions.

Rituals and Festivals

The situation is completely different when it comes to the essential rituals and festivals of the family, caste or settlement. Then there is little freedom, as the priests, participants, timing, completion, and materials are all strictly determined and codified.

Thus, important events and changes in life, such as birth, coming of age, marriage and death must be secured by priests with traditional religious ceremonies, to insure that disaster and ritual impurification do not befall the clan or family. For this purpose, one calls the

For Hindus death requires special purification ceremonies.

family priest, a Hindu Brahman or a Buddhist Vajracarya from the vicinity. Only people of low castes or members of ethnic minorities have their own priests, but these also often try to gain a Brahman for themselves, in order to increase their status.

The birth of a child is an event which carries with it ritual impurification not only for the mother, but rather for the entire house. It therefore requires particular purification rituals. These include prayer as well as washing and dietary restrictions. A more cheerful ceremony is the first feeding of boiled rice to the baby at the age of about six months. This is a festive occasion, and many relatives come together to celebrate the well-being of the child.

During ceremonial initiation rites for the higher castes, boys receive the holy cord. They are then for the first time considered to be fully fledged and marriagable members of their castes. The Buddhist groups also celebrate a similar coming-of-age ceremony, at which time the candidates are taken formally into their orders.

Marriage is the most elaborate ritual. Not only must the majority of relatives be invited, the marriage partner must be chosen with reference to genealogy and caste-specific criteria. For the higher castes, a wedding is very expensive. The family of the bride "pays" with both gifts and money in order to find the most suitable possible bridegroom.

Death is the most impure event. It affects the entire group of relatives to varying degrees, but most of all the oldest son. It is he who is responsible for carrying out the cremation ceremony, and furthermore he must have his hair cut, and sometimes wear exclusively white clothes for one year as well. Years afterward, a ritual must still be celebrated for the deceased on the anniversary of his death, and no significant event can be begun without commemorating one's ancestors.

Whilst most of the rituals surrounding the important events of life are limited to relatives, in many festivals the caste or even the entire community of the settlement comes together to take part in the feast. This applies especially when the towns hold the main festival for their gods of protection. The worship of these gods at regular intervals is especially important in order to hold back the gods of bad harvest, epidemics, earthquakes and other catastrophes.

Nevertheless, the organization of these festivals lies mostly in the hands of a few specialists, who are often united in a religious association called a *guthi*. One can only become a member of a guthi on the basis of religious specialisation, caste membership and place of residence. A guthi exists for almost every ritual obligation; for the payment of sacrificial materials, for the provision of sacrificial animals or for the construction of procession wagons.

While the city or town festivals which are directed towards the goddesses are obligatory as a rule, with other festivals it remains up to the individual whether and in what manner he participates. This applies for example to the number of participants in the *Shivaratri*, which is certainly the largest festival in Nepal. On this day an especially large number of pilgrims – from India as well – seek out the Pashupatinath temple to worship Shiva with fasting and night-time vigils.

A substantial difference exists between the two categories of festival: The town festivals are carried out for the well-being of the community and in these festivals the gods are carried around the settlement. The other festivals are celebrated for personal well-being, and in these one goes to the gods. The town festivals are also bound to certain dates on the calendar, which have much to do with the harvest cycles. In contrast, with family festivals and the taking of religious vows, the best points in time for them are determined by certain auspicious or lucky days of the week or according to the personal birth horoscope of each and every individual.

Modes of Worship

Just as with the festivals, the methods by which the gods are worshipped are also differentiated. The most common way to demonstrate one's respect is the *Puja*. This form of worship can take place very modestly, sometimes as a simple bow with hands clasped together, or perhaps the strewing of rice grains. But the Puja can also be an elaborate ritual, in which flowers, incense, water, lights, powdered cinnobar, food (rice, sweets or fruits), coins, cloth or small umbrellas are brought to the god as offerings.

The gifts must be unused, when possible even new, and undamaged. The rice grains should also be unbroken and not yet de-hulled. The donator usually receives the edible offerings back from the priest. With this the subordination of the believer in relation to the god is expressed for as a rule one may only receive (cooked) nourishment from a superior. The priest also gives back a portion of the cinnobar, at which time he puts a small red point, the *tika*, on the forehead of the temple visitor. In addition a sacred blossom is popularly placed behind the right ear. All offerings must be protected from impurity. Among things considered impure are, for example, bodily secretions (excrement, saliva, menstrual blood), liver, dogs, but also members of the untouchable caste.

The Puja is a sign of respect with which one requests protection and prosperity. It is offered not only to deities, rather also to elders, priests, gurus, a monk or an ascetic. Furthermore in one well-loved festival, the *Bhai Tika*, older sisters proffer various honors on their younger brothers. Here it becomes even

more clear that in Hindu South Asia, status at the individual level depends not only on age and caste membership, but also on one's gender.

Only certain gods accept animal sacrifices and alcohol. To these belong many manifestations of the goddesses, particularly the Eight Mothers and the Nine Durgas, as well as Bhairava, Ganesha and Bhimsen. It would be a serious sacrilege to make such offerings to Shiva or the bodhisatvas. Goats, sheep, chickens, ducks, and in special cases water-buffaloes are used as sacrificial animals. These should also be flawless and, when possible, of male gender. The sacrifices must be taken "of their own free will", attested to by a shake of the head. In this way the animal expresses its wish to be reincarnated as a higher being. Mostly, however, the animal is helped through this process, as a little bit of water is trickled into one of its ears, naturally causing it to immediately shake its head.

Only men from the slaughtering-caste kill the animals, however, not the priests or donors. While the head is intended for the deities and – afterwards – the priests, the sanctified torso is returned to the donor. He then later prepares the meat for a feast.

The rituals with which the animals are sacrificed usually follow carefully worked-out rules from Tantrism. The sacrifice cannot be carried out at all until the participants have received a secret consecration (*diksha*). It is seen as life-threatening to organize a sacrifice if one has not been initiated into the cult of the deity concerned.

In one Tantric ritual, an effigy of a deity is placed on a specially purified spot (*asana*), after which the priest calls upon the deity to occupy it. Then, a likeness of the deity in its most notable characteristics is composed, during which the priest places numerous offerings on ritual diagrams (*yantra*) and with changing hand-gestures *(mudra)* murmers certain

Sacrifices to the Durga at the Dasain festival. Left: Bell and sword – indispensable in Tantric ceremonies.

secret incantations. Afterwards, the animal is sacrificed, and with the blood that sprays out, the slaughterer makes a magical circle around the sacrifice place. Following this the priests distribute offerings to the people who have made the sacrifice, and these in turn give the priests payment, mostly in the form of money. Finally the place of sacrifice is ritually broken down and the deity again released. Such rituals occasionally extend through the entire night.

As members of the higher castes one can also be privately initiated into the cult of a Tantric deity. Only then does one have the right to worship them directly – that is, without priests. In addition there are secret teachings on how one can come as close as possible to the higher nature of a deity. These teachings are connected not only with the correct offerings and the way they are presented, but also with the control of the body – especially breathing – and with the esoteric sexual interpretations of the cult.

Among the popular forms of religious expression are special vows, which are particularly popular amongst women. These are taken to achieve religious merit, to secure the blessings of the gods for this and the next lives, or to put a god into a merciful mood through particularly obliging behavior. Sometimes one fasts for only a day, or one might decide to go on a long pilgrimage. In addition an elaborate fire-sacrifice (*Homa, Yajna*) might be held, or a feast offered for the glorification of a god. It is also possible to organize – rather than merely participate in – the recitation of holy texts or songs.

The entire diversity of rituals and forms of worship in the Kathmandu Valley is, however, not simply a ritual mixture of religions, but rather an expression of the fact that there are many gods – and that several paths can lead to religious salvation.

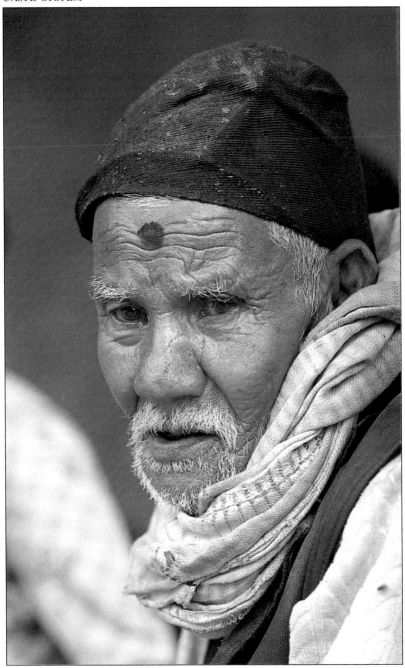

THE CASTE SYSTEM

Since the beginning of this millenium, Nepalese Hill Region has experienced the immigration of Hindu groups the, under whose influence the local ethnic groups have taken on a part of Hinduism with the norm and value systems connected with it. The co-existence of Hindu groups and non-Hindu tribes has resulted in the development of its own caste system, which is however still based largely on Indian tradition.

The membership of the different castes and ethnic groups live – with variations from area to area – either in their own hamlets or in mixed settlements. At first glance you can't distinguish one group from the other. People from different groups meet each other in the same businesses; children from the different castes sit on the same benches in the schools and outdoors, people who are members of the various social groups associate with each other. Only an experienced observer would notice that their seemingly uninhibited behavior is actually directed by many rules and regulations.

The inhabitants of the Nepalese Hill Region are organized into a strict hierarchy. They are classified into superior and subordinate groups, and their rank descends according to their level of ritual purity. At the top of this stratification is the *Tagadhari* caste – ritually the purest Hindus – the male members of which wear the "holy cord". They are also designated the "twice-born" caste, because after their physical birth they come to the world once again – through elaborate rituals of initiation – as a full social member of their caste. The *Brahmans* and

Left: A Newar from Kathmandu with the tika, a religious mark, on his forehead.

Chetris are counted among these. The conducting of Hindu rituals is incumbent upon the Brahmans; the Chetris are predisposed to being warriors and governors – their rank corresponds to that of the Indian *Kshatriya* category. Subordinate to these two castes are the Matawali groups – literally: "the alcohol-drinking castes" to which the non-Hindu ethnicities belong. From the viewpoint of the Hindu all ethnic groups are considered to be castes. However, the members of ethnic groups only see themselves as castes when they have become largely "hinduized".

The majority of groups have come into such close contact with the Hindus that they have taken on several of their rules. Only a few ethnic groups have been able to withstand the continuing process of hinduization; in general the rule applies that the Hindu influence decreases from south to north. The various populations living in northern Nepal are located in the sphere of influence of another "great tradition", namely that of Tibet and especially Tibetan Buddhism.

The Northern Peoples

Far away from the religious and political centers of the Hindu population, the groups from the North have contact primarily with the Tibetan population and Tibetan institutions, and their culture exhibits a diversity of Tibetan characteristics. Some of the Magar ethnic group could be counted among the strongly hinduized groups (not including, however, the Kham-Magar); the Tamang and Gurung find themselves under the influence of both traditions, while the renowned Sherpas have by and large retained the Tibetan Buddhist beliefs and cultural elements. But the cultural practices and religious assumptions within one ethnic group can vary considerably from region to region. The Newar, who, in an urban milieu, particularly in the

53

Kathmandu Valley, have developed their own caste system are considered to be a separate caste in the scattered villages of the Hill Region where they live.

Left: Both father and son are porters. Right: A spicemonger in front of his shop.

The Caste of the Untouchables

The Untouchable castes stand on the very lowest rung of the Hindu caste system; these are the *Kami* (smiths), the *Sarki* (shoemakers) and the *Damai*, who practice two occupations: they are tailors and musicians and accompany many of the significant Hindu festivals with their music. These three groups form the majority of the Untouchable castes in the Nepalese Hill Region. In the urban milieu as well as in the southern Terai strip there is a much larger diversity of ritual specialists or religious healers (*Jhankri*) who are considered Untouchables. In the Kathmandu Valley many of the impure occupations are carried out by Untouchables of Newar ethnicity. Many different Indian castes have settled in Terai. It is a local peculiarity of the Nepalese Hill Re-

gion that the high-caste Hindus perform occupations which are seen in India as ritually impurifying.

Rules and Regulations

The hierarchified structure is founded on the concept of ritual purity. Every person and practically every article and each deed is classified according to this principal. This strict hierarchization has resulted in certain sequestrations. In villages in which several castes live, the houses are built a certain distance away from each other. Only members of the same group occasionally live closer together.

Even slight differences in the appearance their farmsteads can reveal the caste membership of their occupants. Color is no indication of caste membership. Villages where white paint is scarce and expensive can inform you only about the

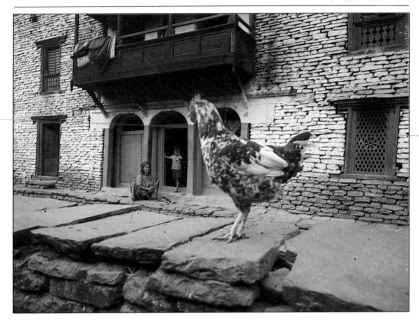

Brahmans are not allowed to eat chicken because they are regarded as impure.

relative affluence of a household. Only in the farmsteads of the higher castes do you find the clay pedestals with the holy *tulasi* plant. The holy images which hang over the house entrances are also primarily found among the high castes. The view into the houses of the high castes is prohibited and therefore blocked. Thus the entrances are never constructed directly on the footpaths, which, in contrast, is a common practice among the lower castes. You can also recognize the caste membership of a house's occupants by their domestic animals, because as a rule, animals are not kept unless one is allowed to eat their flesh. The presence of chickens in a yard permits the assumption that the house's occupants do not belong to the highest caste, because the Brahmans do not eat chicken meat or eggs. Only in most recent times have the Brahman women begun to supplement their private income with chicken breeding, which, however, runs up against the determined resitance of the traditional Hindus. Castes that rank higher than the Magar are not allowed to keep pigs in their yards. These are ritually impurifying for those of higher caste.

The wells from which people draw their water and wash themselves are from time to time accessible only to certain specific groups. The Untouchables are not allowed to use the wells of the higher castes. The Untouchables are prohibited from entering the houses of the higher castes. They are only permitted to stay on the shady verandas, or – if there are already persons of higher caste present – they must sit further away. In many places the Untouchables are also not allowed to set foot into the interiors of the tea shops.

The rules of ritual purity are expressed in many additional regulations. The purest Brahmans, for example, are not allowed to plow. For the cultivation of their fields they must employ people of lower castes. Equally, the higher castes may not

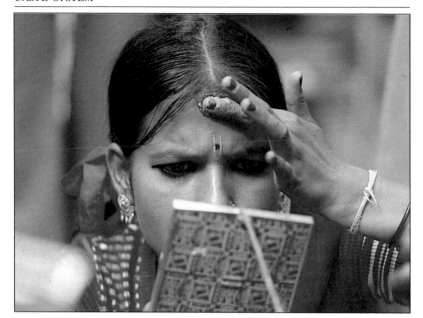

carry the sedan chairs of the bride and bridegroom. These tasks are fulfilled by lower, but still touchable castes. The ideas of ritual purity are also expressed in the regulations concerning food, especially during the transfer of boiled rice, which can only be passed along from a member of higher caste to another of equal birth or lower-caste person. At the larger festivals, at which members of a variety of groups are gathered, the rice is only prepared by Brahman cooks for this reason. The rice is then served first to the Brahmans. Only after this may the remaining groups eat. Whereas the high-caste Hindus have to change their clothing before eating, the Untouchables eat in their everyday clothes. The Untouchables must also keep their distance when other groups are eating. If they are invited to eat at the house of a higher caste person, they must eat outside in front of the door.

The regulations of ritual purity are also manifested during smoking which takes on the aspect of a ceremony. In the Nepalese Hill Region, frequently several

The tika is not only a religious sign, women also wear it as decoration.

men smoke from one cigarette. Since the saliva of a person from a lower caste is impure, the cigarettes are passed from the higher to the progressively lower caste members. Also during the smoking of the waterpipe, the purity commandments are observed. The entire pipe can only be used by its owner and the members of the same caste. Lower caste people must first remove the wooden handle.

Hindu Rites

Veneration towards those of higher castes is expressed by bowing. One bows down low – to the hands of the person of higher standing. One bows down to the feet of religious dignitaries; in earlier times such a bow was also made to the big landowners.

The beliefs of Hinduism are manifested in a multiplicity of ceremonies, which are conducted by the Brahman

A man may not pass his cigarette to another from a higher caste.

priests; the better-educated *Pandits* and the less-learned *Purohits*. Some examples of these ceremonies include purifying rituals such as the *Om*, annual cycle ceremonies like the Dasain festival, or life-cycle ceremonies such as initiation and marriage (both of these rituals can only be conducted by Brahman priests for members of the "twice born" castes), as well as death rituals.

Sacrifice is also a part of some Hindu rituals – according to the deity who is called upon. The Hindus ascribe an especially purifying effect to the taking of a bath in a holy river. For the residents of villages, the religious festivals – which frequently last all night long – are the main occasions for meeting each other.

Children are not recognized as full members of the higher castes. The first years of life are not regulated by the caste prescriptions. Only after their initiations do the young boys become full members

of the caste – "born" for the second time. They may not be married until after this ritual; marriages generally take place within the same caste.

For the women, marriage functions as their initiation. After this ceremony, the bride separates from her parents. She is then adopted by the family of her husband. In the family of the husband, the daughter-in-law has at first a reduced status; contrastingly, in relation to her family of birth she achieves a "holy" status as a result of the merit that her parents and other blood relatives acquire by the "gift of the virgin" (*kannya dan*) to the family of the bridegroom. This "holy" status is manifested for example on the occasion of the *brother's day*, during which sisters visit their brothers and ritually honor them with a *tika*.

The marital status of women is visible from their appearance. Married women wear a chain around their neck as well as red powder (*sindur*) in their hair partings or on their forehead. Even those who are still single may wear a red "beauty-spot".

Widows may not wear any red clothing, no marriage chain and also may not apply a beauty-spot to themselves.

Caste and Profession

In contrast to the Indian caste society, the caste structure of the Nepalese Hill Region does not know a strict classification of professions.

Traditionally, the practice of only the professions alloted to their castes is observed primarily by the Brahman priests and the Untouchable handcraftsmen. The majority of the residents of the Hill Region make their living from agriculture. The remaining professions – for example the maintaining of a tea shop or woodworking and other crafts is performed by members of various castes.

Particularly the higher castes are feeling the winds of change. So, for example, young Brahmans – who have of course learned Sanskrit and are able to direct religious rituals – prefer work in the modern world as teachers. Other high caste men like to occupy political posts. Within one family one can encounter men with different orientations. In spite of far-reaching social upheavals in Nepal, the fact remains that the extensive dominance of the high-caste Hindus (Indo-Nepalese) in relation to the rest of the population persists.

Myth and Reality

No genuine Hindu believer would doubt that the system of castes has existed always, and that it is to be traced back to the creation of the gods. However, there are significant points of reference which allow us to assume that it first came into existence during the Vedic period (1500-500 B.C.); the older Vedic writings – holy Hindu books – do not even exhibit all of the so-called Varna names – the main categories of the Hindu caste ordering.

The origins of the Indian as well as the Nepalese caste systems are today (still) shrouded in darkness. Most would also agree, that – in relation to Hindu Nepal – it is quite impossible to speak of a single caste system.

Considering the diversity of the origins and customs among the Nepalese population it would be possible to speak of several caste systems; that of the Hindus in the Hill Region; that of the Hindus of the Terai; that of the Newar – where one can make yet a further distinction between the Hindus and the Buddhists – and that of the Moslem population, whose religious orientation certainly stresses equality, but has undergone a strong adaptation to the customs of Hinduism. At any rate, the Moslems as a group rate low within the Hindu hierarchy. The principles and regulations concerning ritual purity described above apply – barring certain theoretical and practical distructions of course – for all of the systems already listed here.

When the membership of the high Nepalese castes (Hill Region) speak of the Nepalese society as "one" caste system, in this way they are actually emphasising their own political, economic and ritual dominance which they have been able to establish in the course of a millenium-long historical process. The cradle of the caste system within the Indo-Nepalese population group is today generally considered among scientists to be the Karnali region in distant West Nepal. It is very probable that three migration streams met each other there at the beginning of this millenia: 1) Hindus from the North Indian Plain – as is the assertion of a number of myths, and to which can be traced the origins of Nepal's caste of warriors from the ruling houses in Rajasthan; 2) the Khas, who came here from the West, as well as 3) members of a variety of different ethnic groups which emigrated from Tibet. The Khas are considered the founders of the Jumla Empire (12th-14th

Bathing in the holy Bagmati River is said to have a purifying effect.

century); evidently under their rulership the transition from Buddhism to Hinduism there was completed and a caste system peculiar to the region was established. Furthermore, it is of great significance that groups which had established their dominance in the Jumla Empire after its ruin gradually continued to conquer surrounding areas, and in the process established a great number of principalities between the 14th and 16th centuries.

The Gorkha reign which finally resulted from these conquest invasions began a tremendous militarized expansion in the middle of the 18th century, the battalions of which conquered not only the western territories combining Kumaon and Garhwal (belonging today to India) but also the kingdoms of the Kathmandu Valley, the eastern regions up to the Mechi River, and the southern Terai region. After the military expansion

of the British East India Company in the year 1814, a stop was put to further conquest expeditions, and the borders of Nepal were drawn between the Kali and Mechi Rivers. During the several wars with Tibet the course of the northern frontier was determined in the middle of the 19th century.

It is of great significance for the development of the Hinduist caste system in Nepal that the rulers of such a "unified" empire – who traced their origins back to the above-mentioned houses of the western principalities – achieved political power over the other ruling noble families – in particular the Malla rulers of the kingdoms of the Kathmandu Valley. It was the Gorkha rulers who determined which among the ethnic groups were to be set free in the course of the 19th century.

Contrary to widely held opinion, the caste system was not completely eliminated in the year 1963 – even if modern legislation treats all Nepalese citizens as being of equal birth.

ROYAL CITIES IN THE KATHMANDU VALLEY

KATHMANDU

PATAN

BHAKTAPUR

KATHMANDU VALLEY

KATHMANDU

According to the local chronicles, Kathmandu was founded in the tenth century by King Gunakamadeva. However, in this case one must speak rather of a new religious order in the settlement, which was already in existence – if not yet organized. In any event, it led to the establishment of addional shrines and sanctuaries.

Legends tell how Gunakamadeva had a dream in which the goddess Malakshmi appeared. She charged him with the task of founding the city of Kantipur (an old name for Kathmandu) at the place where the Vishnumati and Bagmati Rivers flow together. The city was to have the shape of a sword (an attribute of the goddess). The king undertook his task as he had been ordered, and for protection, he placed all the important gods around and about the city.

The present-day layout of the old city stems from the 16th century. It was only at this time that Kathmandu gained importance with regard to the older city of Bhaktapur. The rulers Mahendra Malla (1560 to 1574) and Pratapa Malla (1641

Preceding pages: Annapurna II and IV. Night-time on Durbar Square. Left: The Kathmandu pottery market.

to 1674) encouraged much building activity during the Malla period.

The limits of the old city are no longer marked everywhere by the city wall, however the enclosed heart of the city has been extensively preserved. The **New Road** was only constructed after the catastrophic earthquake of the January 15th, 1934, to make the widest possible approach – suitable for parades – to the palace area.

Today the capital city Kathmandu attracts ever larger portions of the population from the whole country. Nonetheless, the city still hasn't suffered the fate of many other large Asian cities, which are in danger of suffocating from the masses of humanity, traffic, slums and hectic construction activities. Kathmandu has no underground sewer system, no adequate water supply, only a few properly paved streets – but above all, it has no money. It may be that this last factor alone has hindered the complete re-shaping of such a traditional city, which has already succumbed to the automobile and is criss-crossed with electricity and telephone wires. To be sure, fashionable concrete buildings and cheap corrugated tin roofs already disfigure the city quite enough, but even so, the old city centers of the Kathmandu Valley have forfeited none of their charm and fascination.

65

KATHMANDU

0   500m

Palace and Durbar Square

One point of attraction of the three royal cities of the Kathmandu Valley is formed by their respective palace areas. In Kathmandu the palace is particularly extensive, rebuilt in 1975 in its present form with the assistance of UNESCO on the occasion of the crowning of King Birendra Shah. This **Durbar Square** (see also the sketch on p. 69) encompasses the entire richness of Nepalese religiosity and culture, and it clearly shows the various types of Nepalese art and architecture. The basic form of the palace, with its courtyards and numerous auxiliary buildings, was first designed by Mahendra Malla (1560 to 1574) and since then it has been expanded and reconstructed several times. Both of the interior courtyards, **Mul Chowk** and **Sundhara Chowk** (off-limits to foreigners), as well as the Palace Garden (**Bhandarkbal**) go back to the rule of Pratapa Malla (1641 to 1674). In 1672 he also had the huge Hanuman statue erected next to the entrance gate, which is perpetually smeared with cinnobar powder and covered with a red cloth. It gave the entire area its name – **Hanuman Dhoka**, who is supposed to protect the palace from ghosts and illnesses.

Pratapa Malla was a cosmopolitan ruler. Evidence of this is borne out by the stone tablet on the main face of the palace, on which the goddess Kalika is revered in fifteen languages. One can admire the ruler himself on the columns in the front plaza, erected in 1670, as well as on the **Rani Pokhri**. Similar columns were modeled on these columns in Patan and Bhaktapur.

Nepal's rulers especially like to immortalize themselves with statues. Eight equestrian statues more or less define the boundaries of the **Tundhikhel Square**, and standing in between is a memorial to the martyrs of the Rana rulership, as documentation of the protests against this

67

despotic period of Nepal's history. Several Shah-kings, among them Prithvi Narayan (1769 to 1775), Tribhuvan (1911 to 1915), and Mahendra (1955 to 1972), are repesented by large and imposing bronze statues.

Undoubtedly the most prodigious testimonial of the Rana period would have to be the **Singha Durbar**, which was constructed in 1903 for the prime minister in the western pseudo-baroque style. Later the Shah government took over the building, all but the main wing of which burned down in 1973. It has only gradually been reconstructed. Since the end of the 19th century, the King himself has lived in the **Narayan Miti Palace** on the northern edge of the old city. The older buildings of the palace were constructed by the Rana princes, the new section in 1969 by Mahendra Shah. The Shah and Rana rulers left behind great monuments in the old King's Palace in Kathmandu. It is an original nine-storied palace tower on the southern edge of the palace grounds which has especially richly carved window frames – behind which the queens are supposed to have once observed the goings-on at the **Basantpur Plaza** from an aristocratic distance.

Nearby is the **Gaddi Baithak**, a long throne-hall which the Premier Chandra Shamsher Rana had constructed and luxuriously appointed in 1908, inspired by a trip to London.

The Votive Temples

The rulers of Nepal have not only immortalized themselves in palaces and statues, but also with temples to the gods, which they have built to commemorate themselves or their close relatives. These were built mostly from contributions and gifts of land to the primarily private communities – the so-called *guthis*. However, since the introduction of a new law which places the guthis under the guardianship of the state, this traditional system has

been almost completely destroyed, with the result that many temples are no longer taken care of.

The Durbar Square is filled with these sorts of votive temples. The Trailokya Mohan Mandir (also called the **Narayan Temple**) which is dedicated to Vishnu, was ordered built by King Parthivendra Malla (1680 to 1687) in memory of his brother Nripendra Malla. In 1689, Riddhilakshmi, the widow of Parthivendra, donated an impressive **Garuda Figure**, which is a copy of another statue dating from the eighth century.

Riddhilakshmi's highly influential minister was involved with this, and he also donated – in memory of himself – a three-roofed **Shiva Temple** in **Jaisi Devai**, a copy of which, the **Maju Deval**, Queen Riddhilakshmi had built on Durbar Square in 1692.

Another such votive temple is to be found in the immediate neighborhood. This is the elongated **Shiva Parvati Temple**, so-named because this god-couple leans out from the wooden windows of its highest floor. In its interior, the temple – which was founded by Rana Bahadur Shah (1777 to 1790) – shelters the Nine Durga Goddesses.

One of the oldest temples in the Hanuman Dhoka is the **Jagannath Temple**, which was also founded by Rana Bahadur Shah in 1797. It is particularly famous for the erotic wood-carvings in its roof-buttresses. The Nepalese sometimes add to their explanation of these sexual scenes the notion that, out of shame, the goddess "Lightning" would spare this wooden temple. But, no doubt, the actual reason for these carvings is to be found in the old fertility cults and in the religion of Tantrism.

One further **Jagannath Temple** was founded in the same year by Rana Bahadur Shah. This stands in the city prison and is only one of many votive temples outside the old quarter of Kathmandu.

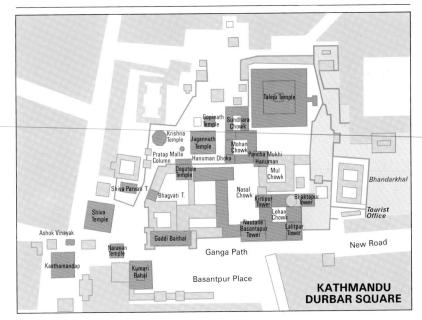

**KATHMANDU
DURBAR SQUARE**

The Seats of the Goddesses

Besides the votive temples, which are mostly dedicated to Shiva or Vishnu, the rulers also secured the assistance of the goddesses, who are so powerful in Nepal. Lording over the northern side of the Durbar Square is the **Taleju Temple**, the largest and tallest temple in the entire Kathmandu Valley. The goddess Taleju, a manifestation of the Durgas, was the goddess of the Malla kings, who worshipped her with blood sacrifices. As a family deity she has still another residence on the Durbar Square: the three-storied **Degutale Temple**, which was erected by Shivasimha Malla (1578 to 1619), but completely renovated by Pratapa Malla (1641 to 1674). According to the chronicles, Ratna Malla (1484 to 1520), the youngest son of Yaksha Malla, is supposed to have brought a magical diagram from Bhaktapur to Kathmandu, in order to obtain power there with its help. Mahendra Malla (1560 to 1574) had the temple expanded. In the process he gave

it three roofs and placed the entire temple on a five-stepped pedestal, so that the goddesses would be visible also in the neighboring cities.

In addition, a living goddess bestows authority on the King. She is the *Kumari*, a maiden who is seen as a manifestation of the Durgas. Every year in the *Indra-jatra* festival, the King is ritually confirmed again in his office. This child-goddess lives the whole year round in the first floor of the **Kumari Bahal**, a Buddhist monastery building, richly endowed with wood carvings, which was constructed in 1757 by Jayaprakasha Malla (1735 to 1768). The Kumari at the Palace of Kathmandu is the most prominent of many living goddesses in the Kathmandu Valley. They are all chosen from particular, mostly Buddhist castes and must appear especially fearless and undauntable. In order to determine this, they are locked in a dark room or they are shown horrible masks of demons, and if they don't cry, this is considered one of several signs of their divine predilection.

69

Once they are chosen, the girls continue to be Kumaris until puberty. They do not all lead as isolated a life as the Royal Kumaris in Kathmandu, who must be carried during their few "excursions" outside of the Kumari Bahal, in order not to touch the impure ground. After their time, the Kumaris receive a pension from the state or their village council. They rarely marry, for it brings bad luck to marry an ex-goddess.

Taleju and Kumari are representatives of the numerous goddesses in the Kathmandu Valley who must be worshipped with blood sacrifices and alcohol. They frequently appear in small groups as in, for example, the Eight Mothers (*Ashthamatrika*) or the Nine Durgas (*Navadurga*), and have their temples on the edges of the cities, from where they can protect the communities. Also associated with them are stories of human sacrifice. Some of the goddess-temples are spoken of only with a shudder, as they are thought of as places where murderous demons carry out their mischief. Among

Town festivals are particularly important for the inhabitants of Kathmandu Valley.

these are the three-storied temple of *Naradevi* (also referred to as *Shvetakali*), in which the goddess is bethroned on two people, and the residence of *Luti-Ajima* (also called *Indrani*), which is located among the northern cremation sites along the Vishnumati River.

Many holy places of the goddess seem insignificant, because their sanctuaries - for example that of *Raktakali* in the **Tangal** quarter of the city – often shelter only a raw, uncarved stone. However, these temples and shrines typically host more festivals and rituals than many a monumental commemorative temple for a more peaceful god. Of *Bhadrakali* it is said that she transformed bread into gold, as, when she had assumed the form of a crying child, a farmer gave her his loaf of bread. The **Lumarhi Temple**, once between fields and meadows, is now located on a busy traffic island south of the Tundhikel Square.

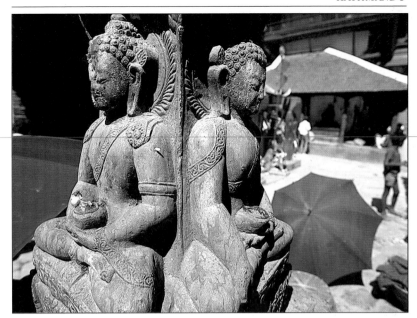

Statues of Buddha Shakyamuni, the "wise man of the Shakya family".

The Little Big Gods

Still another highly-worshipped deity has become a victim of street traffic on Kathmandu's parade ground: *Mahakala*, whose shrine is located across from the military hospital. The god is venerated by Buddhists as protector of the monastery, and is worshipped by Hindus as *Bhairava* (Shiva in his most fear-inspiring aspect, but also a fully independent god).

Scarcely an automobile driver fails to greet this god as he drives past, especially on Saturdays, when multitudes of believers make their pilgrimages there. The reason for this: At one time a priest is supposed to have tried to capture the god in the stone statue forever. Mahakala, however, resisted this idea, because he, as "Great Time"- the meaning of his name – must endlessly circle around the Earth. Finally though, he acquiesced - he would live in the stone each Saturday.

Bhairava is a very popular god in the Kathmandu Valley. His function ist primarily a protective one. He also accepts blood sacrifices. At the Hanuman Dhoka are two of his most famous effigies: a five-meter high statue – the **Kala ("Black") Bhairava**, and, a couple of steps further south, the Sveta Bhairava. The origin and age of the Kala Bhairava sculpture are uncertain, but it was transported to Durbar Square by order of Pratapa Malla in the 17th century. In front of the large, colorfully painted statue, officers of the court had, at one time, to swear their oaths of loyalty and witnesses attest to the truth of their statements.

The **Sveta ("White") Bhairava** (also mistakenly referred to as Akash Bhairava) is in the form of a large, gilded head, mostly hidden behind a grating which is only removed during the *Indrajatra* festival. At this time rice beer sometimes streams from his mouth. The statue was donated by Rana Bahadur Shah in 1795 on the occasion of the *Indrajatra*. Likewise, the huge mask of **Akasha**

71

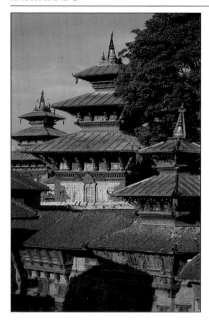

("air, sky") **Bhairava** is fetched from the temple of the same name, which lies near from the turbulent Indra Chowk.

A wild festival, at which much blood and alcohol flows, is held for **Pacali Bhairava** in southern Kathmandu. On the fifth day of *Dasain* he is brought by farm-boys – in the form of a large urn of rice beer – from the old city to his open shrine, where he is represented in the form of a black stone. Next to that is a life-size *betal* (demon) made of bronze, which lies on the ground. Pacali Bhairava is supposed to have hidden himself there after he was caught spending a passionate night with a slaughter-girl of lowly caste.

These small shrines play a major role in the hearts of the local residents. For example, almost every house worships a stone deity made of plaster – kept standing in front of the threshold – in order to ward off demonic dangers and for the elimination of ritual impurification. Almost every household also has its own little shrine in which one demonstrates respect for one's ancestors.

As is true of all Newar cities, the old city of Kathmandu is composed of small blocks of houses (called *tol* in Nepali), in which the people live – separated according to caste and family – in brick houses, some with elaborately carved wooden window-frames and brick roofs that have become overgrown with moss. Only very gradually did these blocks of houses grow together into today's densely-packed urban structure. However, in the numerous city festivals the old lines of separation are still recognizable, as for example between the upper and lower sections of the city.

Each and every *tol* has its protective Ganesh shrine, where now and then the elephant-headed god is called upon for very special purposes. Especially memorable to see among these is the "**Toothache Ganesh**," where one pounds in a nail to alleviate the pain, or at the **Ashoka Vinyaka** or **Maru Ganesh** on the Durbar Square, a small shrine which is worshipped by almost all passers-by in order to ease some ague.

The individual quarters of the city are mostly connected only by very narrow streets in which even a riksha can block up the traffic. Only one large street crosses the old city: the trade route between India and Tibet. Along this traditional route the traders cluster their businesses, offering everything for sale that the market demands – from aromatic spices and rusty old nails to souvenirs for the tourists.

The narrow character of the city is relieved only in the public places. Especially on the **Indra Chowk** and in **Asan Tol**, where the old north-south road crosses a smaller street, a riot of color always dominates the scene. Also in Asan Tol stands the **Annapurna Temple**, which received its present form in 1839 from Rajendra Bikram Shah. Here this highly revered mother-goddess is portrayed as a silver pitcher wrapped in snakes – a symbol for divine fulfilment

The inner courtyard of the Kumari Chowk.
Left: Bhagavati Mandir on Durbar Square.

and fertility, on which the farmers who spread out their goods before the temple, are particularly dependent.

On the plazas one finds numerous rest-houses (called *sattal* or *pati* in Nepali) for pilgrims and traveling traders. These buildings, open toward the street, were also funded by the well-to-do. On the **Maru Tol** alone – south-east of the Hanuman Dhoka – one finds four such *sattals*: **Simhaa Sattal, Lakshmi-Narayana Sattal, Nasa** or **Kavindrapura Sattal** (erected around 1672 by Pratapa Malla for the dance-god Nasadyo) and **Maru Sattal**. This latter resting-house is better-known by its original Sanskrit name, for which verification exists dating from 1143 A.D. **Kasthamandapa**, which literally means "wooden hall", after which Kathmandu is named. The square-shaped three-story building shelters at its center a statue of

the saint Gorakhnath and also serves as an abode for the cult of his followers, the so-called Kanphatta ascetics.

Water Installations

In Hinduism, a bath cleanses one not only of dirt, but also of ritual defilement. It was therefore of religious merit to found such bathing-places. The largest water installation in Kathmandu is the rectangular **Rani Pokhri**, the artificial "Sea of the Kings" which Pratapa Malla had constructed in order to help his wife to get over the loss of a beloved son. In the center of the pond he placed a Shiva temple, which was renovated after the devastating earthquake of 1934 by Jang Bahadur Rana. Another especially wide and beautiful water installation is located just behind the post office. It was named **Sundhara** because the water flows into it through gilded spouts in the stylized form of a mythical water-dragon (*sun* means "gold" in Nepali). The installation was built around 1825 by Bhimsen Thapa at

73

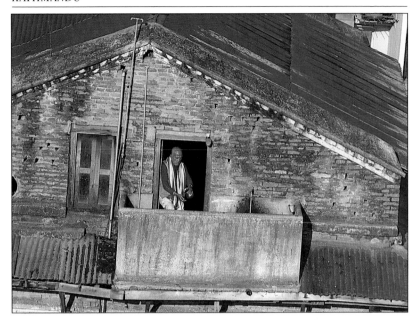

the wish of Queen Tripurasundari. This prime minister also had the nearby tower **Dharahara**, also known as **Bhimsen-stambha** erected in the style of a Mogul minaret. This construction work also came crashing down in the earthquake of 1934, but was later reconstructed – albeit a bit smaller.

The bathing-places on the Bagmati and Vishnumati Rivers also originated largely during the Shah and Rana periods. Both on the **Kalamocan Ghat** and in the Tripureshva section of the city, the Rana princes had them extended and embellished them with numerous votive temples. In front of the **Hema Narayan Temple**, the most prominent of these – Jang Bahadur Rana – is to be seen on a column which is dated 1874.

Buddhist Monasteries and Sanctuaries

In contrast to the temples devoted to Hinduism, Buddhist temples are to be found almost exclusively in interior courtyards. Among their distinguishing

Brahmans at a purification ceremony.

features is a Buddha Shakyamuni statue, at least one Caitya cult object and frequently also a secret deity of Tantric worship in their first stories. Besides these, the temples rarely lack statues of Mahakala or Ganesha and Nasadyo – the god of dance – who is mostly represented as only a hole or slit in a wall. The gate entrances are frequently ornamented with artistic carvings or hewn metal, and on the roofs there is often a sort of bell-tower *(gajura)* visible from a good distance.

The more than fifty monasteries in Kathmandu – called in Newari *baha* (in Nepali: *bahal*) or bahi, according to their size – are differentiated by the type of building, caste and function with which they are associated. The ostentatious monastery buildings, which have lent their names to many sections of the city, no longer shelter any monks, but serve rather as temples and centers for the ritual life of Buddhist groups.

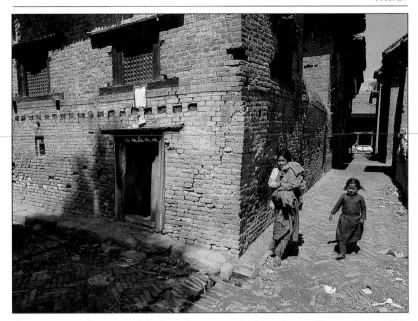

Street scene in the center of Kathmandu.

Many of the monastery buildings conceal treasures of art history, such as rare statues, buttresses and roof pillars (for example the **Yatkha Baha** from the 14th century) or stupas and caityas. These cult-edifices, often privately donated, characteristically have a vertical shaft in their interiors which represents the Buddha, his teachings and the creation of the world. In the **Dhoka Baha** is one of the oldest known votive-caityas, dating from the seventh century and including sculptures of Shakyamuni, Avalokiteshvara and others. The **Sighah Baha** (also called **Srigha Caitya** or **Kathesimbhu**) has become well-known because it is a replica of Svayambhunath Stupa. In **Tukan Baha** in the south of Kathmandu is a caitya with Licchavi statues.

In the **Jana Baha** between Indra Chowk and Asan Tol there is a sanctuary of a special sort – the **Seto** ("white") **Matsyendranath Temple**, which is

watched over by two lion sculptures. It is also named **Sanu** ("smaller") **Matsyendranath** in order to distingush it from the larger **Rato** ("red") **Matsyendranath** located in Patan. Both gods have a lot in common, particularly in that they are also worshipped as *Padmapani Avalokiteshvara* (an especially popular god of protection among the Buddhists) and in the several-day-long festival, during which the gods are carried on procession wagons to a neighboring village. However, everything about the Seto Matsyendranath is smaller, so that one is inclined to believe the legend that the cult in Kathmandu is at least partly an imitation of those in Patan and Bungamati.

PATAN

In contrast to the Hindu-Buddhist Kathmandu and the dominantly Hindu Bhaktapur, **Patan** is a pre-eminently Buddhist city. In the legends of its founding this becomes quite clear: According to these, Patan is supposed to have been founded by the Buddhist emperor Ashoka (268 to 233 B.C.) and his daughter Carumati. The legend has it that Ashoka laid a central stupa and four additional stupas as the corner-points of the city. In fact there are four of this type of stupa located around the old quarter. They indicate the four points of the compass, at the end of the two crossed streets which extend through Patan. The fifth, central stupa is believed to be in the interior of the **Patuko Blocks** northeast of the palace grounds, where, however, there is only a roughly ten-meter-high mound of earth to be found.

It is unlikely that the origins of these so-called **Ashoka Stupas** really can be traced to the great Indian ruler. At any rate, their unadorned forms make anything approaching an exact dating very difficult, and up to this time excavations have still not been permitted. They are usually only flattened-out hemispherical earthen hills constructed during the 19th century. Only the northern stupa has been embanked with cement.

To the present day, little is known about the further history of Patan. The city first became the independent seat of a king under King Siddhi Narashima Malla (1620 to 1661) Under this king and both of his successors – Shrinivasa Malla (1661 to 1684) and Yoganendra Malla (1684 to 1705) – Patan experienced an architectural revival, which even today is still easily perceived at the larger endowment temples and especially the palace area. The conqueror of the Kathmandu Valley, King Prithvi Narayan Shah, laid the city open to plundering, so that numerous valuable art treasures were stolen. The earthquake of 1934 also caused heavy damage to the city.

Monastery Complexes

The original Buddhist character of Patan shows itself especially in its more than 150 former monasteries. Nearly every fourth courtyard entrance leads into one such monastery building. In the majority of the cases these are not shelters for Buddhist monks but secular living-space for Newar families. These are called *Vajracharya* (literally "master of the Vajra") or, after the name of the historical Buddha, *Shakya*. The monasteries represent the center of the religious community (*sangha*).

In the 14th century, Jayastithi Malla introduced – more ore less by force – a system of castes. Also in Patan the ruling families were Hindu, although they tolerated the Buddhist population. However, the influence of Hinduism led to a situation in which the different groups of Buddhists also cut themselves off from one-another. In this way it came about that the membership of a monastery was increasingly decided by relatives, and not through the wish to lead the life of an alms-seeking monk. In fact, membership in a *sangha* means only that one of one's forefathers was initiated as a monk in the monastery. Of course, one only remains a monk during the few days of the iniatiation rites, but one stays a member of the congregation and monastery for the rest of one's life.

As in Kathmandu, tradition also differentiates between the 18 main monasteries (*baha*) and numerous secondary mo nasteries (*bahi*). One of the most well-known monasteries – and the most significant main monastery in Patan – is the **Kva Baha** or **Hiranya Varna Mahavihar**. It has not only the largest congregation, with over two thousand initiated members, it also has an especially rich endowment. Many inscriptions on the monastery, the earliest dating from the end of the 14th century, bear witness to the numerous donations it has received.

As soon as you step into the inner courtyard, you will see why the monastery has also been designated the "**Golden Temple**", as you glimpse several gilded statues and the three gilded copper

PATAN

0   500 m

roofs of the main shrine. In this temple, with its impressive wooden windows, both the high deity Akshobhya (one of the five transcendental Buddhas) and the Buddha Shakyamuni in his basic attitude – touching the earth – can be seen. They are both frequently portrayed with the same iconographic identifying features, so that it is not always possible to tell one from the other, all the more so when – as is also true in Kva Baha – the statue is covered with decorative objects, so that it is no longer clearly recognizable.

In the center of the courtyard stands a further temple with a gilded roof. This is a shrine with the clan-deity of the congregation, a caitya from the Licchavi period. The courtyard is surrounded by a corridor with oil-lamps, prayer wheels, and many sanctuaries, among them three life-size bodhisattva statues in the corners. Apart from the periodically changing guards of the gods, nobody lives in the houses which surround the courtyard. There prayers are said and holy texts are read, or religious songs sung. In the upper floor of the north wing, there are also especially valuable Tibetan frescos to be seen.

One of the oldest monasteries is the **Uku Baha** (also named **U Baha** or **Rudravarna Mahavihara**). Its courtyard is full of votive caityas and a variety of different statues: Manjushri, a Vajra, pairs of animal figures, a statue of Juddha Shamsher – the prime minister at the time of the 1934 earthquake, who also donated a lot of money for the monastery's renovation – as well as a member of the congregation who, in 1716, had a large statue of himself erected in the courtyard. The highest deity of the broad, two-storied main temple is a statue of the transcendent Buddha Akshobya, which is surrounded by many other Dhyanibuddhas or bodhisattvas. South of the Uku Baha stands the great **Yantarivi Caitya** (also called **Yatalibi Caitya**), in which there are said to reside more than fifty Buddhist deities, and was supposedly privately founded around 1684 by a certain Ratna Simha.

Similarly associated with the Uku Baha is the **Mahabouddha Baha** with a temple by the same name, which has become famous as the "**Temple of the Thousand Buddhas**." Here, each of the over 9000 bricks carries a likeness of a transcended Buddha. It is a taller building in the Shikara style, which served as a model for a similar temple in the Indian Bodh Gaya (where Buddha achieved his enlightenment).

The Mahabouddha Temple is supposed to have been founded by a rich coin-minter, and was first consecrated around 1600. This building was also seriously damaged by the earthquake of 1934, however it was possible to restore it to its original form with the help of the memory of the local population. In contrast to most of the other monastery complexes, there are no further shrines in the narrow courtyard, which is so narrow that a view of the entire temple ia hardly possible.

On the other hand, the courtyard of the **Tanga Baha** or **Jesthvarna Mahavihara** is completely overflowing with votive caityas, stone sculptures, prayer-mills and inscriptions. The **Minataha Temple** constitutes the central point of this complex, which is dedicated to Jatadhari Lokeshvara, a form of Padmapani Lokeshvara. This is a richly decorated building in the style of a pagoda, with two roofs. Its age is not precisely known, although the monastery was already mentioned in the twelfth century.

The Macchendranath Temple

The nearby **Macchendranath Temple** is also a sanctuary for a god with many names and faces. Macchendranath is also referred to as *Bungadyo*, because one of the numerous legends about him claims that he originated in the small village of Bungamati. Still to this day, during the

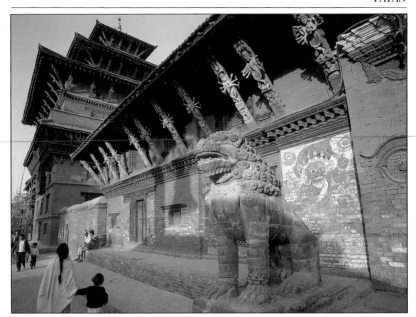

Stone lions keeping watch over King's Palace in Patan.

winter months a figure of this god is brought to the village, which is located ten kilometers south of Patan.

At some uncertain time, this village-god was identified with the bodhisattva Padmapani Avalokiteshvara. In the middle of the 18th century he first received the Hindu name Rato ("red") Macchendranath, in order to distinguish him from the Seto ("white") Macchendranath of Kathmandu.

The Macchendranath in Patan has become a major syncretistic national god of Nepal, because he plays an important role in the fertility of the country. He is supposed to have brought a twelve year long drought to an end, when the great Yogi Gorakhnath meditated on nine snakes, which are considered to be bringers of rain. According to the Buddhists, Gorakhnath had only done this to lure Avalokiteshvara to Nepal, after which , in his unmeasurable benevolence (one of his further names is Karunamaya, "the god filled with compassion") he ended the drought.

The Hindus explain Gorakhnath's behavior rather differently. Macchendranath is also considered to be Gorakhnath's teacher. At the instruction of the legendary priest Bandhudatta, Macchendranath is supposed to have been brought from Assam to Nepal. Gorakhnath stood up to show respect for his guru and had to allow the snakes to escape.

The significance of Macchendranath as a provider of rain is especially obvious in his huge festival. From the beginning of summer by the Newari calendar (the end of April) until the beginning of the rainy season (in June) Macchendranath is paraded through the city on a wagon over ten meters in height. Following him is a smaller temple wagon which is dedicated to Minanatha. At seven precisely determined points in Patan the god-chariots are worshipped by the population. The high-point of the festival is reached when the wagons arrive in the **Jawalakhel** quarter in the western side of Patan. Then, in the presence of the king, the priest shows the believers a black shirt belonging to the god – an important moment in the ceremony, during which it is vital that several drops of rain should fall.

Durbar Square

The square in front of the former King's Palace exhibits less of a Buddhist than a Hindu structure. The Malla rulers also tolerated Buddhist religiosity, but worshipped predominantly Hindu gods themselves. Perhaps the most significant indication of this religious tolerance is to be found in a **gilded window** on the front of the palace. In its center the bodhisattva Avalokiteshvara can be seen, supported by various riding animals, among them Vishnu's Garuda-bird, and surrounded by Hindu gods including Ganesh and Shiva-Parvati. This window is removable, and therein, on certain occasions, the King himself appears – to a certain degree in place of both Buddha and Vishnu.

The Royal Bath in the Sundri Chowk.

The square is divided into two areas – the northern contains the **Durbar Square** with the royal palace and diverse shrines, the southern **Mangal Bazaar** includes numerous businesses and street-vendors. The center-point is also the intersection of both of the major streets which cut across Patan. The impressive, three-level **Degutale Temple** stands in the middle of the old grounds of the royal palace. The Kathmandu-King Shivasimha Malla (1578 to 1619) gave one of his sons the familial-goddess Degutale (one form of the Durgas) to bring with him to Patan, and also charged him with the task of erecting a temple modeled after the Degutale Temple in Kathmandu.

Under Siddhinarasimha (1619 to 1661) the entire royal palace was generously expanded. Included in this work were a few temples, magnificent courtyard-grounds (*chowk*) and several gardens, among them the great **Palace Garden**

Bhandarkhal in the southeast. Under Vishnu Malla, the Durbar Square acquired more or less its present-day form. Three inner courtyards are connected to the Degutale Temple. In the north stands the **Manikeshava Chowk**, which was added around 1660. It occupies the site where an old Licchavi palace originally stood. At any rate, that is what an inscription there from 643 A.D. indicates. Today its courtyard accomodates a small **Archeological Museum**.

In the south is found an octagonal **Taleju Temple** (to which belongs the imposing **Taleju Bell** on the other side of the street, erected in 1737), which is adjacent to the **Mul Chowk** – both built in 1666 by Shivasimha Malla. Finally we find the **Sundari Chowk** with what is quite probably the most beautiful fountain installation in the Kathmandu Valley. A particularly notable feature here is the old **royal bath** of Shrinivasa Malla (1661 to 1684). In the circular depths of the bath there are numerous niches which are decorated with reliefs of primarily Tantric gods. The water flows into the pool from the jaws of a Makara-dragon.

On the western side of the north-south street which cuts across the palace grounds there are several Vishnuist shrines, which were founded mostly as votive temples by the Malla rulers. In the extreme south end, Princess Yogamati had the octagonal **Krishna Temple** – also called **Cyasing Devai** because of its shape – erected in 1723 in memory of her son Yogaprakasha Malla, who met an early death.

Further north is found the three-levelled **Temple of Harishankara** (a combined manifestation of both Vishnu and Shiva). This was also ordered built by Yogamati, this time in memory of her father Yoganarendra Malla (1684-1705), who in his day had two statues – of himself and his son – put up on a tall column in front of the Degutale Temple in 1693. A similar column, namely that of Pratapa

**PATAN
DURBAR SQUARE**

Malla, stands in Kathmandu. Only the King of Bhaktapur, Bhupatindra Malla, had no column to show for himself at the beginning of the 18th century. Out of jealousy he is supposed to have killed a son of Yoganarendra Malla through some secret method – or so it is said in one legend.

The oldest temple on the Durbar Square is the **Car Narayana Temple** from the year 1566. Its roof-buttresses, which feature the various manifestations of Vishnu, are particularly impressive. An unusual building for the Kathmandu Valley is the **Krishna Temple** (also called the **Bala Gopala Temple** after Krishna's child-like manifestation). It was founded in 1637 by King Siddhinarasimha Malla (1619 to 1661). It was modelled on the Islamic architecture of the Moguls and on a similar temple in north-Indian Mathura. Surrounding a **Shikhara Tower** there are small pavilions on three levels which include columns and built-in arcade passages. Inside these there are lengthy renderings of scenes in relief from the great

81

Indian epics *Mahabharata* and *Ramayana*. The reliefs are also partly explained in the Newari language. The gilded **Garuda Bronze** in front of the temple was also contributed by Siddhinarasimha Malla. This temple is also the highest holy place for the ever increasing adherents of Krishna-worship, who distinguish themselves in the singing of their especially devout religious songs. In August and September the king also participates in the celebration of Krishna's birthday.

Besides Vishnu and Krishna, there are also several shrines on the Durbar Square dedicated to Shiva. Again, Siddhinarasimha Malla founded the huge two-storied **Vishvashara** (called **Vishvanath Temple**) in 1627. Most probably the ruler is portrayed as one of the two riders on the stone elephants at the east entrance.

Many of the buildings in the northern section of Durbar Square are closely connected with another legend concerning the founding of Patan: An ugly grass-cutter from the Lalitvana Forest, who was a great worshipper of the goddess Mani-

yogini, is supposed to have found a fountain of youth at this spot. When King Biradeva heard news of this event, he founded at the same place the city of **Lalitpur** (= Patan), in which he built a pond for the water-providing serpents, and on which he had erected various shrines, all of which were named after goddesses whose names begin with "Mani" (literally "jewel" or "precious stone"). In fact, even today several of the buildings and sanctuaries still carry these names. For example, the large fountain installation across from the Vishveshvara Temple received the name **Manidhara**. On the stairs to the accessible fountains there stand two pavilions. The one to the north is assigned a special function. This is the **Manimandapa**, at which astrologers gather every year in order to determine the most auspicious moment for the beginning of the Macchendranath procession. One can also see a stone throne in the hall, which Yogendra Malla had built in 1701 – as is indicated by an inscription on the back.

The three-leveled **Bhimsen Temple** in the northern part of the square dates back to the time of Shrinivasa Malla. It is rectangular and was not built on a pedestal – as is frequently the case with temples which are dedicated to Bhimsen and Bhairava. The temple is also not placed directly on the ground but is on the first floor. It was almost completely destroyed by a fire in 1862, but then it was again restored. It is said of Bhimsen that, at the time of Yogendra Malla, he threatened anyone passing by with annihilition. Therefore, the king asked his guru to do whatever he could to appease the god. The priest declined, and so the King appointed his brother to do the job, thus calming him down.

Kumbheshvara Temple

The **Kumbheshvara Temple**, in the north of the city, is considered the oldest

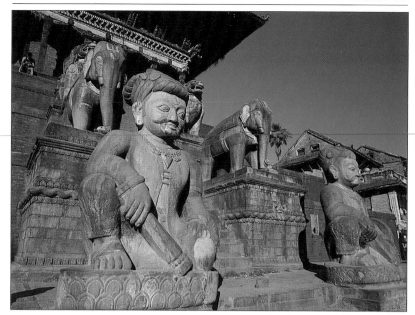

Left: Temple carving in Patan. The wrestlers at the entrance of Nyatapola temple.

temple in Patan. Jayasithi Malla (1382 to 1395) founded the shrine which is dedicated to one of the forms of Shiva, however since that time the building has been repeatedly expanded, and was even increased to five stories in height from its original two. As a result, the Nyatapola temple in Bhaktapur and this Kumbheshvara Temple are the only pagodas with five roofs.

Next to this temple one can see an artificial pond which – or so it is told – is fed with the holy water of Lake Gosainkund in the Himalaya Mountains. At the time of the full moon in the month of Shravana (July-August) a bath in this pool is supposed to be particularly profitable. At that time hundreds of pilgrims stream by to worship the four-faced *linga* in the temple.

In addition, a small temple is erected in the middle of the pond with a further *linga* especially for this occasion. Here,

as also at other Shiva-dedicated temples, the men of the higher castes exchange the holy beads which they receive at their initiations.

BHAKTAPUR

The third-largest city of the Kathmandu Valley is **Bhaktapur** ("city of the pious"), which is also named **Bhadagaon** ("rice-village"). It is located about 16 kilometers east of Kathmandu on the old trade route between India and Tibet, which is still today a vital artery cutting through the city. There are approximately 50,000 people residing in its heavily-populated old quarter, a large portion of whom are Newari Hindus. The majority of these are farmers, even though they have a rather urban appearance.

Of the three royal seats in the valley, Bhaktapur is the least disturbed by modern life. New buildings have been constructed only reluctantly, and motorized traffic generally stays out of the city. As a result, even today Bhaktapur offers one a

BHAKTAPUR

0   500 m

rare glimpse into a very nearly intact city of the Middle Ages.

The Nepalese-German **Bhaktapur Development Project** was an influential contributor to the preservation of Bhaktapur's historical character. The Project combines measures for the improvement of the quality of life (water supplies, sewer systems and road construction) with the renovation and restoration of selected buildings. One goal was – and still is – to avoid sacrificing tradition to unnecessary modernization.

According to legend, Bhaktapur is supposed to have been founded, with 12,000 houses, by King Anandadeva Malla (1147 to 1166), after which he turned his sovereignty over Kathmandu and Patan over to his older brother, Narendradeva Malla. However, in reality Bhaktapur is the product of several small settlements which grew together, and which in the course of time have expanded – especially during the rules of the Malla Kings Jayasithi (1382 to 1395), Yaksha (1428 to 1482), Jitamitra (1673 to 1696) and

Bhupatindra (1696 to 1722). In 1768 Bhaktapur lost its independence, when it could no longer hold its own after heavy battling with the troops of Prithvi Narayan Shah. The city is clearly separated into two sacrally contrasting areas: the upper city to the east and the lower city to the west. During certain festivals, as, for example, in the *Bisketjatra* in springtime, the people from these areas meet in heavy ritual battles.

Just as in the other Newar cities of the Kathmandu Valley, the public plazas represent the center points of the 24 quarters of the city. In Bhaktapur these are especially distinctive and often give the quarters their names. Things are especially lively on, for example, **Potters' Square**, where the potters' wheels spin perpetually and half-completed earthenware stands drying, ready for the kiln.

Durbar Square

In contrast to Kathmandu and Patan, the old palace is not located in the center of the city, but rather on its northern boundary. As a result, the front plaza is integrated to a lesser degree with the life of the city. The beginnings of the palace complex extend back to Yaksha Malla (1428 to 1482), however certain individual buildings and sculptures are older (see sketch on p. 86).

One of the earliest is dedicated to Taleju, the goddess of protection of the Malla kings, who had already been brought to the city at the beginning of the 14th century. In a high court, the **Mul Chowk**, she received her seat and temple. This is closed to non-Hindus, but you can catch a glimpse of the wooden tympanon above the entrance, two golden windows in the interior courtyard, wall murals all of which date from the 17th century, and the statue dated 1708/9 of King Jitamitra Malla alongside his wife. Surrounding the Mul Chowk there are several auxiliary courtyards and the **Nag Pokhri**, which is the royal bathing pond.

Access is gained to the temple grounds through a richly ornamented **Golden Gate**, the **Sundhoka**, in the royal palace. It was built into the face of the palace by the last king, Ranajit Malla, in 1753.

This same ruler also had a life-sized statue erected on a column in front of the gate, which portrays his father **Bhupatindra Malla** kneeling in reverence before Taleju, under the latter's patronage and protection. In its fundamental characteristics, the palace again has its origin with Jaksha Malla, and it was brought to completion under Bhupatindra Malla. The facade of the east wing – which is constructed of red brick and features 55 black, artfully-carved wooden windows – stands in stark contrast to the white-plastered west section, with its Islamic ornamentation and its gate, over which two large lion-statues stand watch. The **Bhaktapur Museum** is now accommodated in the west wing. It has on exhibit a collection of Newaric statues and Tibetan scroll-pictures (thangkas), as well as

mural paintings from the 17th century.

There are comparitively few monuments standing on the front plaza. It is clear from earlier drawings, that at one time the plaza was substantially more built up than it is now. Here too, the earthquake of 1934 caused heavy damage and destruction. In the west side of the palace grounds one can see some evidence of this destruction in the only provisionally reconstructed remainder of the **Shiva Temple**, which was originally much larger. In more recent times, a rectangular resting-house has been reconstructed, with German assistance, after its historical model on its original location.

Also found among the preserved or restored sanctuaries on the palace plaza is a replica of the Pashupatinath temple in Deopatan – the **Yaksheshvara Temple.** It is named after its founder, Yaksha Malla. He began construction of the temple in 1478, apparently so that he could worship Pashupati without having to travel the long distance to Deopatan. This temple was destroyed by the 1934 earthquake, and wasn't restored until 1968.

Not far from there stands the **Vatsala Temple**, built in the Shikara style. This goddess has her primary seat in the Pashupatinath Temple of Deopatan. Jagatprakasha Malla (1643 to 1672) had this temple erected in Bhaktapur. Still two further temples feature the north-Indian Shikara tower: a 1696 temple, probably founded by Bhupatindra Malla, which is believed to be dedicated to the goddess *Siddhilakshmi* and the stairs of which are bordered with various animal statues, and another **Durga Temple**, the builder and year of construction of which are unknown. The large double-levelled temple on the extreme west end of the plaza is locally designated as the **Narayan Temple.** However, it actually houses a cult illustration of Krishna. The constructor and year of founding of this building are unknown, but judging from the style it comes from the later 17th century.

**BHAKTAPUR
DURBAR SQUARE**

Taumadhi Square

Unlike the Durbar Square, **Taumadhi Square** is located in the center of the city, surrounded by old Newaric residences. Here there is alway a colorful riot of traders and passers-by. Two temples influence the character of Taumadhi Square: the Nyatapola Temple and the Bhairava Temple.

The **Nyatapola Temple** is the largest temple in Bhaktapur. It stands on a five-stepped pedestal, on the corners of which are four Ganesh shrines. The five-storied pagoda roof, at over thirty meters in height, towers over all the other buildings in the city. Apparently in competition with the gigantic Taleju Temple in Kathmandu, King Bhupindra Malla had the temple erected in 1703, which he dedicated to his god of protection. No one, with the exception of priests, is allowed to set foot inside its sanctuary, in which this goddess is worshipped with Tantric rituals. Accordingly, the temple is not named after the secret goddess, but

simply means "five-storied temple." The ascent to the temple is flanked by pairs of statues representing guardians and deities: first, there are two legendary wrestlers who are supposed to be ten times as strong as ordinary men, then lions, elephants and the mythological lion-clawed griffins. Finally, the series is completed by two Tantric guardian goddesses.

The three-storied **Bhairava Temple** was also founded by Bhupatindra Malla, in 1717. It is a rectangular building, in which the god has his seat in the top level. The actual cult-idol is kept in the interior, which is closed-off to foreigners. However, one can catch a glimpse of a comparable Bhairava mask between the first and second roofs.

One such mask is also taken from the Bhairava Temple and carried in a large procession wagon during Bhaktapur's huge **New Year's Procession**, the *Bisket-jatra*. Following this wagon is another in which the goddess Bhadrakali is transported. Both of the wagons stand on

The magnificent entrance to the Bhaktapur Palace: the "Golden Gate".

Taumadhi Square on the border between the upper and lower cities. At the beginning of the procession, men from both the city-sections play tug-of-war. At this point it is not unusual for heavy fighting to break out between the members of the different quarters, which have old rivalries. Most often, the struggle is won by the men of the higher social strata from the upper city. Only when the wagons have reached the square in the south is the new year brought in, with the ritual erection of a tall tree.

The large, somewhat elevated platforms on Taumadhi Square give also a sign of the sorts of festivals of which Bhaktapur has a good number. Normally these platforms serve as places for the sale of fruits, vegetables and fowl, however on certain days they become stages for rituals and religious festivals.

In the south-west section of the square there is a single-storied house into which the **Cafe Nyatapola** has been installed. Originally it was a residence and, in all probability, also the quarters of a local deity. Further south there is an adjoining temple courtyard, the **Narayan Chowk**. In it is located a two- storied pagoda, the **Tilmadhav Temple** (also called the Narayan Temple), which is dedicated to Vishnu. This place of worship was already mentioned in inscriptions dating from 1080, but the present form of the temple originated, as is also true of the Nyatapola and Bhairava Temples, in the earlier 18th century. In front of the entrance are three pillars featuring attributes of Vishnu, with his riding-mount **Garuda** in the center, surrounded by his discus and his conch.

The Tacapal Quarter

One further major square is located in the Tacapal Quarter on the eastern section of the old trade route that cuts through Bhaktapur. The center of this section of the city is represented by the three-storied **Dattatraya Temple**, which originally functioned as a place for assemblies as well as a wayside rest-house. The name of the temples means trinity, and accordingly, its sanctuary houses statues of the god-trio Brahma, Vishnu and Shiva-Mahadeva.

King Yaksha Malla is supposed to have had this wooden building constructed in the 15th century, which was then restored by his successor, Vishva Malla, in the middle of the 16th century. The front-building to the west as well as both of the wrestler figures – copies of the lower pair of statues in front of the Nyatapola Temple – come from the year 1860, as do the three columns with Garuda, discus and conch.

Another sanctuary, the rectangular two-storied **Bhimsen Temple**, is found in the west of the square. It is dedicated to the god *Bhimasena*, who is very popular because of his power. He is the idolized hero of the *Mahabharata* epic, and in Nepal is also the protective god of many castes of craftsmen. Adjoining the Bhimsen Temple to the rear is the largest fountain installation in Bhaktapur.

Located to the southeast behind the Dattatraya Temple is the **Pujari Math**, a house that originally served for the reception of sectarian pilgrims and the directorate responsible for alterations to temples. However, it was renovated in 1971-72 and transformed into a **Museum for Art Handcrafts**. The Pujari Math is especially well-known for the rich, finely-nuanced wood-carvings from the 18th century that grace its doors and windows. Particularly beautiful among these is the **Peacock Window** which faces the alley on the east side of the building.

Temple Groups

The number of shrines and temples that one also finds in Bhaktapur at thresholds, in every backyard and each street intersection is scarcely countable. However, these seemingly insignificant holy places frequently receive more attention than – for example – the great monuments on Durbar Square. Every morning each household demonstrates its membership to its section of the city, as a someone of the household, most frequently a woman, seeks out the nearest seat of the gods in the quarter. This might be a small enclosed shrine, or it could simply be an uncarved stone on the edge of a street. It may be dedicated to Ganesh, Bhairava, or the Divine Mothers. To these, prayers are said requesting assistance for the day. However, fulfilment of some concrete wish – the birth of a son, success in an examination, or luck in a game – might also be requested. In addition, the street-deities are also visited for protection against ritual impurification. The Hindus think of events such as birth and death as temporarily impurifying. Only certain gods and demons accept such defiling things as hair clip pings, umbilical cords and death-clothes. These deities reside mostly in the so-called **Chvasa Stones**, one of which is associated with every household. These can be recognized as lotus-shaped stones in the street pavements at intersections of public places.

Each quarter of the city is also assigned one of the various cremation places in the south of the city along the **Hanumati River**. When someone dies, his corpse is carried along precisely predetermined "death-paths" through the old city to the cremation place of his caste. At these so-called *ghats*, such as the **Kalighat** and **Hanumanghat**, are mostly only small shrines to the gods, votive temples and resting-houses.

Besides the individual gods for each section of the city there are groups of gods which protect the entire city. To these belong especially the Navadurghas and the Asthamatrika. The Nine Durghas have a common house, the **Navadurgha Temple** as it is called, in the eastern part

Entrance to the Dattatraya temple in the Tacapal quarter of Bhaktapur.

of the old quarter. In it masks of the gods are kept, which are employed by certain castes for rituals which occur mostly at night, always at different spots in and around Bhaktapur, where they dance for the protection of the city.

The Asthamatrika – which means "Eight Mothers" – have their shrines scattered around the core of the city. Several of these seats, such as, for example those of *Mahakali* and *Mahalakshmi* have been greatly expanded. The Eight Mothers are also expressions of old protective principles, according to which the gods must send their protection in the direction of the heavens. In this way the diversity of the world is brought into accordance with a cosmic order. In autumn during the *Dasain* Festival, many of the residents of Bhaktapur go to each of the Asthamatrika shrines for eight consecutive days, where they pray to the goddesses for a good rice harvest.

The goddesses do not only have their permanent homes in their shrines at the edges of the city, each has also a *Dyoche* – or god-house – inside the city. There, statues of them are kept, which one only has a chance to see during parades. These god-houses don't always turn out to be quite as large as the Mahakali Dyoche, but are often indistinguishable from normal residences.

THE KATHMANDU VALLEY

The Kathmandu Valley – which at about 25 kilometers in length and 15 in width is scarcely bigger than many a medium-sized city – has for ages been a point of intersection between two of the great cultures of Asia – the Indian and the Tibeto-Chinese. Only all too gladly do pilgrims, monks, and traders or threatened clans from the neighboring regions settle in the Valley – in order to wait out the snow thaw in the north, or the dangers of malaria in the swampy lower spurs of the Himalayas during the

VALLEY OF KATHMANDU

0   5   10 km

rainy season. The valley basin is surrounded by massive mountain chains, offering protection from enemies, and at an elevation of about 1,400 meters it has a mild, subtropical climate.

Little is known about the earliest settlements. They must have only been small villages comprising scarcely more than a couple of houses. In these lived Tibeto-Burmese speaking clans or tribes – the ancestors of the Newar, who now represent the majority of the population in the cities of the Kathmandu Valley.

For a long time the local rulers had only small areas of power. It wasn't until the reigns of Kings Jayasithi Malla (1392 to 1395) and especially Yaksha Malla (1428 to 1482) that the Valley was politically united. However, under Yaksha Malla's son, the empire again broke up into the three kingdoms of Kathmandu, Patan and Bhaktapur. With this came the beginning of a great period of cultural blossoming in the history of Nepal, for which we can thank many fantastic monuments and other unique objects.

What is found in Kathmandu, Patan and Bhaktapur in concentrated form appears again in the other towns which are scattered throughout the entire Valley. The smaller villages are for the most part not as diverse as the old royal cities. Their significance may lie rather in a single sanctuary, a particular caste structure, or their special location. Such is the case in, for example, **Banepa**, which was still a politically important city during the Malla period, and now has only a couple of small Vishnu temples and a temple to Candeshvari to show for itself. In the village **Chapagaon**, the Vajravahari Temple attracts believers. It is dedicated to a manifestation of Vishnu as a boar. Its central cult-image apparently comes from the fifth century.

In **Harisiddhi**, the temple of a goddess by the same name – who is said to demand human sacifice – and the mountain-based seat of the goddess Vajrayogini in **Shankhu** both have a special force of attraction, which extends far beyond the village limits. However,

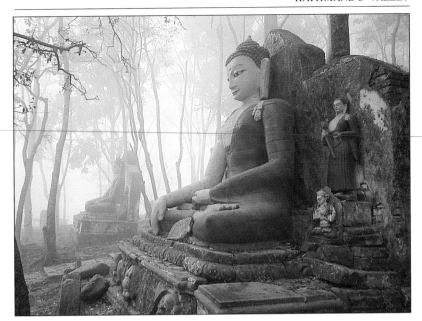

Statues of Dhyanibuddha Akshobhya on Svayambhunath Hill.

Thimi is unsuitably called "the city of potters". Although this caste has achieved an outstanding position there, the city, which is located between Kathmandu and Bhaktapur, offers a most exceptionally complex scene of religious buildings – among them a ritually important Balkumari temple from the 16th century.

Many of the hamlets on the cliffs or on the surrounding mountains have become well-known less because of their religious significance than for their location. They offer a most rewarding view on the Himalayan mountain-range or over the Kathmandu Valley. From the Newar city of **Dhulikhel** (30 km away from Kathmandu) you can gaze over the entire areas of Langtang, Helambu and also toward the east out to Makalu. The view from **Nagarkot** (15 km. northeast of Bhaktapur) also provides the beholder with an overwhelming panorama including mountains like the Annapurna Mas-

sif, the Ganesh Himal and the Lhotse. In springtime, when the tree-height rhododendrons are in bloom, it's worth a climb to the **Shivapuri** (2563 m.) to the north of Kathmandu, or to **Phulchowki** to the south which is accessible to traffic and from where one can overlook the entire Kathmandu Valley. The southern **Godavari** is also worth a day-trip because of its botanical gardens.

Svayambhunath

The fame of the most significant stupa in the Kathmandu Valley – that of **Svayambhunath**, which rises up over the valley basin on a hill to the west of the capital – reaches as far as Tibet. According to the legend, *Manjushri* – a bodhisattva and god of wisdom – found a lotus flower there as he was cutting through the surrounding mountains with his sword in order to drain the lake which once covered the valley. A Manjushri Temple, which the Hindus worship as the seat of Sarasvati – the goddess of wisdom and

Sleep – *niva home*
– sunrise

91

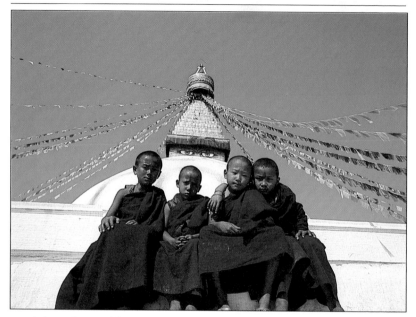

art – is located west of Svayambunath.

Even though the earliest inscription comes only from the year 1129, the **Svayambhunath** stupa must be considered one of the oldest religious places of the Valley. It has been renovated over and over again, most extensively after its partial destruction, suffered during the Islamic invasion in the middle 14th century. This is recorded in an inscription from 1372 A.D. the basic features of the stupa as it stands today almost certainly come from this time. The best approach to the stupa is from the east, up a staircase with 365 steps, which is bordered by several votive caityas and Akshobhya statues from the earlier Shah period. When you have reached the top, you will find yourself observed by one of the eyes of Buddha, which are painted on all four sides of the stupa's tower. They are a part of the complex symbolism of this sacred building: on the square ground-plan, an upwardly-inclined hemisphere is raised – the body of Buddha and symbol of his consummate perfection. Surrounding the

Young Tibetan monks in front of the Bodhnath stupa.

cupola is a balustrade with 211 prayer mills, each of which carry the holy mantra *Om mani padme hum* (Oh, you jewel in the lotus blossom).

The five *Dhyanibuddhas* or *Tathagathas* are also inserted alongside watchful riding animals in the recesses of the stupas: in the east are *Akshobya* on an elephant as well as *Vajrocana* on a lion; in the south *Ratnasambhava* on a horse, in the west *Amytabha,* who is the most worshipped of these, riding a peacock; and in the north, *Amoghasiddhi* on the heavenly bird Garuda. Between these transcendental Buddhas – embodying the five cosmic elements of earth, water, fire, wind and ether – are niches for their female aspects, the *Buddhashaktis.*

Thirteen shields, donated by the monasteries in the area, project from the tower, representing self-regenerating discs, which symbolize steps on the way to perfection and enlightenment. A central element of the stupa is a wooden post in the interior, which must be renewed regularly in great rituals.

The stupa is surrounded by resting houses for pilgrims, souvenir shops, Tibetan monasteries (*gompas*) from which loud prayers and muffled fanfares ring, and five special shrines, which represent three elements (wind, earth and fire) as well as two mystical snakes. Among the larger buildings there is also a much-attended temple which is dedicated to a goddess who gives protection from smallpox and childhood illnesses: *Hariti*, or, as she is called by the Hindus, *Sitala*.

Again, it was King Pratapa Malla who to a considerable degree gave shape to the grounds. From him came the large bronzen *Vajra* (Tibetan *Dorja*) dated 1667, which is on a large mandala to the east of the stupa. A *Vajra* is, in the mythology of Hinduism, a thunderbolt weapon of the gods. However in Buddhism it is rather a diamond scepter as a symbol of the absolute. Pratapa Malla also erected two sacred buildings in the style of the Hinduistic Shikara temple: **Pratapapura** and **Anantapura**, which, of course, are named after himself and his favorite wife – but are dedicated to the goddesses of Vajrayana Buddhism.

The countless votive caityas and sculptures which surround the Svayambhunath are evidence of the popularity of the stupa. These are for the most part not very old; in contrast to the equally popular Hinduist Pashupatinath sanctuary, astoundingly few holy places originated during the Licchavi period. Even the three life-size **Dipankara Statues** could not have been erected before the late Malla period.

Bodhnath

Next to the Svayambhunath Stupa, that of **Bodhnath** (also called "**Baudha**") is the most significant Buddhist sanctuary of the Kathmandu Valley. With a diame-

ter as well as a height of 40 meters, the **Bodhnath Stupa** is also the largest sacred structure of its kind in the Valley. It is located about eight kilometers north east of Kathmandu on the old trade and pilgrimage road between Tibet and India. On this building too, a pair of Buddha's eyes painted on the stupa's tower can be seen from a good distance. However, the stupa is becoming increasingly hidden by tall houses which have been settled in primarily by Tibetans.

Also, ever larger numbers of Tibetan monasteries are to be found there. Residing in one of these is the *Cini Lama* – after the Dalai Lama and the Panchen Lama the third-highest dignitary of the Tibetans. In general, the Bodnath Stupa is place of worship predominantly for Tibetans and Sherpas but rarely for the Newar Buddhists.

From the point of view of architectural history, the three-leveled substructure on which the hemisphere and the thirteen shields are raised is worthy of note. Apparently its builders were attempting to unite two cosmological ideals: the terraced mountain and the hemisphere.

There is anouther stupa located not far from the Bodnath Stupa in the village of **Chabahil**. It is substantially smaller, with a diameter of 14 meters. This stupa has become famous because for a legend: The Indian Emperor Ashoka (3rd century B.C.) and his daughter Carumati are supposed to have founded it. However its true age is just as uncertain as the stupa in Bodhnath. Ritually the Chabahil Stupa has become largely insignificant, however in the village itself there is a highly worshiped **Ganesh Temple** to be found, surrounded by several very old sculptures and relics from the Licchavi period.

Pashupatinath

Pashupati, one of the manifestations of Shiva, was already a god of protection for rulers in the earliest written testimonies

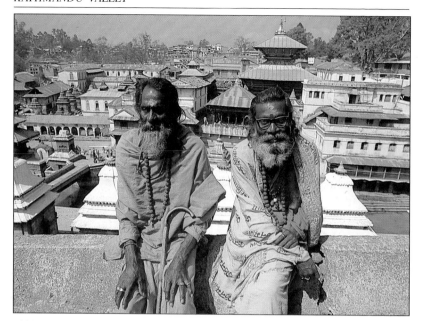

of Nepalese history. Still today the king closes the speeches he makes from his throne with the declaration: "May the god Pashupati protect us!"

The **Pashupati Temple**, in the small, idyllically situated city of **Deopatan** on the west bank of the Bagmati River, has therefore become the most significant holy sanctuary of Hinduism. In the morning and evening numerous believers stream into Deopatan, devotional sellers offer images of gods, flowers or pieces of incense for sale, and lodgings for pilgrims. Additionally there are the *ghats* – bathing grounds on the banks of the Bagmati – on which corpses are also cremated.

According to a popular myth, in this place Shiva, in the form of a gazelle, is supposed to have hidden himself from the other gods and his spouse Parvati. This act threatened the safety of the world, and so everyone looked for Shiva. When Parvati finally found him in the **Mrigasthali Grove** on the east bank of the Bagmati, he attempted to flee across

Two ascetics, devotees of Shiva, in front of the Pashupati Temple.

the river, whereupon his gazellehorn broke into four pieces. So he stayed where he was and henceforth became worshipped as "Master of Animals" (Pashupati) and the four-faced *linga* (phallic symbol and sign of Shiva).

The main temple is closed off to non-Hindus, but from the west road and from the other side of the river on the Mrigasthali Hill you can get a glimpse of the temple courtyard: The pagoda-shaped Pashupati Temple was erected anew at the end of the 17th century by King Bhupalendra Malla – after the previous building was completely consumed by termites. In front of it to the west are standing two large bronze **Nandis** (Shiva's bull and riding-mount).

Around and about this two-storied temple, countless further temples have been erected. Kings, members of royalty and rich traders are always wanting to immortalize themselves with votive-

The Pashupatinath ghats are always brimming with life.

lingas near the protective deity of the land. Particularly outstanding among these are the **Pancadevala Temple-Grounds** of the Shah Kings, south of the Pashupati Temple, but the Rana rulers also left behind their traces: A chain of lingam-shrines stands on the east bank of the Bagmati; south of these there is a predominantly Vishnuist temple complex with a **Ram Temple** from the 14th century; located in the **Mrigasthali Grove** there are over sixty further small lingam-templets. The grove is also the site of the Shikara Temple of Goraknath (a foundation of the Kanphata Sekt which is also housed there), around which apes play.

The old temples and shrines of the goddesses are even older and more ritually significant. The **Seat of the Guhyeshvari** in the northeast is mentioned as early as the 11th century in handwritten manuscripts, even though the temple of today was first laid out by Pratapa Malla

(1641-1674). According to the legend, Parvati had thrown herself on a sacrificial fire after Shiva had been harshly rejected by her father in his desire to become her husband. Shiva then took the corpse of his beloved over his shoulder and, as he then headed off through the country, parts of her body fell to the ground. Her *guhya* – literally the "hidden" or "concealed", but also "anus" or "vulva" – is supposed to have fallen off in Guhyeshvari.

The **Temple of the Goddess Vatsaladevi** – which is located west of both bridges over the Bagmati – also enjoys great popularity. Human sacrifice is brought into connection with it. Frescoes are painted onto the exterior walls of the temple, and on the east side jackals are even pictured with human limbs sticking out of their maws.

Each year in March/April, Vatsala is carried in a huge city-procession to the Pashupati Temple, where they then ram the temple with her processional chest: it is said that Shiva refuses her because in her rituals she accepts alcohol and blood

95

offerings. Nowhere else in the Kathmandu Valley is the latent conflict between the pure, vegetarian and the more savage original Tantric Hinduism more openly contested than here.

Roughly 150 meters further south stands a temple of the Nine Durga Goddesses, the **Rajarajeshvari Temple** from the early 15th century (on the way there you find one of the oldest **Buddha Shakyamuni statues** of the Kathmandu Valley, dating from the 7th century).

In the west of the city, on the other side of the Ring Road, there is a yet more important goddessshrine: the **Jayavagishvari Temple**. Painted onto its north side is a large portrait of Bhairava, which must be renewed every twelve years.

Changu Narayan and
Budhanilakantha

Just as Svayambhunath and Bodhnath are the centers of Buddhism and the Pashupatinath is the middle-point of Hinduism, Changu Narayan and Budhanilakantha represent the cultural-historical high-point of Vishnuism.

Changu Narayan (also named Dolagiri) stands on a hill roughly four kilometers north of Bhaktapur. This location was already mentioned in the year 464 A.D. on a column inscription before the main temple – the oldest transmitted inscription in Nepal. The content of the inscription is most informative – in it the son of King Manadeva's disuades his mother from her wish to have herself burnt as a widow.

The temple itself in its present form originated at the beginning of the 18th century. Located on the west side are bronze portraits of the founder, Queen Riddhilakshmi, and her young son Bhupalendra Malla (1687-1700). However, the son was no longer there in 1704 for the festive dedication of the temple. The central religious symbol of the temple shows Vishnu (Narayan is another name

for Vishnu) riding on the heavenly bird Garuda. This sculpture, from the fourth century A.D., is not always to be seen since the temple is usually closed, but facsimiles are located all over the Kathmandu Valley, starting already with a statue on the forecourt from the ninth century. The life-size Garuda in the form of a human on the west side is quite probably a portrait of King Manadeva.

The temple – which is surrounded by resting houses – alongside several more recent votive shrines with *lingams* and Vishnuist sculptures (Krishna and his female companion Lakshmi) houses still further precious treasures on Nepalese sculpture art. One **Vishnu Trivikamra statue** from the 8th century represents Vishnu in his form as a midget: When the demon Bali promised him as much land as he could measure with three (*tri*) strides (*vikamra*), Vishnu grew to the size of a giant and stepped through the underworld, the earth and heaven.

Apparently originating from the same workshop is the nearby **Vishvarupa Statue**, which represents Vishnu as Emperor of the World, surrounded by his spouse and numerous accompanying figures. One **Narasimha Statue** from the 13th century portrays Vishnu as "half man, half lion", as which he cleverly killed a demon who was terrorizing the whole world.

A Vishnuist religious symbol in the north of Kathmandu, which has become known under the name **Budhanilakantha,** is worshipped even more than Changu Narayan. It shows Vishnu in the middle of an ocean – symbolized by an artificial pond of water – as he sleeps on a coiled snake. This is also the form that Vishnu rests in after each cyclical destruction of the universe. He also slumbers, however, during the four months of hottest summer. When he wakes up in the autumn, thousands of devotees stream to Budhanilakantha in order to greet him with flowers and fruits.

Changu Narayan, the oldest Vishnu shrine in the Kathmandu Valley.

The King, who is considered to be an incarnation of Vishnu, is refused entrance to Budhanilakantha. The five-meter-long picture – of which there are several facsimiles in the Kathmandu Valley – is supposed to have been dedicated by Vishnugupta in the 7th century.

Dakshin Kali

One of the most popular goddesses in the Kathmandu Valley is *Kali* or *Camunda;* in Nepal they are iconographically hardly to be told apart from each-other. This goddess of death is often represented as an emaciated, hollow-eyed and withered figure, with flat breasts hanging downward, bejeweled with chains of human bones, snakes around her neck, and dancing on a corpse. She likes to dwell around cremation places or other similarly dark locations outside of settlements.

One of her most popular manifestations is known as "Kali of the South", **Dakshin Kali**, from which direction she protects the valley from this cardinal direction. Her little shrine is hidden in a gorge on a mountain brook, surrounded by statues of other mother-goddesses. This was once actually the seat of a pre-Hindu goddess, who – as is so frequent in the Kathmandu Valley – was only gradually identified with the great goddesses of the Hindu pantheon.

While the location of the Dakshin-Kali – off the beaten track – once helped to ensure that she would only be visited by initiates, now every Saturday hundreds of automobiles proceed up the little mountain road from Kathmandu, in order to worship the goodness with bloody animal sacrifices.

On the way there one passes **Kirtipur**, a city of the Middle Ages with around ten thousand inhabitants; since 1959 also the seat of the **Tribhuvan University**. The city turned away the first attack of Prithvi Narayan Shah, for which this ruler is said to have later had the noses and ears of all the male inhabitants cut off. It offers countless holy places and sanctuaries – a three-storied **Bagh-Bhairava Temple** and the **Cilanco Stupa** next to its monastery building are especially worth seeing.

A little further up the road, a short visit to **Pharping** is probably well worth your while. This is a little mountain village with a **Temple of the Goddess Vajrayogini** from the 17th century; a rock sanctuary – named **Sheshnarayan** – with a Vishnutrivikrama statue from the 14th century and, on the ridge of the hill, a hermitage which is considered by the Hindus as the sanctuary of Gorakhnath (a footprint found in the stone here – typical of this saint – originated in the year 1390). However, the Tibetans believe this place to be one of Padmasambhava's resting places.

Also located on the way to Dakshin-Kali is the village of **Chobar**, which has become famous because of the **Bagmati Gorge**, which the legendary Bodhisattva Manjushri is supposed to have chopped

A Newar woman hard at work in the fields near Kirtipur.

out with his sword, in order to let the lake which once covered the Kathmandu Valley flow away.

In the village itself – which is located on a nearby knoll – the **Adinath Temple** from the 16th century is particularly interesting.

The main holy object of the temple consists of an apparently local figure with a red face and wide-open eyes – a little like the Red Macchendranath in Patan. It represents the Bodhisattva Avalokiteshvara. However the name "Adinath" is also carried by Shiva, to whom several other sanctuaries in the same location are also dedicated.

And so, at the entrance to the Kathmandu Valley, with the many myths and legends which have been woven around it, we find an ever-increasing, magnificient religious diversity and a variety of cultural traditions, which is unparalleled in South Asia.

Accomodation in:
KATHMANDU

LUXURY: **Soaltee Oberoi**, Tahachal, Tel: 272550. **De l'Annapurna**, Durbar Marg, Tel: 221711. **Everest, New Baneswor, Tel: 220567. Yak & Yeti**, Durbar Marg, Tel: 413999. **Shanker**, Lazimpat, Tel: 410151. **Sherpa**, Durbar Marg, Tel: 222585.
MODERATE: **Shangrila**, Lazimpat, Tel: 412999. **Blue Star**, Tripureswor, Tel: 211470. **Malla**, Lekhnath Marg, Tel: 410620. **Dwarika's Village**, Battisputali, Tel: 414770. Kathmandu, Maharagunj. **Ambassador**, Lazimpat, Tel: 410432. **Woodlands**, Durbar Marg, Tel: 222683. **Yellow Pagoda**, Kanti Path, Tel: 220337. **Hotel Crystal**, New Road, Tel: 223611. **Vajra**, Bijeswari, Tel: 224545. **Gautam**, Jyatha, Tel: 215014. **Kathmandu Guest House**, Thamel, Tel: 413632. **Mandap**, Thamel, Tel: 413321.
INEXPENSIVE: **Lhasa Guest House**, Jyatha, Tel: 211147. **Tushita Rest House**, Kanti Path, Tel: 216144. **New Gajur**, Jyatha, Tel: 212621. **New Ganesh**, Bhote Bahal, Tel: 220296. **Shakti**, Thamel, Tel: 410121. **Sita**, Chhetrapati, Tel: 214978. **Star**, Thamel, Tel: 411000. **Tibet Guest House**, Chhetrapati, Tel: 214383. **Yeti Cottage**, Thamel. **Tara Gaon Resort**, Boudha, Tel: 410409. **Ratna**, Bagh Bazar, Tel: 224809. **Manaslu**, Lazimpat, Tel: 410071. **Blue Diamond**, Jyatha, Tel: 213392. **Mount Makalu**, Dharmapath, Tel: 224616. **Panorama**, Khichapokhari, Tel: 221502. **Himalayan View**, Jyatha, Tel: 414770. **Maya Guest House**, Boudha, Tel: 414866.

PATAN

MODERATE: **Narayani**, Pulchowk, Tel: 521711. **Himalaya**, Sahid Sukra Marg, Tel: 523900. **Summit**, Kopudol, Tel: 521894.
INEXPENSIVE: **Oasis**, Patan, Tel: 522746. **Aloha Inn**, Jawalakhel, Tel: 522796.

BHAKTAPUR

INEXPENSIVE: **Nyatpola Guest House**, Taumadi Square. **Golden Gate Guest House**, Durbar Square.

NAGARKOT

MODERATE: **Flora Hill**, Tel: 223311. **Tara Gaon**, Tel: 410409.
INEXPENSIVE: **Niva Home**.

DHULIKHEL

MODERATE: **Dhulikhel Mountain Resort. Himalayan Horizon.**
INEXPENSIVE: **Dhulikhel Lodge.**

Hospitals

Kalimati Clinic, Tel: 270923. **Bir Hospital** (Kanti Path), Tel: 221988. **CIWEC Clinic** (Baluwatar), Tel: 410983. **Kanti Hospital** (Maharaganj), Tel: 411550. **Maternity Hospital** (Thapathali), Tel: 213216. **Teaching Hospital** (Maharaganj), Tel: 412303. **Teku Hospital**, Tel: 211344. **Nepal International Clinic** (Hitti Durbar), Tel: 412842.
Patan Hospital (Lagankhel), Tel: 522278.
Bhaktapur Hospital, Tel: 610798.
At the Red Cross on the Exhibition Road (Tel: 228094) AIDS tests can be performed.
Each embassy has its **confidential doctor** – please inquire!

Pharmacies

Most medications can be obtained without a prescription. They are less expensive than in the West.

Nightlife

Casino Nepal in Hotel Soaltee Oberoi. Open 24 hours a day all week long. Ask in the hotel about free transport.
The Galaxy, discotheque in the Everest Hotel open every day from 21:00-2:00 hours except Mondays. Entrance only for members and guests of the hotel – admission: 400 rupees per couple.
The Damaru, discotheque in Hotel Woodlands. Except for Tuesdays open from 21:00 to 1:00 hours. Non-member admission: 350 rupees per couple.
Take a look in the larger hotels for special offers.

Culture

Besides performances for the Nepalese in the Royal Nepal Academy and the Rastriya Nach Ghar (National Dance Theater) there are various dance and musical groups in Kathmandu:
The New Himalchuli Culture Group: At the Hotel Shanker, Lazimpat. From seven to eight in the evening. Tel: 410151. Entrance: 75 rupees per person.
The Everest Cultural Society: At the Hotel De'l Annapurna, Durbar Marg. From 19:00 to 20:00 hours. Tel: 220676. Entrance: 90 rupees per person.
Nepalese and Indian musical pieces and ghazals are performed in the Everest Hotel and in the Ghar-e-kabab Restaurant, Durbar Marg, and in the Moti Mahal, Durbar Marg.
The Oberoi, Yak & Yeti, Everest, Shangrila, Shanker, Himalaya, Vajra, and Kathmandu Hotels as well as in K.C.'s Restaurant in Thamel have specially announced programs.

Restaurants

Especially in Kathmandu – here and there in Patan – there is something for all tastes. In Bhaktapur as well as Dhulikel and Nagarkot you can get Nepalese, European and Chinese dishes in the better-known hotels. Here are some special recommendations:

NEPALESE: **Bhanchha Ghar**, Kalamadi (near Durbar Marg). **Nanglo**, Durbar Marg. **Third Eye Restaurant,** Thamel (diagonally opposite the Hotel Star; the owner earlier had the legendary Yin Yang Restaurant). **Nepali Kitchen**, Chhetrapati. **Sun Kosi**, Durbar Marg. **Tushita**, Kanti Path.

INDIAN: Is especially tasty at the **Ghare-kabab**, Durbar Marg. **Third Eye Restaurant** (the chicken chilli is delicious), Thamel. **Shanker Hotel**, Lazimpat. **Everest Hotel**, New Baneswor. **Oberoi**, Tahachal. **Ambassador** (especially the tandoori dishes), Lazimpat. **Moti Mahal**, Durbar Marg. **Shiva's Sky**, New Road.

TIBETAN: The oldest restaurant in Thamel is the **Utse** – Tibetan, Mongolian and Chinese cooking. Also among the oldest restaurants are the **Tashi Tagkai** in the Kathmandu Guest House in Thamel and the **New Om**, Chhetrapati.

CHINESE: **Nanglo** – Chinese Room, Durbar Marg. **Third Eye Restaurants**, Thamel. **Omei Restaurant**, Jyatha.

KOREAN: **Arirang**, Durbar Marg.

JAPANESE: **Fuji**, Kanti Path (small park). **Koto**, Durbar Marg. **Kushi Fushi**, Durbar Marg. **Sakura Ya**, Lazimpat (with beautiful garden). **Himalaya Hotel**, Sahid Sukra Marg.

EUROPEAN: **K.C.'s Restaurant**, Thamel (outstanding steaks, salad, pastries and pizzas). **Third Eye Restaurant**, Thamel. (very good vegetable and meat dishes). **Nanglo**, Durbar Marg. (try out the tomato soup and sizzlers). **La Dolce Vita**, Thamel (good Italian food). **Ropes Everest Hotel**, New Baneswor. **Gorkha Grill Oberoi**, Tahachal. **Garden Restaurant Summit Hotel**, Kupondol. **Aloha Inn**, Jawalakhel.

GOOD BREAKFAST RESTAURANTS: **K.C.'s Restaurant** (sometimes they have fresh waffles). **Mike's Breakfast**, at the Yak & Yeti Hotel, Durbar Marg. **Nanglo**, Durbar Marg. **Annapurna Coffee Shop**, Durbar Marg. **Mona Lisa**, Thamel.

Shopping

KATHMANDU: The most important shopping districts are in Thamel, the Durbar Marg, Indra Chowk, New Road and on the Durbar Square. In addition many wares from India/Kashmir are offered by the business- oriented Kashmiris. In the meanwhile there are even chic designer fashions on the Durbar Marg and in Thamel. More recently tourists have also been glad to buy – besides the traditional handicrafts – contemporary artworks of Nepalese painters and sculptors.

BODHNATH (near Kathmandu): Primarily Tibetan every-day items, textiles, jewelry, thangkas (painted religions-scrolls) and rugs.

BALAJU INDUSTRIAL AREA (near Kathmandu): Factories processing silk and cotton with their own shops – they have also especially beautiful Pashimi-shawls and scarves.

SVAYAMBHUNATH: particularly Tibetan articles and thangkas.

PATAN: At Durbar Square, in Jawalakhel (Tibetan camp with carpet weavery) and in the Industrial Estate,Lagankhel (woodcarvers, bronze and metal casters).

BHAKTAPUR: On Taumadhi Tole, Durbar Square and Dattatraya Plaza (cooperative for the preservation of traditional crafts with beautiful products such as wood carvings, masks, textiles, pottery works and puppets.

THIMI (near Bhaktapur): Pottery workshop and mask maker.

KIRTIPUR: Textile workshop, weavery.

Public / Entertainment Parks

There are several very attractive public parks in the Kathmandu Valley, which the locals like to visit for a picnic on holidays.

Gokarna-Safari Park, behind Bodhnath (elephant and horse riding are possible); **Balaju Garden** with 22 dragon-headed water-fountains, on the way to Trisuli (with public swimming pool); **Thankot-Tribuvan Park**, on the street to Pokhara (flower garden); **Godavari Botanical Garden**, behind Patan (with splendid parkgrounds, conservatory and ponds near the Jesuit School, below the Phulchowski Mountains).

One popular excursion destination is the **Zoo** in Patan, near the Tibetan camp of Jawalakhel.

Museums / Art Galleries

National Museum of Kathmandu: This is located in the quarter of Chhauni near the Svayambhunath Stupa. Objects of historical significance – i.e. weapons, clothing, and an art gallery are on display. Open daily except Tuesdays and holidays from 10:15 to 15:45. Minimal admission, plus 3 rupees per camera.

Tribhuvan Museum Kathmandu: This is located in the Hanuman Dhoka Palace at Durbar Square. The life of King Tribhuvan and his successors is portrayed. In addition there is a coin collection. The entrance ticket is also valid for the

Basantpur Tower. Cameras are not permitted. Open daily except Tuesdays from 10:30 to 16:30.

Museum of Natural History: Located behind Svayambhunath, outstanding collection of fauna and flora of Nepal. Opening times from 10:00 to 17:00.

Nepal Association of Fine Arts (NAFA): In Naxal, with exhibitions and sale of contemporary Nepalese art. Opening times from 10:00 to 17:00.

~~Siddhartha Art Gallery: In Kanti Path~~, with contemporary art especially of Sashi Kala Tiwari, Manohar Man Poon and Jagdish Chitrakar. Opening times from 12:00 to 19:00.

The Gallery Palpasa: In Kantipath, with contemporary art; one of the oldest galleries. Opening times from 12:00 to 19:00 Sunday through Friday.

B.B. Thapa Art Gallery: In Hotel Soatee Road, Kalamati; with classical and naive paintings of Buddhist themes.

Art Museum in Bhaktapur: Is located in the Palace of the 55 Windows at the Durbar Square. With fascinating old sculptures and paintings from the Newar. Opening times from 10:00 to 17:00.

Hermitage Art Gallery and Studio: Behind the Bodhnath Stupa; it is a non-profit making art center with painting classes held weekly and studios which can also be used by foreign visitors. In addition it is also possible to hold concerts and symposiums.

Festivals

BHAKTAPUR New-Year's Festival, *Bisket Jatra*, Carriage Festival.
A one week festival in the entire valley. The goddess Bhadrakali and the god Bhairav are paraded through the city on temple carriages – mid-April.

Gai Jatra, Dance of the Dead – mid-August, day after the full moon.

Bhimsen Jatra – end of August, day before the new moon.

Sakimala Punhi – November, full moon, evening.

THIMI: New Year's Festival – mid-April.

PATAN: *Rato Matsyendranath Jatra*, Carriage festival, symbolic bringing-in of the rainy season – second half of April until June.

Matya Puja – August/September, second day after the full moon.

PATAN, KIRTIPUR: *Krishnasthami*, the god Krishna's birthday – end of August.

KATHMANDU VALLEY: *Buddha Jayanti*, Buddha's birthday – May, full moon.

KATHMANDU: *Seto Matsyendranath Jatra*, carriage festival in honor of the god by the same name – end of March.

Ghode Jatra, horse-race at the Tundikhel Square, on the next day a sword-fight based on the ritual conflict among the goddesses of Kathmandu – March/April, new moon.

Indra Jatra, festival in honor of the god Indra, the living goddess Kumari, and the king – September, full moon.

NEWAR CITIES: *Gathamuga*, spirit exorcism – end of July, the day before new moon.

Gumla, Buddhist procession month – beginning of August, after the new moon.

PASHUPATINATH: *Tij*, fasting festival of women – August/September.

Shivaratri, night of the god Shiva – end of February.

Bala Chaturdasi, night festival of lights for the dead – November/December.

BUDHANILAKANTHA: *Haribodhini*, the awaking the god Vishnu from his cosmic sleep – October/November.

BODNATH: *Magh Purnima*, festival of the thousand lights – February, full moon.

Lhosar, Tibetan New Year – beginning to middle of February.

Trekking Offices

Alpine Trekking Expedition Service Ltd.,Durbar Marg, Tel: 2- 12736. Ama Dablam Trekking Ltd., Thamel, Tel: 4-10219. Annapurna Mountaineering and Trekking Pvt. Ltd., Durbar Marg, Tel: 2-12736. Himalayan Rover Trek, Lazimpat, Tel: 4-12667. Himalayan Horizon,airport area, Pokhara, Tel: 253. Himalayan Explorer, Jyatha, Tel: 2-16142. Lama Excursions, Durbar Marg, Tel: 4-10786. Mountain Adventure Trekking, Thamel, Tel: 4-14910. Natraj Trekking, Kantipath, Tel: 2-16644. Summit Nepal Trekking, Kopundol, Tel: 5-21810. Sherpa Trekking Service, Kalamadi, Ghantaghar, Tel: 2-16243. Sherpa Society, Jyatha, Tel: 2-16361. Sagarmatha Trekking, Thamel, Tel: 4-13239. Yeti Trekking Ltd., Kantipath, Tel: 2-16841.

Rafting Agencies

Great Himalayan Adventure, Kanti Path Himalayan Encounter (in the Kathmandu Guest house), Thamel, Tel: 2-16144.

Himalayan River Exploration, Naxal, Tel: 4-13928.

Journeys White Water Rafting, Thamel, Tel: 4-10093.

Great Himalayan River, Durbar Marg, Tel: 4-10811.

Tourist Information

See travel information at the end of book.

SUMMITS AND LAKES

POKHARA
BEGNAS AND RUPA LAKES

POKHARA

The small city of **Pokhara** has a completely different atmosphere from the capital city. Pokhara has about 50,000 inhabitants, and lies in the heart of a 900-meter-altitude valley by the same name, some 200 km west of Kathmandu. If you want to get some relief from the screeching traffic and restless agitation of the Kathmandu bazaars, then you should come here and set off for the shore of the Phewa, Begna or Rupa Lake, where in clear weather, lying back under banana fronds, you can enjoy a unique mountain panorama. The summits of the Annapurna and Dhaulagiri Massifs are mirrored in the lake; the view of the "Nepalese Matterhorn"– Macchapuchare – is especially impressive. It is also called the fish-tail-mountain because its curiously-shaped peak looks like one, but it can't really be recognized as such until you engage in one of the exhausting but exhilatring treks which start from Pokhara into the interior Himalayan valleys. There were originally seven fresh-water lakes – called *pokhari* – located in this valley, from which its name was also derived. The largest of these is the five

Preceding pages: Macchapuchare and Annapurna seen from Lake Phewa.

kilometer long **Phewa** (**Fewa**) **Lake**, which at its narrowest point measures 100 meters across and at its widest two kilometers. Located at its southernmost side, along the city-section of **Pardi**, there is an artificial dam with a hydroelectric generator, which was put back into commission a few years ago.

Picturesque villages, gently rolling chains of hills with terraced fields of rice, subtropical forests and the unique silhouette of the Himalayas – whose gigantic mountains are only fifty kilometers away and seem so close that you could grasp them – are the great attraction of this place: On the left juts the **Dhaulagiri** (8,167 m), followed by **Annapurna South** (7,295 m.) and **Annapurna I** in the background (8,091 m), then the pyramid-like tower of **Macchapuchare**, one of the holy mountains, whose peak has never been conquered (6,997 m), **Annapurna III** (7,556 m), **Annapurna IV** (7,525 m), and next to it **Annapurna II** (7,937 m). Further to the right from there you can also recognize in good weather the **Lamjung Himal** (6,981 m.), east of it the **Manaslu** (8,156 m) and finally the **Himalchuli** (7,893 m).

One legend purports that at one time in the place of Phewa Lake there lay a beautiful valley, which was inhabited by gracious and well-to-do people. However, over time they became ever more un-charitable and inhumane. The gods, who didn't want to believe this, sent down to the valley one of their number in the shape of a beggar, in order to test the people there. Nowhere did he receive any charity; everyone pushed him away. Only one poor old couple had compassion for him. Blazing with fury, the gods decided to annihilate the valley. Only the two poor people were warned; they fled to some high ground located nearby. Even while they were still on their way they became aware of a thunderous dinhuge masses of water deluged into the valley and completely inundated it.

Like so many legends, this story has a real backgroud. In all probability, a tectonic quake, which occur frequently in Nepal – or natural erosion – unleashed a catastrophe about 600 years ago, which led to a glacial lake pouring into the valley and also partially covering the plain with water.

History of Pokhara

In spite of its central location and the ideal climate, the valley has never gained the cultural and political significance of Kathmandu and its neighboring cities, although there is nevertheless one of the most important trade routes between India and Tibet located here. Rather, Pokhara crystallized in the course of the centuries into a marketplace – it was the gathering place for the surrounding population, such as the Gurung, Newar and Magar. Especially when the mountain inhabitants from the interior valleys of the Himalayas come here to spend the winter, the mule caravans of the Thakali and the Baragaonli populate the bazaar streets, and everywhere the Lopa from Mustang offer for sale dried herbs, spices and fossils from the upper Kali-Gandaki River.

It can be assumed that the first settlers in the valley were Gurung, whose origins are just as unclear as the history of the valley. Like the Magar, it is also said that the Gurung have an astounding ability to adapt themselves to changing religious, geographic and cultural circumstances. They were originally known as goat and sheep herders, and still today many of the Gurung living in the surrounding higher villages often keep a dozen or so goats or sheep. Almost every village has a herd of some 200 to 300 animals. From April to September they are pastured on high-altitude meadows, where the weather is cooler, and the variety of grasses and herbs far greater. In October the herds are driven down the hills – sometimes all the way to Terai, in order to sell them profitably for the Dasain Festival which occurs in October. Today most of the Gurung live as farmers and livestock breeders in villages, whose comfortable financial situation comes from the pensions of the men who have served as Gurkha soldiers. As a result, the jewelry of their women is also particularly elaborate and sumptuous.

Political impulses brought the Rajputan princes out of India in the 14th century, with whom Chetris and Brahmas fled into the Pokhara Valley. Then, from the little village Kaski-Kot north of Phewa Lake, the fore-fathers of the conquerer Prithvi Narayan Shah pushed further forward to Gorkha – from where the Kathmandu Valley would later be conquered. The resulting integration which followed, of the Kaski – or Pokhara – region into the Kingdom of Nepal brought an economic revival. Then the Newar from the Kathmandu Valley came and settled in Pokhara, building multistoried houses and temples and establishing artisan workshops. The one-time settlement took on an increasingly urban character. When the trade route to Tibet was closed off in 1959 after the flight of the Dalai Lama, many of those Thakali employed as middlemen between India and Tibet had to seek a new place of residence. A few of them settled in Pokhara

to Mahendra Cave

Seti Gandaki

Shining Hospital

ROHATEPANI

Bagmati

Pritvi Narayan Campus

Bhalam Khola

Bindu Basini T.

Annapurna Regional Museum

DHORAPANI

Bhimsen Tole

Nalamukh

Nadipur

Patan

PARSYANG

Police Office

Mahendra Bridge

Post Office

BASAR

Museum

Ram Krishna T.

Nayar Bazar

Ramipawa

Malepatan

Phewa Lake

BAIDAM

Fewa Hotel

Ratna Mandir

Manswara

Gandaki Zonal Hospital

Simakhaur

Birauta Chok

Bus Stop

Ram Ghat

Kantipur Hotel

Barahi Bhawani T.

Immigration Office

Tourist Office

New Crystal Hotel

Fishtail Lodge

Dragon Hotel

Pardi Birauta

Seti Gandaki

Devin's Fall

Pardi Bazar

POKHARA

Airport

0   500m

PARDI

as clever businessmen and hotel owners, which has contributed decidedly to the city's economic development.

The main attractions in Pokhara are the shores of Phewa Lake along the **Baidam** and **Pardi** sections of the city. In contrast to both of the other larger lakes located in the direction of Kathmandu – Lakes Begnas and Rupa – this area is accommodating to tourists. Countless little souvenir businesses – primarily owned by Tibetans – restaurants, small hotels and lodges in all price classes; boat, bicycle and more recently wind surf-board rental shops are all to be found here. Earlier – when Nepal was still more the dreamland of hippies than it was of trekkers, and Freak-Street in Kathmandu still housed genuine freaks – **Pokhara Lake Side** was *the* secret tip. Only a few little lodges and hotels such as the **Swiss Hotel** (still in existence) existed at that time, and the "long term guests" rented small cottages near the lakeshore for themselves. There is also a row of good, clean restaurants located here, at which the cooking is by

far more rich in variety and tastier than it is in the larger hotels, such as, for example, the **Fishtail Lodge** operated by the Annapurna Hotel, or the **New Crystal Hotel** at the airport.

The scenario around and about the big old "newspaper tree"– from which the fast and comfortable **Swiss Bus** still begins its journey toward Kathmandu or the Indian border – also offers the most up-to-date and direct information about the surrounding trekking regions. You will always find somebody who has just arrived back from **Manang**, or someone who announces that the Annapurna Base Camp is overcrowded. Agents at the lake or directly at the airport offer the opportunity to book an organized trekking tour, river rafting or an excursion into the Chitwan Park at the last minute.

The swimming possibilities all around the lake are really excellent – as long as you don't plunge into the cool water right where the locals wash and do their laundry. But here too, the water was much cleaner ten years ago – when there weren't so many tourists!

A rewarding side-trip might be a brief visit to the little **Bahari Bhawai Temple** – on a small island not far from the lake's edge. Bahari is though of as a manifestation of the goddess Kali; on festival days animal sacrifices are also offered to her here. If you still have a little more time, you should take a trip to the the other side of the lake and climb up the hill there. About half-way up there is a little hut where mostly fish but also other delicious tidbits are offered. The view over the lake and out to the ice-giants of the Himalayas is overwhelming. However, be careful during the monsoon season! Within the shortest time, a storm can brew up over the lake, and you should make sure that you can get back to the Baidam shore in time. Also located in the neighborhood of the boat docks is the **Royal Inn** which is shielded from the usual hubbub. For several years, a rumor has persisted that a

The summit of Macchapuchare, one of the sacred mountains of Nepal.

large portion of the Baidam shore – also called Lake Side in the common parlance – is going to be transformed into a park, in order to hold at a distance from the idyllic area around the Inn both the hippie tourism – which is still to some extent in existence – and the constantly growing individual tourism, with all its unwelcome side-effects.

The departure point for many trekking tours is the former **Shining Hospital**, which can be reached either by taxi or the city bus. The hospital – which was for a long time the only one within a radius of several days' hiking – has now fulfilled its function and has been replaced by a modern hospital in Pokhara. On the large plaza in front of the Shining Hospital, jeeps and carriers await new customers. Here you can find porters, but you will have to bargain for the price of the tour yourself. You can drive up to the village of **Suikhet** on the road to **Baglung**,

which has meanwhile been rebuilt. The "classic" Annapurna tours begin from Suikhet.

Pokhara City

Since the end of the 1960's, this little city has developed rapidly, following the completion of the overland roads from Kathmandu to Pokhara and from there on down to **Sunauli** at the Indian border. Pokhara became the administrative center of the Gandaki zone (one of Nepal's 14 administrative zones); Within the shortest time, schools, hospitals and administration buildings were built. Flights connecting the city with Kathmandu take place several times daily. Since the middle of the 'eighties an additional road connecting to **Baglung** in central Nepal has existed, this one under Chinese management. From a sleepy market spot, Pokhara has meanwhile developed into a typical bazaar city, unfortunately featuring unplanned residential blocks – as a sign of overly-hasty growth.

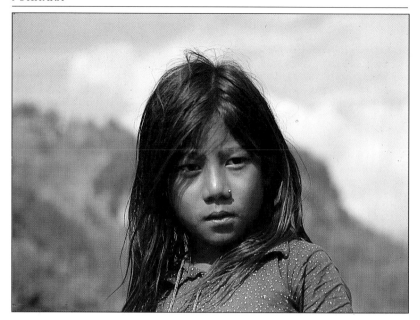

A young girl from the Pokhara Valley.

Pokhara is divided into three zones: the **Bazaar**, the area around the **Airport** and **Baidam/Lake Side** on the shore of Phewa lake. The **Tibetan Centers** are particularly interesting and significant in recent history. These were originally conceived of as refugee camps for the Tibetans who were driven out of their homeland in 1959 by the Chinese. At that time Nepal put land and building materials at the disposal of the refugees, so that they could build a new home for themselves here. Three Tibetan settlements are located in the Pokhara area: in the north, **Hyengja** lies on the trekking route into the mountains, and in the area of the huge bus station as well as behind the airport there are two further Tibetan villages with carpet weaveries, artisan workshops, schools and health stations. In the meantime many of the Tibetans who have settled here have managed – through skill and hard work – to achieve a moderate degree of prosperity; some of them have even established their own souvenir businesses. These can primarily be found along the lakeshore in Baidam and Pardi. The **Seti Gorge** is counted among the particular natural beauties in this area. At its narrowest point it is only 4.5 meters in width. Here, in the course of millenia, the Seti River has gnawed its way to a depth of 45 meters into the valley floor. You can get a good view into the gorge from the **Mahendra Bridge** (Mahendra Pul) in the Pokhara Bazaar. The 1,590 meter high **Kanhu Danda Hill** stands in the northeast of Pokhara; it can be reached from the Bazaar over the Mahendra Bridge.

About seven kilometers north of the Bazaar you can get to the **Mahendra Cave,** a stalagmite cave which to date has been only slightly researched and is therefore only partially accessible. Take care – it is unlit.

In the Bazaar itself you might take a rewarding little excursion to the **Bindu Basini Temple**, located on the northern edge of the city. Sundays and Tuesdays

Women setting young rice in a paddy.

an enthusiastic crowd gathers here to offer their sacrifices to a goddess – an incarnation of Parvati, the spouse of Shiva.

There is a striking difference between the tourist-populated lakeshore promenade of Phewa Lake, and the Bazaar section of the city, which has now become relatively hectic. Today it is impossible to imagine that until 1961 even primitive ox-carts were unknown here and, at first, had to be brought in by airplane.

Begnas and Rupa Lakes

The **Begnas Lake** is not yet so frequented, but is just as beautiful. It is picturesquely located at the foot of a hill, nestled in among rice and mustard fields, citrus trees and papaya groves. You can get there by public bus in a half-hour ride from Pokhara over the road to Kathmandu – the **Prithvi Rajmarg**. From the bus station on the southwestern shore of

the lake there are two possibilities to gain access to the terrain. Either you set off to the left directly to the lakeshore, where you can cross the lake with a row-boat, or perhaps an indigenous log canoe, or you turn to the right in order to reach a knoll in a one-and-a-half-hour hike, which takes you past village-like settlements of Chetris and Gurung. From the top of the knoll you have a lovely panoramic view over the three-square-kilometer Begnas Lake and the somewhat smaller **Rupa Lake** which is connected to it. Everywhere along the way, you will meet curious villagers who aren't accustomed to seeing foreigners in this still relatively undiscovered region. There are two possibilities from here: either choose the same route back, or proceed by way of a medley of twisting paths down to the edge of Begnas Lake.

The residents of this touristically untested area are very helpful and – for an appropriate payment – will gladly row you back to the exit point near the bus station, which is still far away.

109

POKHARA
Accomodation
LUXURY CLASS: **Fish Tail Lodge**, Lakeside Pardi, Tel: 20071.
MODERATE: **Dragon Hotel**, Pardi, Tel: 20027; managed by Thakalis, especially beautiful garden. **Mount Annapurna**, Airport Side, Tel: 20027, under Tibetan management. **New Crystal Hotel**, Airport Nagh Dungha, Tel: 20035.
INEXPENSIVE: **Fewa**, Lakeside Baidam, Tel: 21051. **Ashok Guest House**, Damside, Tel: 20374. **Garden**, Damside, Tel: 20870. **Mona Lisa**, Damside, Tel: 20836. **Tragopan**, Damside, Tel: 20189. **The Kantipur**, Lakeside-Baidam, Tel: 20887. **The Hungry Eye**, Lakeside-Baidam, Tel: 20908.
There are many small lodges and hotels of varying quality, especially in Pardi and Baidam.

Hospitals
Gandaki Zonal Hospital, in eastern Pokhara, in the quarter of Ranipauwa. However, in case of serious illness, fly to Kathmandu!

Museums
Annapurna Regional Museum: Vivid portrayal of Nepal's plant and animal world. The butterfly collection is especially worth seeing. On the first floor is a presentation on the Annapurna Conservation Area Project. Located in the Prithvi Narayan campus in northern Pokhara. Hours: daily (except Saturdays) from 10:00-16:00.
Regional Museum: Small museum on the surrounding area. Between the bus station (China Chowk) and Bazaar. Hours: daily (except Tuesdays) from 10:00-16:00.

Telecommunication / Post
The post office is located in the area of Mahendra Pul in Bazaar. Opening times: Sunday to Thursday 10:00 to 16:00, Friday 10:00 to 15:00. Meanwhile most of the hotels and lodges have got telephones. Calls to foreign countries can be made from the luxury and middle-class hotels.

Restaurants
Besides the restaurants in the larger hotels there are countless places to eat in Pardi and Baidam-Lakeside. Try out the cake at **The Hungry Eye**, Baidam-Lakeside. Besides European cuisine the **Dragon Hotel** offers preferable Nepalese and Indian dishes. In **Mount Annapurna** you should ask for the Tibetan momos. On the lakeshore street after Baidam is Woody Pumpernickel's "German bakery". There are whole-grain breads, fresh curds and delicious cookies. Next door in the **Phewa Restaurant** the mousse au chocolate is especially recommended.

Getting There
Flights: The Royal Nepalese Airline offers daily flights to Pokhara and vice versa. The prices change fast. Most recently the fare was US$ 50. Flight time is around 35 minutes. Book in plenty of time! With flights from Pokhara to Kathmandu sit on the left side–because of the mountain view. Daily flights are also offered from Pokhara to Baglung (from there you can get to the Jomosom/Muktinath trekking path) and several times a week there are flights to Jomosom.
Bus: With the Swiss Bus or a corresponding firm you can ride for 120 rupees from Kathmandu to Pokhara in 5-7 hours. Boards behind the post office at Bhimsen Tower. A night bus also departs from there for about 50 rupees. With the Local Bus (40 rupees), which starts from the central bus station opposite the Tundikhel Square the drive takes 8-10 hours. In Pokhara most of the busses to Kathmandu or to Bhairahava/Butwal up to the Indian border depart from the bus station on China Chowk. Tickets can be obtained at hotels or directly at the bus station–purchase in good time! **Auto/Taxi**: Rental cars and taxis to Pokhara cost about US $50: Attention: Inquire about the road conditions, which are often very poor.

Tourist Information
This is located opposite the airport, Tel: 20028. Open from Sunday to Thursday, 9:00 to 18:00, on Friday until 16:00.

Visa Extensions / Trekking Permits
The Immigration Office is found by going from Baidam along the lakeshore street, left at the first big intersection in Pardi. Open: Sunday through Friday 10:00-16:00, in summer to 17:00.

Shopping
On the lakeshore street there are countless souvenir shops – particularly from Tibetans. There are also two larger Tibetan camps with carpet weaveries, souvenirs are also sold: **Tashi Palkel** is located near Devin's Fall in the south of Pokhara, and **Hyengja** is about an hour's walk north of the city. You can also get there by group jeep or taxi (if the new road to Baglung is drivable). At the lakeshore and in the Bazaar you can also buy so-called *saligrams:* these are fossils which are found in the river- bed of the Kali Gandaki.
In the Bazaar behind the post office you'll find the photography shop Bishwa Shakya – Zenith Photo – where you can buy beautiful posters and

panoramas. Ask in the **Mount Annapurna Hotel** about the Tibetan artist Herm Lutup. He paints impressive pictures with Tibetan motifs.

Various

Bicycle and Motorcycle Rental: It is possible to rent bicycles and motorcycles. Motorcycles can also be rented between China Chowk (bus station) and Bazaar. Repair shops are also located there. The prices are higher in Pokhara than in Kathmandu.

A **camp-site** with toilets is located in Baidam-Lakeside directly on the lakeshore.

Boat Rental: A boat costs about 10RS, with rower c. 30RS.

In the larger hotels folk-dance groups appear from time to time. Watch for the corresponding announcements. In the **Dragon Hotel** in a hall especially devoted to this purpose, the performances are especially impressive.

Taxis: Group taxis and taxis drive everywhere. You usually have to dicker about the price.

Ponys: Ponys can be rented at Pony-Trek opposite the airport for around 150-200 rupees per day. Tel: 20253.

Jeeps: Jeep trips can be arranged by the larger hotels. Ask about this at reception, and get information about the prices.

Buses: A bus goes back and forth between Bazaar and the lake.

Many hotels have nice roof terraces, from which one can get a lovely view of the mountain panorama. Don't neglect to catch the sunrise! In good weather from left to right are Dhaulagiri (8167 m) far in the distance, then Annapurna South (7219 m), Annapurna I (8091 m), Macchapuchare (fish-tail mountain) (6997 m), Annapurna III (7556 m), Annapurna IV (7525 m), Annapurna II (7937 m), further right to the east the Lamjung Himal (6985 m), Mansalu (8156 m) and way to the right, Himalchuli (7893 m).

Excursions

Because Pokhara is very spread out it's worth renting a bicycle. Besides the **Mahendra Cave** in the north of town or **Devin's Waterfall** in the south by the dam you can also reach the Begnas and Rupa Lakes. From the bus station out to Begnas Lake it's about 13 kilometers–first on the road to Kathmandu, then after about ten kilometers turn left on the gravel road that leads directly to the village of Begnas. Then walk the rest of the way to the lake.

From there you can either hike further along the shore or take a boat trip to the opposite shore. From there it takes about 30 minutes to climb up the **Pachbaya Hill**, from which you have a wonderful view of the Begnas and Rupa Lake. In 2 hours you can hike from here back to the village of Begnas on a path which gets wider as you go. Soft drinks and tea are available along the way. You can also take a taxi or a bus to Begnas Lake. The **Kandu Danda Hill** is a 1,560 meter lookout mountain located northeast of Pokhara. From there you can easily make out how the Seti River dug its way deep into the valley over centuries. In good weather the view of the Dhaulagiri and Annapurna Massifs is overwhelming. On the eastern peak of the mountain there is a fortress ruin (**Kanhu Kot**) from the 18th century. The hike up the Kanhu Danda takes about four hours there and back. Begin at the Mahendra Bridge, which leads you over the Seti River and hike eastwards up to the Buddhist monastery that is visible from a long way off. Just short of it, a path to the left leads up to the mountain. **Sarankot** is 1,600 meters high, northwest of Pokhara directly above Phewa Lake. A day-trip to this viewpoint is quite breath-taking, because you have a steep hike up the mountain, however the view is full compensation for the hardship you must endure. You will also find an old ruin of a fortress and a temple. Restaurants and tea shops edge the trail, which begins in the Pokhara Bazaar at the Bindu Basini Temple. You reach the top in around four hours. On the way back you can climb straight down the mountain to Baidam-Lakeside in about two hours, a beautiful path past small settlements with a great view of Phewa Lake.

GORKHA (Gurkha)
Accomodation

INEXPENSIVE: **Hotel Gorkha Bisauni** below the bus terminus. The hotel also has a simple restaurant.

Getting There

Buses from Kathmandu to the 138-kilometer-distant Gurkha take off daily from the central bus station (across from Thundikel Plaza). The ride takes about 6 hours and costs some 30 rupees. Busses from Gurkha to Pokhara put the 110 kilometer stretch behind them in about 4-5 hours. The ride costs 25 rupees.

PALPA / TANSEN
Accomodation

Half-way down the stretch between Pokhara and the Indian/Nepalese border is the high village of **Palpa/Tansen**. *MODERATE:* **Hotel Srinagar**, Tel: 20212, with adjoining restaurant. Small treks in the surrounding area are possible; they can be organized by the hotel management.

ON OLD PILGRIM TRAILS

ANNAPURNA

MUKTINATH

MANANG

ANNAPURNA / MUKTINATH TREKKING

By far the most well-known hiking routes in Nepal among trekking tourists are the **Jomosom/Muktinath Trail** and the well-trodden path to the **Annapurna Base Camp.** Apart from the beautiful landscape and mountain scenario along the deepest valley on earth, going by the Dhaulaghiri and Annapurna Massifs, the hiker walks for part of the time down one of the oldest trade routes between the Indian subcontinent and trans-Himalayan Tibet. It is especially interesting to come into contact with the various inhabitants of the central hill regions and the adjoining valleys of the Himalayas. Although the paths here are truly overflowing – particularly in October and the late spring – and the local residents have been used to foreigners and their apppearance for many years, they still show as great an interest in their foreign guests and their ways of life as they ever did.

There are now sufficient small lodges and hotels along both trekking routes and we needn't go into detail about them. The *bhatti-shops*, in which one is invited to linger and drink tea, can also be found

Left: Ulleri on the Muktinath trek marks the end of a long climb.

everywhere along the hiking paths. One can carry on conversations in broken English in most of the villages. Nevertheless it is still advantageous to pick up a few of the most important Nepali words and phrases.

Most of the population of this region knows Nepali, although the individual ethnic groups such as the Magar, Gurung, Thakali and the residents of Mustang – the Baragaonlis and the Lopa – speak their own languages.

In spite of the flight from the land which is also to be observed here in Nepal, in the last few years many of these ethnic groups in the Annapurna-Dhaulagiri area have either stayed or come back. To some, the ever-increasing number of tourists is an amusing enough attraction to settle down here; for others, the government or foreign partners have taken pains to provide the population with better living conditions. This must be said in order to make clear to the new arrival that the conditions – in comparison to the past – have improved substantially. There are now several smaller hydroelectric generating stations in many villages. The electricity they produce has greatly improved the quality of life of the local people.

In places where there is still no electricity, an installation of appropriate size

ANNAPURNA TREKKING

0   5   10 km

is at least planned in the next few years. Many Nepalis have a tendency to postpone things of importance – in general they say: *bholi, bholi* ("tomorrow", which here has the meaning of *soon*) or *khe garne* (what should one do?). However, in the area of **Thak Khola** along the **Kali Gandaki**, where the Thakali live, or in the region of **Ghandrung**, the settlement-area of the Gurung, this manner of speaking is less common than elsewhere in Nepal. Improved water facilities, enlarged and hardened hiking trails, supervision of the forests assigned to their villages and more schools make this district stand out visibly from the other rural areas of Nepal.

Organization and Self-Initiative

One contributing element of this is, the partially well-organized village communities and ethnic groups, which in general tend to favor not so much Hinduism, but Buddhism and the various ancestor and demon cults, which allow a

Sometimes trekking requires considerable courage and persistence.

greater degree of freedom in their personal lives. An organization must also be mentioned which in the last few years has been much talked about as an exemplary project for environmental and cultural protection. This is the **Annapurna Conservation Area Project**, which has been active since 1986, especially in the area of Ghandrung.

The project is working under the **King Mahendra Trust for Nature Conservation** in Nepal, and – with its planning and individual projects – has contributed decidedly to the improvement in the quality of life of the population. It is worth emphasizing here that this is not a governmental institution. As a result, better conditions were created to coordinate the plan with the needs of locally affected populations.

The intention was not to establish a Nature Reserve, in which the local residents are normally excluded from all con-

Winter landscape on the way to ABC, the Annapurna Base Camp.

siderations, sometimes even re-settled to other another section – or *out* – of their native area.

Trekkers shouldn't be too surprised if they are asked to leave behind a fee (most recently 200 rupees) for the Annapurna Project when they are at the immigration office in Kathmanu or Pokhara. The money is piped directly to the Project for new kerosene depots, health projects or other efforts. In the area of the Annapurna trail you will come across information boards over and over which request that you keep the surroundings clean, not only to set a good example for the local residents, but particularly for other hikers!

The Annapurna Conservation Area Project will shortly be extended to the region along the banks of the Kali-Gandaki River up to the villages of Jomosom and Muktinath and beyond the Thorung-La Pass to the area of Manang.

Trekking Routes: Prerequisites

Those who don't want to undertake the roughly one-week-long tour to **Jomosom** can also fly there – either with the regular flights of the Royal Nepalese Airline (depending on the season, from Kathmandu as well as from Pokhara) or with charter flights – which, however, are normally expensive. Find out about the most recent flight times and prices – they change constantly – when you arrive at the Royal Nepalese Airline office or at one of the numerous trekking agencies. If you only want to make one of the journeys by plane, it's recommended that you fly out and return by another method. In Jomosom, which possesses a little grass-overgrown landing field, a regular tumultuous scramble rules the place. If a booked flight should get called off because of bad weather – which happens frequently – by no means rely on being put at the top of the list of passengers in the next flight! The crew working for the Royal Nepalese Airline in Jomosom is frequently

117

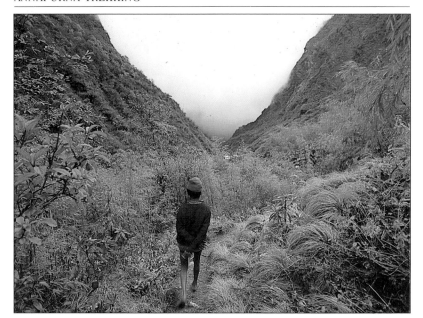

"utterly overworked" and tends to react in rather unfriendly fashion. This is partly because strangers to the village were transferred here, most of whom are also high-caste Hindus, who behave in a correspondingly arrogant manner – unfortunately also toward the locals.

Hikers who want to set off on one of the two major treks can put the first few kilometers out of Pokhara behind them by jeep. These can be rented behind the old **Shining Hospital** next to the exit of the village. You should find out about the price beforehand at your lodgings. In general, it is also recommended that you find out what the current price is, for carriers for example. Prices change very rapidly, and you shouldn't – as a result of a misunderstanding – be paying very much more than the population settled in the villages pays. Otherwise the locals will suffer from future price-increases.

The jeeps drive by the **Tibetan Camp Hyengja** – where there is a rug weavery and expensive souvenirs – to **Suikhet**, where there are several tea-houses. The

On the ABC trek you finally cross the timber line at Hinku.

one-hour drive ends here. Soon the road to **Baglung**, which is being built by the Chinese, will be finished, so that you can have yourself driven to the little village of **Lumle**. On from Suikhet, the climb up to the village of **Naudanda** takes roughly one hour. A beautiful high mountain ridge runs out from here toward the west. At this point the trek in the direction of Jomosom and Muktinath actually begins, for now you have finally taken leave of the Pokhara Valley. The Phewa Lake is located on the other side of the ridge. From there you can push on to **Naunanda** by way of the village of **Sarankot**. A little bit further on from there is the path to Gandrung and the Annapurna Base Camp.

Annapurna Base Camp

To take the shortest path into the Annapurna Base Camp you should turn right

Clouds hide the Annapurna mountain after mid-morning.

just after Suikhet, and from there on choose the climb over the opposite mountain ridge to **Dhamphus**. From there it takes about four days' march to get to the 2,000 meter altitude village of **Chomro** (**Chomrong**). The path leads at first to **Landrung**, with the remarkable houses of the Gurung; from there you climb down into the valley over a bridge and then again steep uphill over carved stair-steps to **Gandrung.** This village, which is the center of the Annapurna Conservation Area Project, offers an exquisite view of the Annapurna Massif with the great flank of the Annapurna South, the Hiunchuli and the so-called Fish-Tail Mountain – the holy mountain Macchapuchare.

Gandrung (Gaandruk) is an affluent Gurung village, the wealth of which was built up step by step by the British Gurkha soldiers through their pension payments. After about three more hours

you progress from Gandrung to **Kimrong Khola** (**Kyumnu**). From there it is only one more hour to **Chomro**, a Gurung village which for some time has also been the location of a kerosene depot.

In the high tourist season the population consumes almost a thousand liters of kerosene for the purpose of cooking per month. The use of the depot was connected with difficulties in the beginning, because many of the residents thought that using kerosene burners instead of wood stoves would spoil their food. However, once they realised how it could simplify their work in the kitchen the depot began enjoying great popularity among the people of the entire area. By the way, in Chomro you should remember to find out if the little tea-houses and lodges at Macchapuchare and at the Annapurna Base Camp are in service in spring and autumn. Otherwise you must be sure to pack sufficient provisions for the further two to three day long tour. In addition, you should also inquire whether

The valley between the Dhaulagiri and Annapurna massifs.

or not there is a danger of avalanches, which is often the case – especially in springtime.

From Chomro you reach, in about three hours, the mountain pastures of **Kuldi-Garh** (2,499 m). From here on the path continues through dense, humid bamboo rain-forest, and after about five hours you get to **Hinko** (3,100 m) under an immense cave-like rock overhang, where during the season a "tea-shop" is located. Beyond Hinko, after leaving the timber-line behind, comes a stretch where there is a danger of avalanches. Ice avalanches break off Hiunchuli, which are often noticed only too late. From the cave you proceed on past several tea shops in the two to three hour long ascent up to the **Macchapuchare Base Camp**, at 3,750 meters altitude, where a cabin is also located. The west flank of Macchapuchare, which up to now has never been ascended, towers above you. The mountain scenery here is particularly impressive, but the most intoxicating view of the imposing moutainous giants is to

be had at the Annapurna Base Camp, which is another hour's distance at 4,130 meters. Those who decide to set off still somewhat higher will experience an unforgettable panorama – from left to right the Hiunchuli (6,441 m), Fang, Annapurna I (8,091 m), Annapurna III (7,555 m), Macchapuchare (6,997 m.), the Tent Peak and the Fluted Peak. Beware of taking your ascents too rapidly. With the slightest hint of nausea you should descend immediately. Altitude sickness has already cost some people their lives.

On the return hike you can reach the village of **Ghorepani** (2,800 m) from Khola and Gandrung by way of a broken path over the **Deorali Pass**, which lies on the trekking route to Jomosom. Located about half way there is a guest-house in **Thante** which is managed by a veteran of the Gurkhas. You should give some consideration to taking a guide with you

Beyond Jomosom the barren landscape is like that of nearby Tibet.

from Gandrung to Ghorepani. On the next day you can undertake a rewarding one hour ascent from this village onto the 3,200 meter-high **Poon Hill**. From Ghorepani you can get back to Naudanda and on to Pokhara in a one or two day hike down the valley via **Birethani**.

Jomosom Muktinath Trek

You should estimate two weeks for the way there and back; for the trek around the Annapurnas a good 20 days. From the 1,458 m altitude **Naudanda** you can reach **Khare** (1,646 m) in three hours. From there on you continue to **Chandrakot** (1,646 m), for which you need just short of one and a half hours. Here you are only one more hour's distance from the first check-post, where you must present your trekking permit. In three hours from there you will reach the village of **Tirkhedunga**, and then the path

up begins to get more and more exhausting and burdensome. It will take you at least another hour to get to the little village of **Ulleri** (2,073 m), and from here on begins the steep ascent to the top of the pass over **Ghorepani** (2,600 m), which takes at least three hours. From Ghorepani, where primarily Gurung and Magar, but also Chetris and the so-called untouchable castes such as the Damai, Sarki, and Kami live, you have a beautiful panoramic view, especially when you climb up **Poon Hill** (see above). In three or four hours from the top of the pass the trail goes down again – passing by the inviting small village of **Sikha**, on to the river bed of the **Kali Gandaki**, where **Tatopani** (1,189 m) is located, the village with the hot sulphur springs. It is a pleasure, after the fatiguing descent, to take a bath here. If the forced march should have exhausted you, you will be able to relax a bit in this village and enjoy some pumpkin-cake, a local speciality imported by the Americans, and delicious citrus fruits.

121

amine trekking permits. It's a good three hours from Dana to **Ghasa** (2,012 m), on the way to which you pass by the **Rupse Khola Waterfall** and the little village of **Kabre**.

The climate – which up to now has still been of a pleasant subtropical sort – starts to change here. The region becomes drier, pine forests replace deciduous ones, and a different vegetation starts to develop. The human settlements look different as well. Flat, layered-stone buildings border the edges of the trail. This is where the original area of the Thakali begins. And this is also the location, at **Kabre** (1,707 m), of the most deeply-cut river canyon in the world, through which thunders the Kali Gandaki River. The river breaks through at a height of 1,700 meters, clamped in between two 8,000 meter peaks of the Himalayas – to the right is the majestic Annapurna Massif and to the left towers Dhaulagiri.

The area of Thakuri influence extends from Ghasa up to Jomoson here in the southern part of the Mustang district, the capital of which is Jomoson. Following the long, drawn-out village of **Ghasa** along the old pilgrim and trade route to Tibet is the village of **Lete** (2,438 m) which you can reach in three hours, then **Kalopani, Larjung** and **Kobang** (2,560 m), two to three hours' distance from Lete, and finally **Tukche**, at which you arrive after an hour's hike. As soon as you get behind Kalopani the valley begins to broaden enormously; the Kali Mandaki begins to meander a bit and an increasingly drier landscape with conifer and pine forests arises. Now there is no longer a trace of the glorious trader history of the Thakuri to be found. Besides agriculture and livestock breeding they have acted as toll-collecting *Subbhas* since the middle of the 19th century, and as traders between Tibet and India. However, the times when one trader's caravan after the other paraded through these villages are over.

Here the trek meers the old traders' path that leads south to the Indian border along the river. Even today you still come across the heavily-loaded mule caravans, or run into a pilgrim on the path to the sanctuary in Muktinath. Tatopani used to be one of the places where the Thakalis from Thak Kola – located further north in the Mustang district – stayed for the winters. Many of them now possess farms and hotels here. However, many of the lodges have disappeared since a flood – caused by a glacial lake in Tibet which suddenly drained – devastated the village two years ago, carrying half of it along with it. Very popular among hikers are the good food and cosy, homelike living-quarters, for which the Thakali are famous throughout Nepal.

Also in **Dana**, the next village – a good hour's distance from Tatopani – the influence of the Thakalis holds sway. Here there are impressive palatial houses with artistically-carved wooden balconies. Dana was earlier a toll station for traders, which was managed by Thakalis. Today a check-post is located here in order to ex-

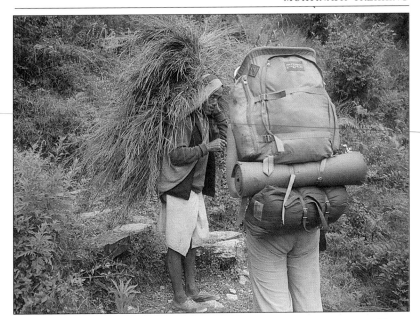

An encounter between two worlds on the path. Left: Porters at rest.

Tukche was the main point of re-loading in its day, where you can still admire the palatial stone buildings and the carefully attended mani walls of the rich traders of days gone by. But there is otherwise nothing left of the industrious activity from back then to be found. The mule caravans which once transported salt and grains out from Tukche now rapidly leave the village behind them, setting their courses for **Marpha**, which is now the largest and most important village besides Jomosom.

After the closure of the Tibetan-Chinese border in 1959, trading activities suffered badly. A portion of the Thakalis from Tukche and its surroundings emigrated to more southerly regions. As a result the ornamental little town of **Marpha** (2,600 m) has since the end of the 1960's become ever more widely renowned for its fruit and vegetable cultivation, thanks in particular to the govern-

ment-sponsored **Horticulture Farm**. The farm, known all throughout Nepal, is especially famous for its *rakshi* (spirits) distillery, which makes use of the apricots, pears and apples that grow in this area. In the meantime there are already two further distilleries, in Tukche as well as **Syang**, which is located further north.

The Thakali – Masters of the Valley

The influence of Tibet has led – in addition to a distinctive ancestor-cult – to a syncretism of animistic conceptions connected with the Bön tradition and Lamaism in the forms of the Nyingma School (old school) in the region between Ghasa and Jomosom.

The Thakali were segmented into the Tamang-Thakali (from Ghasa to Tukche), the Marpha Thakali (in Marpha) and the Yhulkasompa-Thakali (Syang, Chimang, Thini). The Tamang-Thakali were certainly known throughout Nepal. These laid particular emphasis on being the only ones to be named Thakali, for this name was connected with the power and political influence which they earlier had, as traders of salt and grain.

Looking toward the summit of Annapurna I from the base camp.

To this day their name is connected with a corresponding prestige, because after their re-settlement after 1959 the Tamang-Thakali either took over influential posts in the Nepalese administration, or they built up large businesses and hotels. The orientation toward Nepalese order of society which is influenced by Hindu has, in the meantime, manifested itself above all in the migrated Thakali in such a way that the role of ancestral worship, which had once been of central importance in the life-cycle of the Tamang Thakali, was pushed ever-further into the background. Also, today the Tamang-Thakali are still in competition with both of the other Thakali groups in the Mustang district, who are principally occupied with agriculture, livestock breeding and fruit production.

In contrast to the Tamang-Tamali, the life-style of the Yhulkasompa-Thakali is much more traditional. It is, for example,

thoroughly rewarding to deviate from the trekking route in order to seek out the very beautiful village of **Syang** on the path to Jomoson, which can be reached in one or two hours. You will find prayer banners with mantras written on them, mani-walls, and chortas everywhere. Perhaps you might also – after payment of a small donation – get to take a peek inside of the monastery. Sometimes there is a monk sitting here who paints thangkas (cult scroll-paintings).

By **Jomosom** (2,743 m; district capital) at the latest you will have ascertained that the climate is indeed becoming constantly harsher, and that the landscape is often reminiscent of a desert-like wasteland. The village is divided into several sections. First of all you come across the airport which has a variety of accomodations for those unfortunates who must often wait for days for a flight. You frequently hear stories of tourists being

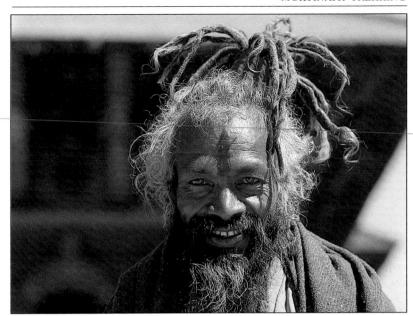

A happy sadhu at Muktinath, the end of his pilgrimage.

stranded here, cursing and mourning their confirmed booking on the flight home out of Kathmandu. Adjacent to the airport grounds there are administrative buildings primarily for the army which is here to secure the border to Tibet and China – seven days' distance. Also, a recently constructed check-post is located in this area. The actual heart of the village is connected to this section by a bridge over the Kali Gandaki. On the other side of the bridge there are several especially attractive hotels. There is also a small bank next to a hospital.

Muktinath – Goal of the Pilgrims

Through the Kali Gandaki Valley, which becomes increasingly windy (the wind kicks up about 10.00 a.m.; before any aircraft can land and take off), the path continues through the gravelly riverbed and then up steep rock ridges. If you're lucky you might find a thousands of years-old ammonite fossils, but you can also buy them directly from traders. Our goal is the pilgrimage village of **Muktinath** (3,800 m), which is around five hours' distance from Jomosom. There are two ways of getting there. You can hike from Jomosom to **Kagbeni** (3,800 m) in two hours, with a short break in the so-called *eklai bhatti* (the only resting house anywhere in the area). Kagbeni is the last accessible village to foreigners before the restricted area of northern **Mustang** – the kingdom of Lo. From here we have the fatiguing ascent to the valley of **Baragaon**, in which Muktinath is also located. Another trail leads over a steep knoll behind the *eklai bhatti* directly into the high-altitude valley. Passing the village of **Khingar** (**Khyenghar**) you reach **Ranipauwa**, a small settlement from which it takes only a few minutes to get to the holy village, which is located in a little poplar forest.

The population here is plainly distinguishable from the Thakali, in both lan-

125

guage as well as appearance and living habits. They are named Baragaonlis – people from Baragaon – and are of Tibetan origin, but they prefer to call themselves Gurung. It is assumed that the southernmost outpost of the Tibetan kingdom was once located here. The chequered villages are reminiscent of pueblos, and the red-plaster Buddhist gompas – visible from quite a distance – exert a magical power of attraction on the visitor. The living conditions here are as harsh as the climate.

Muktinath was already mentioned around 300 years before the era of the *Mahabharata* epic. Hindus as well as Buddhists make pilgrimages to this village, where Brahma – the creator-god of the Hindus – made a sacrifice "by setting a fire on the water". And, in one small Buddhist gompa, you can actually see slender natural gas flames rising from the ground with jets of water. The Buddhists believe that the great master teacher Padmasambhava (eighth century A.D.) – who bought the Tantric Vajrayana Budd-

The village of Jharkot is only a few minutes walk from Muktinath.

hism to Tibet – used to meditate here. They will be happy to show you his supposed foot prints.

Over the Thorung La to Manang

The crossing over the **Thorung Pass** is the only connecting path between the two large valleys of the **Kali Gandaki** and the **Marsyandi Khola**. In March, when even up here at 4,000 meters the fierce winter begins to slowly let up, the first caravans of porters follow the exhausting trail over the pass, still deep in snow. In October, when the heavier snowfalls start, the Thorung La again separates the two valleys.

Out of Muktinath it's a steep ascent up to the top of the pass – at just short of 5,400 meters. Even if you have now gotten accustomed to long foot marches, reaching the top still presents quite a challenge. You should be correspond-

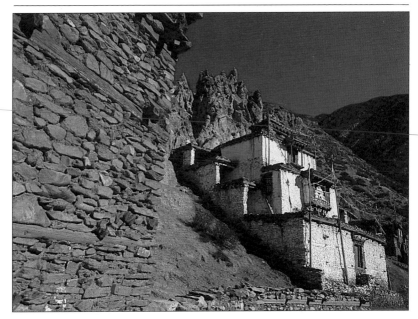

The Braga Gompa, high and remote in the Marsyandi Valley.

ingly more careful and follow the old mountain-climber's rule of "ascending slowly". Beginning at the latest from Muktinath you will find yourself in high altitude regions, in which – independent of physical condition, age or other factors – altitude sickness can break out. Headaches are the first sign of this insidious illness, which – if you disregard it – can have deadly results. False heroic courage is completely out of place here. The only thing to do is descend to a village at lower altitude, in order to become more acclimatized, and then starting to attempt the climb again.

Crossing over the pass requires two days of hiking, primarily because of the altitude. Thus it is recommended to spend the night either at about 4,200 meters in a little tea-house or at about 4,800 meters on a well-located meadow. On from here there is a stunning view of the summits of Dhaulagiri and Tukche Peak (6,920 m)

Between the little tea house and the **Thorung La Base Camp** there are no established lodging possibilities. A tent, or at least a bivouac sack is an indispensable necessity here. Besides the cold temperatures at night, the sun at these altitudes is not to be underestimated. A good pair of sun-glasses and sun protection creme are therefore absolute musts.

On the next day you arrive – after a steep and laborious ascent – to the 5,400 meter Thorung La. From here you have an incredible panorama over the summit of Annapurna, the Chulu and Pisang Mountains, and the Thorung Peak. The descent continues to the Thorung La Base Camp or – still about two hours further – to a large camping area. From this point on you will again find tea-houses and lodges.

On the next day, you will leave the upper Marsyandi Valley (**Manangboth**) and arrive in the large village of **Manang** with its pueblo-style stone houses.

The Manangi are famous and infamous traders, whose routes today often lead

127

A Nepalese kitchen needs little equipment.

them even as far as Hong Kong or Singapore. Their splendid stone houses are decorated with the colorful prayer-banners of the Buddhists, which flap gaily in the wind. The view of the gigantic **Glacier Dome** is also very impressive. Furthermore, its exceedingly slow movement down the mountainside is accompanied by clearly audible sounds.

The houses in the next village, **Braga**, picturesquely perched on a cliff, are also entirely made of stone, which insulates them against both heat and cold. The large, conspicuous roof terraces, which are aligned to the south and very useful in winter, are where the whole life of the village population runs its course – especially during the colder times of year, when the people gather what few warm rays of sun they can. Braga also possesses a large gompa – thoroughly worth seeing – the origin of which is traced back to the poet and yogi Milarepa.

From Manang to Pokhara

The path moves on further through the Marsyandi Valley, while the mighty ice-giants of the Annapurna group are still in your field of vision. The trail leads through fir and juniper forests, passes by the **Manang Airport** – to which the Royal Nepalese Airline flies – and continues further to the large village of **Pisang** at the feet of the **Pisang Peak** (6,091 m).

By this point at the latest you will have noticed the remarkable difference between the Kali Gandaki Valley, which is quite accomodating to tourists, and the Marsyandi Valley. The reasons for this are the later opening of this area to tourists and the remote location. You can clearly see the difference between the old and heavily-travelled caravan route and the secluded Marsanyi Valley. Even after so many years of voluminous tourism, not much has changed.

The next day, the trail leads you further down through the valley along the river, going past the former Tibetan Khampa encampment of **Badang**, where today there is an apple plantation. The next larger village is **Chame**, in the area of which there are also hot springs (*tato pani*).

Down from here to the village of **Tal**, the residents are followers of Tibetan Buddhism, and decorate their houses with colorful prayer-banners. The next station on this trekking route is **Shyange** or, somewhat further, **Khuldi.**

If you don't want to take the dusty path along the street over **Besisahar** to **Dhumre**, you can hike west from Khuldi directly to Pokhara in two or three days of solidary walking. On this path you come through the villages of **Nalma Pedi**, **Thisanku** and **Dhal Besi**. Through the **Begnas Valley** you finally reach the **Rupa** and **Begnas Lakes**, before you meet up with the Kathmandu-Pokhara Road again.

ANNAPURNA / MUKTINATH

In almost every village you will find very simple accomodation, which is indicated by signs. However, in the **Gandrung** area and with the Thakali in **Tukche**, **Marpha** and **Jomosom**, besides the really good and wide variety of food, the sanitary facilities are also better than elsewhere. To some extent there are even solar-energy or electric water heaters for a delightful bath!

Festivals

In November – *Dekhyop* mask-dance in the buddhistic Nyingmapa monasteries of Tukche and Marpha. In March – *Torungla* bow-and-arrow festival among the Thakali in Tukche. In August – *Yartung* riding festival and competition in Muktinath. In September - *Shyopen Lhawa* village festival of the Thakali in Kobang. (The dates vary - inquire!).

Hospitals

It is recommended to bring along bandages, water disinfection tablets, medications against joint pain and diarrhea illnesses, sun protectants, elastic bandages, cold, flu and inflammation reducing medications, light analgesics, and antibiotics. You must consult your physician beforehand. Don't distribute any medications to the population.

Telecommunication / Post

Radio installation in **Jomosom** (airport, army base). Postal station in **Gandrung, Tatopani, Tukche** (the postcards we sent even arrived!).

Trekking Season

The best times are in October and November as well as March through May. Because the monsoon rains only partially reach Thak Khola and the Muktinath region, you can even have a very good hike during summer. Attention: There are leeches in the area of Gandrung and the lower-lying valleys during this time.

Bank

There is a bank located in **Jomosom**; teller windows open according to the usual business hours. Attention: Always inquire concerning the next holidays, because then the bank is closed.

Restaurants

Tatopani is known for its citrus-fruit plantation. In several hotels there is outstanding pumpkin-cake and fresh peppermint tea. Tatopani is particularly well-suited for a couple of days' relaxation. The distilleries in **Thak Kola, Marpha, Tukche** and **Syang** are famous.

If you hike from Tukche to Marpha, located shortly before the entrance to the village is a horticultural farm where, under the management of the legendary Pasang Sherpa, the widest variety of vegetable and fruit types (pears, apricots, apples) is grown. The Marpha brandy which is produced here is prized throughout Nepal. In Tukche at Nirjal and Mana Sherchan you can get - besides apple and apricot brandy – also orange brandy (oranges from Tatopani). In **Syang** ask after Bishnu Hirachan's distillery.

Shopping

In the Tibetan camp shortly before **Marpha** there are souvenirs and carpets. In Jharkot and Muktinath shawls and scarves produced by the indigenous population out of yak and goat wool are offered for sale.

Various

The center of the Annapurna Conservation Area Project is in **Gandrung**. Hot springs are found in **Tatopani**. Army base in **Jomosom** - in case a helicopter is needed. From about 10:00 A.M. there is a strong backwind from Marpha to Muktinath; on the return trip you're walking into it. For this reason get up early. Between Larjung/Kobang and Jomoson there is electricity.

Getting There

By aircraft to Jomosom (grass landing strip). Flown several times weekly using a Twin-Otter machine from Pokhara (c. 30 minutes) and Kathmandu (c. 50 minutes); very dependent on the weather and actually very uncertain – the flights often depend on the "good will" of the RNAC officers; inquire about the most recent departure times (they change a lot) and the latest prices at the RNAC in Kathmandu (1990 from Pokhara US \$35, from Kathmandu US \$58). From Kathmandu you can get to Pokhara by bus or airplane, beginning your trek from behind the Shining Hospital at the exit of the village. Go there by group taxi or the public bus - or drive with a jeep to Phedi/Suikhet from Pokhara.

Worthwhile Excursions

Leaving Muktinath you can take the Thorung La Pass (5,270 meters - watch out for altitude sickness) to Manang on the trekking route by the same name, take this on down to the overland road which reaches to Dumre. From **Tukche** up the 5,200 meter high Dhampus Pass; bring along food, fuel, tent. From **Lete** to the Annapurna Base Camp North over a 4,900 m pass (Thulo Bugin). From **Thini** (gaon) near Jomosom to the Meso Kanto Pass (5,100 m) where you can see the Tilicho Lake. Pay attention to altitude sickness. Be ready to discontinue at any given time for the sake of your health. Poon Hill with observation tower, 300 meters above Ghorepani, 45 min. ascent. There you got a panoramic view – from west to east: Gurja Himal, Dhaulagiri, Tukchep Peak, Nilgiri, Annapurna, Macchapuchare, and Lamjung Himal.

1 Far Western
2 Mid Western
3 Western
4 Central
5 Eastern

CHINA

Jumla
Dolpo

Annapurna
Pokhara Pokhara
Langtang
Helambu Solu
NEPAL Kath.Khumbu Eastern
Kathmandu Valley Nepal
Terai

Lucknow

Biratnagar

BANGL.

Patna

Allahabad
Varanasi

Rajshahi

INDIA

TRIP INTO THE
MIDDLE AGES

JUMLA
DOLPO

The Jumla and Dolpo districts of west Nepal have remained, almost completely spared from the ravages of the modern tourist trade, so that you might feel – so to say – transported into the Nepalese Middle Ages.

On the one hand this is very attractive, however on the other hand, the trip requires a lot of preparation. If you do not go on a promoter-organized trekking tour, then in making your travel plans you can count on having to be completely on your own, and correspondingly well enough equipped for self-sufficiency. That means you will have to bring along everything from your tent to your toothbrush and soup-cubes.

The accomodation and shopping possibilities in this area are exceedingly limited, and even in the district capitals of Jumla and Dolpo there is hardly anything to be found. During certain seasons even the local population obtains some of its provisions by airplane, because the basic staples on hand – such as rice and wheat – are inadequate for their nourishment.

Do not be misled by such high-sounding names as "hotel" or "lodges" – these, almost without exception, offer only primitive accomodation which should

Preceding pages: The deep-blue Phoksumdo Lake near Dolpo Pa.

only be entered into with a corresponding pioneer spirit and plenty of insect exterminant. The accompanying "restaurants" often serve exclusively tea and chapatis; at certain times of the year even getting *dhal bhat*, the national dish (rice with lentil sauce, one of the most commonly prepared foods), becomes a problem for the traveler.

Once you have left the district capitals, any hope of seeking out a lodge or restaurant will be in vain. Making yourself understood to the population presents yet another problem. Almost nobody here speaks English, so that you would be well advised to pick up a few phrases of Nepalese or, among the Dolpo, Tibetan, so that you will be able to conduct at least the most essential conversations.

Note should also be taken of the climatic peculiarities of this region. The imposing Dhaulagiri Massif as well as its western spurs, which separate the region from the Indian low plains, are in effect a weather boundary, by which the influence of the monsoons is substantially reduced. As a result the area is relatively poor in precipitaion, with cold to very cold winters. However, in contrast to most of the other regions of Nepal, this sort of weather can also blow in during the summer. The climate of Dolpo in particular is highly reminiscent of that in

Tibet. The best times for travel here are May, September and October. Nevertheless, before you make up your mind to take a tour through the Dolpo region, you must be appropriately acclimatized, because you'll be staying at some very high altitudes. Altitude sickness has even forced some very seasoned walkers to make a hasty retreat. Unless you prepare yourself in this manner your life could be in danger.

Arriving

Because of the isolated location of the entire Jumla region, flight is the only recommended way to travel. Otherwise you will have to take a wearying bus journey and make the final approach to your destination on foot, which in itself could really qualify as a separate trekking tour.

For the flight connections a RNAC 20-seater Twin-Otter aircraft is employed, but it can only fly when the weather is good.

There is a direct flight once a week, but the connection via Nepalganj is better. It flies from Kathmandu as well as from Jumla several times daily (except in the monsoon season). You can only fly to Dunai/Juphal via Nepalganj; from Nepalganj to **Juphal** there are two flights a week.

For the Courageous

The fastest way to get to Jumla over land is by public bus, from Kathmandu via Nepalganj to **Surkhet** (travel time about 46 hours, and the bus will be crowded). From there it takes seven or eight day on foot, via the villages of Dailekh and Kalikot.

The best way to get to **Dunai**, the district capital, is to take the bus to Pokhara (travel time about twelve hours) and from there to take the eight to twelve day hike by way of Baglung, Dhorpatan and Lake Puphal.

From Jumla to the Rara Lake

Jumla (2,347 meters) – which is situated among green fields of grain in the Tila river valley – is, despite its administrative importance, a small and not exactly clean town with only about 4,000 inhabitants. There is only one lodge and a small number of shops at which the shopping opportunities are primarily limited to the autumn, when, after the harvest, a selection of grains, fruits and vegetables is available.

The population of Jumla consists predominantly of Thakuri, a sub-caste of the Chetri, of which the king (Birendra Shah) is also a member. As such we are concerned here with Hindus, who as members of the second-highest caste are actually not allowed to let us "untouchables" into their houses or offer us other accommodation.

The walk to **Rara Lake** takes about four days. If you should require the services of carriers, they can be hired in Jumla, however you should know that they are normally very poorly equipped and are not exactly fluent in the English language. After you have presented your trekking permits to the local police in Jumla, turn eastwards, past the landing strip and on up to the confluence of the Tila with the **Chaudbise** river. From this point on the going gets steep over the village of **Ghursenigaon** (2,590 meters) until **Padmara** (3,017 meters), a village which is reached after a good march of about six hours.

The next day you climb further up the mountains and before long find yourself high above the dense evergreen forests. Shortly after crossing the **Khali-Langna Pass** you will reach a fork in the path. The path that leads up from the south is a faster and more direct connection to Jumla than ours, however it is certainly the more difficult route because you have to make it over the **Danphe Pass** (3,688 meters). Through a dense mixed forest

CHANGLA HIMAL

6776

5949

5550

Maquan He (Matsang Tsangpo)

Paryang

5950

CHINA
LINE
NEPAL

C H I N A

6078

2062

6712   6562

Mengri

Shey-Phoksumdo

5660

Karnali
Rara Lake

Jahri
Gumgarhi

Rara
N.P.

SISNE HIMAL

6596

KANJIROBA

Phopagaon

National Park

Langu

Tingjegaon

Sirpa

Chauta
Pina
Bumrad

6883

Kanjiroba

Ludku

4160

Khali-Lagna Pass

Padmara

6525

KANJIROBA HIMAL

Ghursenigaon

Jumla

Kurari

Kagmara Pass Kanjelaruwa

5931

Gothigaon

Kunrigaon

Munigaon

Chaurikot Rimi
Triprikot

6612

Kagmara
5960   Pungmo

Numla Pass

Ringmo

Do

Naphukhona

Kaigaon

Bolangna Pass

Basia Pass

5459

Lunh

Tibrikot

Rohagaon

5264

Dunai

Tarakot

Khanigaon

Kakkotgaon

5382

5606

6581

5922

D H A U L A G I R I

7660

H I M A L

Dumjafa
2637

Jajarkot

Jumlikhalanga

Royal Dhorpatan

8167
Dhaulagiri

2102

Musikot

Padmi

4688

J 4773

Bega

Rukumkot

Hunting Reserve

Beni

2537

Baramelo

3583

Dhorpatan

Baglung

Sallyan

2828

Jelbang

Thapagaon

3531

Lawamjula

2059   N   E   P   A   L

2786

Khumkhani

2446

Ramkot

Tulsipur

Swargdwar

Pyuthan

2143

Tamghas
2339

2570

Ghorahi

Sandhikharka

955   1818

2277   1688

Tansen

**JUMLA DOLPO
TREKKING**

0   20 km

with imposing birch trees – whose bark has found application in this region as a paper substitute – you hike down to **Sinja Khola**, and, soon after crossing it, arrive at the little village of **Bumrad** (six hours). The next stage leads us via **Chauta** and the **Ghurchi-Lagna Pass** (3,444 meters) in seven hours to the settlement of **Pina** (2438 meters).

Shortly after Pina you arrive at another fork in the path. After leaving the main path, which leads to **Gumgarhi**, you turn to the left and come finally to **Rara Lake** after an interesting five-hour-long hike, that takes you through the small village of **Jahri** (2,530 meters).

The entire region surrounding the lake was declared a national park in 1975. Here it is less the panorama of the steep ice-giants which makes the visit seem so rewarding, than the overall beauty of the landscape. Fir trees, spruces, Scotch pines, cedars and rhododendrons form a large and sprawling forest, in which bears, wild-cats, wolves and red deer are still to be found. The most beautiful of the many camp-sites lie along the southern shore of the lake.

In the process of establishing the national park, the Nepalese government undertook a step which has since given them much cause for regret. The population that was living around Rara Lake was resettled. They were offered land in Terai – the flat-land in the south of Nepal instead. However, this did not turn out to be to the advantage of the dislocated people. Today they are living in Terai under somewhat worse conditions than before in Jumla.

Although this region is not a traditional and important destination for pilgrims – such as Muktinath, for example – there are certainly a few stony witnesses to the past, such as, for example, the **Malla Stones** – stone pillars with *Devanagari* inscriptions, which originate in the twelfth century, when the Malla kings ruled over western Nepal. Located on the eastern shore of Rara Lake there are the so-called petrified foot-prints of the god *Thakur,* who is supposed to have shifted the outlet of the lake from here to the west. To commemorate this occasion a ceremony occurs each year in July or August.

For the return path to Jumla there is an alternative route which leads west of the one already described. It leads downwards to the **Khatyar Valley** and further over a 3,800 meter mountain ridge-top to the settlement of **Ghorasain** (3,800 meters, six hours). From here on it is still about four hours to **Sinja** (2,438 meters), which was once a summer residence of the Malla kings. A two days' march with about 16 hours' worth of hiking time still separate us at this point from Jumla, which will finally be reached through the **Jaljala Valley**.

From Jumla into Dolpo

At the end of 1988 and in May 1989 a section of a district was opened for tourism by the Nepalese government which is among the most interesting regions of Nepal. This is the **Dolpo**, a region which belongs legally to Nepal, but whose inhabitants, as fas as their descent, culture and language are concerned, are Tibetans. As a result of their isolated location, the approximately 4,500 *Dolpo pa* – as the inhabitants of this plateau (which lies between 3,300 and 4,500 meters in altitude) are named – have been able to preserve their traditional way of life to the present day. One special aspect of their culture is that the ancient and rather animistic rites of *Bön* – the old pre-Buddhist primitive religion of Tibet – are still alive, with their partly shamanistic ceremonies.

The Dolpo was already settled by Tibetans in the tenth century. These gave the land the name *Bä Yül* – "hidden country". Up to about 1800 it belonged to Tibet, but it was obliged to pay tributes to

Trekkers and porters need resilience on the journey to Dolpo.

the neighboring kingdoms of Lo and Jumla. It wasn't until after the subjugation of these kingdoms by the Gurkha dynasty that Dolpo became a part of the Nepalese kingdom. Even so, the influence of Kathmandu remained insignificant, and it took until 1963 before the government made direct links with the *Dolpo pa*.

Although, it only takes two and a half days from Jumla to reach the border of the Dolpo district, it takes seven to push into inner Dolpo, which as already mentioned is so especially interesting. Leaving Jumla one turns first to the east and passes the Thakuri settlements of **Gothigaon, Kunrigaon** and **Munigaon** (seven hours). Further up-river along the Tila River which becomes ever narrower, one finally arrives after three hours at **Naphukhona,** the first village with a purely Buddhist population.

Make sure you pay a visit to the **Nyingma Monastery** above the village!

Through birch, fir and rhododendron forests you proceed to the **Barbaria-**

Lagna Pass (3,810 meters, four hours), which forms the boundary of the Dolpo district. After a steep descent the valley broadens out, and above the **Bheri River** you move along the scattered settlements of **Chaurikot, Rimi** and **Kaigaon** (seven hours foot-march; only poor camping possibilities).

Those who shy away from the technically easy, but fatiguing and burdensome path over the **Kagmara Pass** (5,115 meters) can cross over the Bheri at **Kaigaon** and reach the Shey Phoksumdo National Park (see p.140) in four or five days by way of the considerably lower **Bolangna Pass,** via the villages of **Tibrikot, Dunai** and **Rohagaon.**

If you decide to take the Kagmara Pass anyway, you will be confronted with a fantastic high-mountain world, the view of which is rich compensation for the difficult of the climb. Via **Hurikot** you hike first of all along the Bheri – in untouched

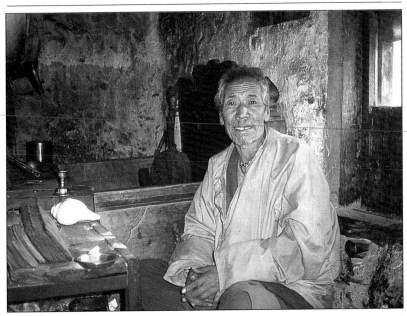

A cheerful and serene monk in the monastery at Ringmo.

nature – up to the river's fork. After that the way leads for a short while up the chilly waters of the **Jagdula River**, which you soon cross. Passing by a lonely military station (3,100 meters, four and a half hours) you next come into the **Garpung Valley**. Climbing steadily, you leave the forest region and arrive after about five hours at a wide 4,100 meter altitude plain, which must be crossed. Turning into the last side-valley to the right, you see the Kagmara Pass directly before you.

In springtime it is recommended that you spend the night at the foot of the pass, in order to begin the march very early the next morning, because the snow fields that await you on the other side of the pass must be crossed while they are still frozen hard. It takes two and a half to three hours to reach the top of the pass. From there one has a great view of the ice-giants of the **Kanjiroba Himal** and the Kagmara group with the **Kagmara I** (5960). With the breathtaking view of the western walls of **Kanjelaruwa** (6,612 meters) you start down the easy path into the **Dorjan Khola Valley**.

Keep an eye out for the famous blue sheep (*bharal*) and snow grouse which are often to be spied along the way!

After five and a half hours you come again to regions, at an altitude of 3700 meters, where suitable camping spots can be found. Three hours later you will once again come across the first traces of human civilization – initially in the form of meager, isolated fields and huts, then in the form of houses with their charac-teristic flat roofs on which cloth is woven, yarn is spun or laundry is washed. Located in the ground floor of these houses are stables and supply rooms which are connected to the living rooms by wooden ladders. These are made of roughly-hewn tree-trunks which are sawn through lengthwise and into which steps are then notched. Meeting the first residents you will believe you have really been transported to Tibet: you will be openly and heartily welcomed in **Pungmo**, and everything that seems unusual to them will be touched, ogled and commented on.

We found the red and white painted entrance halls particularly memorable, as well as the interior wall-paintings several of which show a strong Bön influence. The deities are identical to those of Tibetan Buddhism, only the names are different, and the left-turning *svastika*, one of the symbols of the Böns, shows up over and over. You shouldn't neglect participating in a *puja* in the monastery of **Pungmo** – in exchange for a small donation you will be given permission to enter.

From Pungmo you need another hour to the entrance of the **Shey- Phoksumdo National Park**, where your trekking permits will first be checked again. There you can also get information about the park, and there is also a small museum devoted to local fauna.

After payment of the appropriate fees you can enter the national park, and, in a three hour-long hike which includes some very steep climbs, reach the village of **Ringmo**. On the way there are beautiful views of the eroded landscape opposite you, and also of the waterfall which forms the outlet of the Phoksumdo Lake.

This deep-blue lake, located directly below Ringmo, is surrounded by high, glaciated mountains and shelters a small *gompa* (monastery) on its south-eastern shore, which houses an aged monk who still practices the old rites, which are similar to shamanism.

In the smoke-blackened prayer chamber there are numerous amulets and dried herbs hanging from the ceiling, which he uses for healing illnesses. His art is based on methods of naturopathy, however it includes elaborate and secret gesticulations which are of great meaning to the *Dolpo pa*. In serious cases the healer visits the patient at night, puts himself into a trance, during which he inhales the smoke of a juniper or rhododendron fire, and besides dispensing the natural medicines he also tries to entice the spirit of the sick person – which had earlier been kidnapped by evil spirits – back into his body, through singing, dancing and prayer. This "treatment" is not without a price – a religious healer doesn't live on fresh air and love either.

Because of the beautiful view of the **Kanjiroba Himal**, a hike around the lake is strongly recommended. You should figure on one day's hike along the western shore to make it to the north-east section. There is little point in going further in this direction because shortly after the lake you reach the boundary of a *restricted area*, which as a tourist you may not cross. The famous **Shey Monastery** and the **Crystal Mountain** still cannot be visited at the moment.

From Ringmo on you can proceed along one of two paths:

Direct Descent to Dunai

First take the same route back to the entrance of the national park. From there you can reach **Dunai** in a two-day march. The path there takes you first along the luxuriant banks of the **Dorjam Khola**, and then, upriver for five to six hours of constant up and down. Finally, you leave the forest zone, and after another five to six hours reach the district capital Dunai, which is located in an open hill territory. When the weather is clear one has a beautiful view of the massive silhouette of the Dhaulagiri Himal.

Over the Basia and Numla Pass

This variation is certainly more interesting, though it takes four or five days longer. It leads from Ringmo in a southeasterly direction up to the **Basia Pass**. This approximately 5,100 meter altitude

Salt is still carried on the backs of persevering goats.

pass has to be crossed just as does, on the next day, the **Numla Pass** at about the same height. The path is certainly simple enough for the beginner trekker, and offers a lovely view of the Dhaulagiri group, however, because of its altitude, it is very fatiguing, so that the walking times depend very strongly on your physical condition and acclimatization – and the weather. In spring you can count on a lot of snow on the passes.

Finally you make it into the broad, high valley of **Tarap**, in which about 1,500 *Dolpo pa* live in four villages.

The two most important villages are named **Thakya** (4,200 meters) and **Do** (4,090 meters). As a result of the climatic conditions, only a small crop of potatoes and barley is possible, which at the present time is no longer enough to meet the basic needs of life.

Most of the *Dolpo pa* are therefore forced to live as semi- nomads, and spend the long hard winters together with their herds of livestock – primarily goats, sheep and yaks – in lower-lying areas. The salt trade with Tibet represents another important source of income.

In the Tarap Valley there are many beautiful gompas (monasteries) to be admired, which are partly bound to the Buddhist Nyingma tradition of the Bön beliefs. Observe the unusual construction of the **chortas**: a remarkable feature is the additional wooden roof between *harmika* and *bumpa*, which is found only in the Dolpo region.

Beyond the village of Do, one leaves the central area of Dolpo and arrives within two or three days by way of the wild, cavernous Tarap Valley to **Khanigaon** (2,800 meters; police check- post) or **Tarakot**, where the majority of the residents are once again Hindus. All of the regions east of the settlements between Thakya and Tarakot are still closed off to tourists. This means that crossing over to **Jomosom** through the valley of the Barbung Khola or via Chharkabhot-

In the upper regions yaks and tzos are kept as domestic animals.

gaon was, as of the beginning of 1989, still not officially possible.

From Tarakot you can reach **Dunai** in a strenuous day's hike. The town doesn't have much to offer and is only a stop on the way to the airport of **Juphal**, which is located two and a half to three hours from Dunai.

With a total area of 3,555 square kilometers, the **Shey-Phoksumdo National Park** is the largest in all of Nepal. It was founded in 1984, after the Nepalese government became aware of the unique character of both the culture and the landscape of this region.

There are approximately 3.000 people living in the area of the national park, of which the majority belongs to ethnic groups of Tibetan ancestry.

There are also a few Brahmans and Chetri. All of the residence must, of course, follow the special rules of the park, as a result of which conflicts arise

again and again. For example, no open fires are allowed, and hunting and fishing are forbidden, as is the felling of trees. For heating and cooking only broken branches and dead trees can be used. The wood that is used to build houses even has to be paid for, and carries a high price-tag indeed: 430 rupees for every cubic meter.

Each family is only allowed to make use of their own private land and soil. This means that housing construction, agriculture and even livestock breeding are not permitted on the land of the national park. But because the families' own property is no longer sufficient for their living needs (due to longer life-expectancy and lower child mortality rates with the same number of births, division of the private lands through inheritance) they have tried to find other sources of livelihood.

Yet, wool production, weaving work, and a larger amount of livestock breeding haven't solved the problem. So it often happens that the locals disobey the law and, for example, allow their animals to graze freely on national park land, which of course causes serious damage to the younger trees.

One of the most important functions of the park directorate is therefore to check on the observance of the laws. Further jobs include the maintenance of the paths as well as the observation of the wildlife, including blue sheep, wolves and the snow leopard.

There are long-term plans for the installation of new, wider paths, which will also be accessible to horses, and it will be possible to bring more materials into the park. The construction of a lodge is also planned which should one day serve to accomodate tourists.

With the Langtang Valley standing as a visible organizational example, the actual goal is a large increase in tourism , which is also, naturally, supported strongly by the Dolpo residents themselves.

JUMLA / DOLPO
Accomodation

Neither Jumla nor the Dolpo region has made adjustments to trekking tourism. Therefore there are lodges for an overnight stay in only a few villages. So bring along your own tenting equipment, food and other provisions.

In **Dunai**, the capital of the Dolpo region, there are three simple lodgings.

In **Jumla**, the capital of the Karnali zone as well as the Jumla district, there is one small lodge, as is also true of **Juphal** in the Dolpo area, where there is also a landing strip.

N.B.: When staying overnight in the **Rara** or **Shey- Phoksumdo National Parks**, a fee of 100 rupees per person must be included in your calculations; this must usually be paid together with the entrance fees for the national parks. (As of Summer 1989)

Hospitals

Except for a small, primitively equipped hospital in **Jumla** there is no medical care in the entire Jumla and Dolpo region.

Telecommunication

There is no telephone network in the entire region. There is the possibility in **Jumla** and **Dunai** of sending a telegram from the telecommunication office, however you cannot rely on the receiver actually getting it.

Carriers

These can, in principle, be hired everywhere. However, keep in mind the language barrier, and the fact that the local carriers are not thought of as very reliable. The daily pay in summer 1989 was about 80 NRs per carrier with a load of between 20 and 30 kg.

Various

Interesting Nyingma or Bön monasteries are located in Naphakuna, Pungmo, Ringmo and the High Valley of Tarap. You must request permission if you want to see the monastery from inside!

Jumla is the capital of the Karnali zone as well as the Jumla district. It has approx. 4,000 inhabitants and lies at 2,347 m altitude. Besides various authorities, a hospital and a school, there is a telecommunication office and even a landing strip.

Dunai, with about 2,500 inhabitants, is located at 2,200 m altitude. It is the capital of the Dolpo region with the corresponding authorities, a school, and the district police office.

The only landing strip in the Dolpo region is located in **Juphal**, about two hours away from Dunai.

The entrance and main administration of the **Shey-Phoksumdo National Park** is located in Sumdua at Pungmo. The entrance fee costs 250 rupees per person.

The headquarters of the 106 sq.km **Rara National Park** is found in Hutu at the northern end of Rara Lake, the largest lake in Nepal.

Trekking Permit / Restricted Areas

Make sure when proposing the route for your trekking permit that it doesn't run through one of the restricted areas – in other words, forbidden zones for foreigners.

The entire Jumla district is open, while in the Mugo district the whole eastern part starting around Rara Lake is off limits.

In the Dolpo district – up to the summer of 1989 – the 5 panchayats (counties) of Phijor, Saldan, Tinje, Chharkabhot and Mukot – or the whole east and north sections of the Dolpo district - were still closed.

If you are not sure, consult the State Secretary of Border Security at the Ministry of Home Affairs in Kathmandu, where the present situation can be precisely explained to you.

Getting There

The fastest way to **Jumla** over land is by public bus via Nepalganj to Surkhet (Birendranagar) – travel time about 46 hours. From there it's 7-8 days by foot over the villages of Dailekh and Kalikot.

To **Dunai**, the district capital of Dolpo, the best way from Kathmandu is by bus to Pokhara and from there 8-10 days' hike through the villages of Baglung, Dhorpatan (2,700 meters, has landing strip) and past Puphal Lake on up to Dunai.

For the flight connections a 20-seater Twin Otter aircraft is used: there is only one direct flight from Kathmandu to Jumla per week – the connection via Nepalganj is better, which is flown several times daily from Kathmandu as well as back from Jumla (except in the monsoon season). One way to Nepalganj cost 530 NR, connection on to Kathmandu several times daily at US $90 (as of summer 1989).

From Kathmandu to Dunai/Juphal you can only fly via Nepalganj.

From Nepalganj to Juphal there are two flights a week – one way 530 NR, on from there to Kathmandu several times daily US $90. The RNAC is located at the Juphal Airport.

Worthwhile Excursion

From Jumla (2,340 meters) you can take a beautiful 3-4 day tour up to the 3,000 meter altitude **Rara Lake**, which at 13 sq.km is Nepal's largest lake, in the middle of high mountains.

YOGIS, YAKS AND YOGHURT

HELAMBU

GOSAINKUND

LANGTANG

Helambu and Langtang are the two trekking areas located closest to the capital city. They stretch between the chain of hills which forms the northern border of the Kathmandu Valley and the main range of the Himalayas or the national frontier with Tibet.

Helambu is the name of a region which more or less corresponds with the **Malemchi Khola River** area. Langtang is the designation of the high valley north of Helambu – the **Langtang Khola**, which joins the Trisuli River at the villages of **Syaubensi** and **Bhote Kosi**. The lower course of the river is a veritable El Dorado for hard-core river rafting enthusiasts.

Helambu and Langtang are well suited for the hiker with a tight time budget because they are easily reached from the Kathmandu Valley. A choice of routes which combines both regions is certainly very rewarding, but at least fourteen days of pure hiking-time must be allowed. The crossing from Helambu to Langtang – or the other way around – leads either over the **Laurebina Pass** (4,609 m) and the lake grouping of Gosainkund, or over the difficult **Ganja La** (5,200 m). Certainly in many respects, both regions stand be-

Preceding pages: The Langtang area is famous for its colorful festivals.

hind the spectacular Solu Khumbu or the surroundings of Annapurna in their spectacularity. In the northern-bordering mountain chains of the Langtang Himal and the Jugal Himal there are no eight-thousand-meter peaks, and "only" one seven-thousand-meter peak each – the **Langtang Lirung** (7,245 m) and the **Big White Peak** (7,083 m). Furthermore the relatively well-known cheese factory in Langtang can hardly be considered a major touristic attraction.

The attraction of this region lies more in its diversity: the hiker can acquire a "profile" – from the densely populated Kathmandu Valley to the limitless solitude of the eternal snows on the mountains very near to the Tibetan border.

Such a profile encompasses not only the differentiated and altitude-dependent forms of vegetation and human economic activities from the valley level on up to the mountain flanks and high plateaus (called *lekhs* by the Nepalis). Those who have already know a bit about the ethnic variety of Nepal will ascertain that here, in an almost improbably ideal manner, the various altitude levels are inhabited by completely differentiated ethnic groups. At the same time the Helambu region is the furthest western extension of the settlement area of the famous Sherpa people.

144

HELAMBU

The village of **Tarke Ghyang** (2,560 m) is on a significant section of the most important route in Helambu. Tarkhe Ghyang is attractive primarily as the center of a sub-group of the Sherpas. They differ in their dialect from their famous ethnic cousins in Solo Khumbu. At one time the Rana kings took their harem-girls from the Sherpas in Helambu because the women there were famous for their beauty. The sight of the orderly arrangement of crowded parallel rows of stone houses, with their roof silhouettes of white prayer banners and fine vapor of smoke – fed by countless open stove-fires in the interiors – will never be forgotten by the visitor.

Each visitor to Tarke Ghyang should enjoy *tsampa* and butter-tea at least once in the serene silence of a Sherpa residence. In the common living, sleeping and cooking room sometimes an almost pedantic cleanliness and order dominates. Also worth seeing in this village is the **Temple in Bhutanese Style** with its impressive demon frescoes in the entrance area. It originates from the early 18th century, and was not reconstructed to its present form until 1969.

To get to Tarke Ghyang there is a whole series of route variations, with which a round trip can be put together according to available time, season of the year, individual preferences and the equipment you have brought with you. In addition, from the Langtang Valley you can cross over into the Gosainkund region in the west and the Ganja La to the north.

As a rule, **Sundarijal** – north-east of Kathmandu – is the starting point for a trek into Helambu. The path winds its way predominantly through humid oak and rhododendron forests on up to the **Shivapuri Lekh**, which here demarcates the northern limits of the Kathmandu Valley. After about five hours this day's stage

of the journey ends in **Pati Bhanjyang** (1,767 m). Here, on the other side of the Shivapuri Lekh, you find yourself in the middle of a densely-populated area of Tamang villages. The crops here are especially broad in variety (particularly millet and fruit trees), giving the classic Nepalese terraced landscape here an especially attractive appearance. On your excursion through Pati Bhanjyang you must get a glimpse at the beautiful red-brown plastered Tamang houses with their large, shady verandas.

Behind Pati Bhanjyang the path splits, offering two very contrasting tour variations. The first and simpler path leads in an eastern direction, down into the valley of the **Malemchi Khola**. Further on the path follows the Malemchi up-river along its eastern bank. You reach Tarke Ghyang in three relatively short day-stages, with overnight stays in **Tala Marang** and **Thimbu** (from Tala Marang a broad and more-or-less even-running path leads down to **Panchkal** on the Kathmandu-Kodari road in about seven hours).

The trail up-river from Tala Marang proceeds initially through really low altitudes – here you might be rather overwhelmed by the heat and sun in the warmer seasons. Perhaps you can find some refreshment with a swim in the cool water of the Malemchi or in one of the truly frequent tea houses along the trail. The higher you get up into the valley, the more noticable the changes in the settlements and the human physiognomy. In **Kiul** and **Thimbu**, alongside the Tamang you already encounter Sherpa families.

The climb up from Thimbu to **Kakani** (also accessible by road) is attractive in landscape, but also fatiguing. It brings you past some of the especially beautiful chortas and caityas, taking you finally into the region predominantly settled by Sherpas.

The other trail from Pati Bhanjyang into Helambu proceeds almost exactly in a northern direction onto the range of

HELAMBU/LANGTANG TREKKING

0   5   10 km

mountain ridge-backs which represent the watershed between the two river systems of the **Malemchi/Indrawati Khola** (in the east) and the **Tadi Khola/Trisuli Ganga** (to the west).

On this route you should allow three – probably four – days to get to Tarke Ghyang. Between November and January you should plan for snow on the upper section before Thare Pati; the path is passable, however, with the help of a guide who knows the area. In good weather you have a splendid view of the mountain world. The first day's stage of the journey leads over **Chipling** and the Tamang village of **Gul Bhanjyang** (2,141 m) into the Sherpa settlement **Kutumsang**. On past Kutumsang there are no further permanent settlements until Malemchigaon. The only possible overnight accommodation consists of half derelict stables (*goth*), and with a little luck you might get a warm meal in one of these *goths* in **Thare Pati**.

Thare Pati is at the same time the starting point for a tour in the region of the **Gosainkund Lekh** (see below). In order to make the descent down to Malemchigaon, you must first of all walk back along the ridge for a long while. The path down leads you through a magical forest of rhododendrons hanging with lichens. In the Sherpa village of **Malemchigaon** (2,593 m) you first find yourself again in an area of land used for agriculture. On the opposite side of the valley you see Tarke Ghyang at roughly the same altitude. In order to make it over there, however, you must cross the Malechmi Khola, which flows 700 meters below you. An infrequently-traveled variation into Helambu is the descent to the lakes of **Panch Pokhari** at about 4,000 meters altitude, which can be reached in four days via the villages of **Shermatang**, **Yangri** and **Yarsa**. In two further, very lonely days from there you meet the Chinese Road (Kathmandu-Kodari) at **Baliphi**.

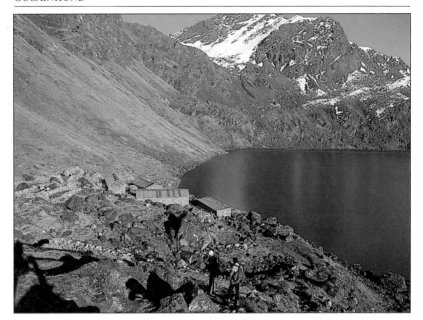

GOSAINKUND

The Gosainkund Lake. Right: A young woman from Helambu.

The **Gosainkund Lekh** is a relatively easy way to pass between the upper Helambu and the Langtang Valley. It is, however, also a destination for those trekkers who want to experience the mountain world around the holy lakes of Gosainkund. Every year at the full moon between the middle of July and the middle of August tens of thousands of Hindus make a pilgrimage to these lakes in order to take a ritual bath in the cold mountain waters. According to a legend the sources of the lakes had their origin when the god Shiva rammed his trident into the rocks above them.

Coming from Kathmandu, the shortest access leads either via **Pati Bhanjyang** and **Kutumsang** (Helambu) or via **Dhunche** (Langtang). The trail over the Gosainkund Lekh is as follows: The base for the crossing of the **Laurebina Pass** (4,609 m) is **Thare Pati** (around 3,400 m), an uninterrupted collection of half-derelict stables (*goths*), which offer a

place to stay overnight in cases of need. During the high trekking season several of the cabins of the Sherpas from the village located nearby are opened for business. The next overnight accomodation after Thare Pati is the pilgrim shelter on the **Gosainkund Lake** (4,381 m) – scarcely to be reached in a single day's march. The path proceeds behind Thare Pati initially at the same altitude past several spring-fed brooks of the Tadi Khola. In this section you can shelter from bad weather under several overhanging cliffs (*gopte*). The path up to the Laurebina Pass is not difficult itself, however it rises in altitude more than 1,000 meters. You will find outstanding camp sites on the foundations of several abandoned *goths* at around 4,000 m height. After crossing over the pass there is a breathtalking view of a portion of the Gosainkund Lakes (i.e. **Surja**, **Gosain**, **Sarasvati**, **Bharain Kund**) and of the mountain world of the Langtang and the **Ganesh Himal**. From the pilgrim huts on Gosainkund you can reach the **Sing Gompa** on the same day. This is the first permanent settlement since Malemchigaon or, respectively, Kutumsang, both of which lie a four days' journey behind you. The village of **Sing Gompa** is arranged around a monastery, a government cheese dairy offers several simple places to stay. With the descent to **Syabru** on the next day, you arrive at the connecting point with the Langtang trek. In **Dhunche** (1,960 m), one more day's journey on, you can get on the bus to **Trisuli Bazar**.

LANGTANG

The valley of the **Langtang Khola** has been a part of the **Langtang National Park** since its authorization in 1976; with 1,700 sq.km the largest protected zone of the Himalaya states. The national park, with its especially varied fauna and flora, also encompasses the upper Helambu (north from Tarke Ghyang), the Gosainkund Lekh and the Jugal Himal further to the east. The destination of the majority of the treks in the Langtang Valley is the village of **Langtang** (3,500 m) and **Kyanjing** (3,850 m) – the summer settlement which belongs to it. These are located in a wide arid valley on the other side of the tree line and framed by splendid mountain scenery.

The inhabitants of the upper Langtang Valley describe themselves – as do the Sherpas – as the *bothya*, a group with Tibetan origins. They are, however, not difficult to tell apart from each-other, both from their appearance and their way of life. The main economic pillar of the *Langtang Bhotya* is the keeping of yaks and tsauris. The herds wander in a seasonal rhythm from the forest underneath **Ghora Tabela** all the way up into the furthest valley of the Langtang Khola, at an earlier time even up into the Tibetan

Highland. Therefore, located everywhere in the upper section of the valley are only seasonally occupied summer settlements. A modest amount of agriculture (around the village of Langtang) contributes to self-sufficiency, with the cultivation of potatoes, barley and buckwheat. Evidence of Tibetan Buddhist tradition is everywhere in the upper Langtang Valley. Countless mantras chiselled in stone accompany the hiker on the long mani-wall between Langtang and Kyanjing. The gompa in **Kyanjing** and the chortas strewn about everywhere are also among such religious manifestations.

An attraction of a different sort is the **cheese dairy** in Kyanjing – not only because of its delicious yoghurt and the swiss cheese which you can obtain there. The dairy was constructed in the mid-fifties, a short time after the valley was visited for the first time by a foreigner (H.W. Tilman). The dairy in Kyanjing was the first of numerous mountain cheese-dairies in Nepal. The initiator was a Swiss dairy economist and developmental as-

149

sistant. The primary goal of the project was to find new methods of preserving and marketing the cheese from the remote high valleys. The increasing influence of the Chinese in Tibet gradually closed access to a portion of the traditional summer pastures on the other side of the border, and in addition, one of the most important markets for the sale of clarified butter (*ghee*), into which the milk had until then been processed. The hard cheese now produced henceforth is taken by carriers in the direction of the capital city. From Kathmandu, the greater portion of this cheese is then e ported to India.

For the trekker it is rewarding to spend a few days in the upper Langtang Valley. Here there are almost no limits to what you can discover. You'll need about five hours for the ascent to **Tsergo Ri** (5,033 m) over the high meadow of **Yala** (eastern Kyanjing) with spectacular mountain views. If you have in mind to cross over the **Ganja La**, enjoy the outstanding view of the pass from Tsergo Ri and brace your body for the altitude adjustment. The short tour to the small summit immediately north of the lodge in Kyanjing is also well worth your while. A daytrip leads you to the cabins of **Lansisa**, nestled on the edge of the **Langtang Glacier**. It is also possible to rent a horse for this excursion.

Coming out from Kathmandu you find the lively little trading center of **Trisuli Bazar**. This is one starting point for a visit to the Langtang Valley. The 73 kilometer long connecting road between Kathmandu and Trisuli was constructed in the 1960's in connection with the erection of what was then the largest hydroelectric plant, located north of Trisuli. In the mideighties the lower section of what was originally the Langtang trek was opened up with a road to Dhunche. It leads on further over the Trisuli River to the feet of the Ganesh Himal at over 4,000 m altitude. Zinc and lead have been

discovered there, which are now to be extracted. The local residents cannot expect much to come from the construction of this road: it is feared that wood will be plundered from the forest-rich area, and there is an almost insoluble problem with the enormous erosion which occurs where the road has not been competently built to match to the steep terrain conditions.

Leaving Dhunche (1,960 m) you can reach the Sherpa village of **Syabru** (2,100 m) by way of Bharku, in about seven hours. Syabru's houses seems to hang like a chain of pearls on a mountain ridge. If you plan an excursion to the Gosainkund Lakes you must either leave the main path to Langtang between Dhunche and Bharku, or, coming out of Syabru turn in a southerly direction towards **Sing Gompa**. On your way from Syabru in the direction of Langtang, you can make it down to the Langtang Khola in about one and a half hours. Then you follow the river through dense, humid forest for about two hours and finally cross it at a massive bridge.

On the considerably drier south bank you will reach, after about one and a half more hours, a collection of tea houses and lodges, among these the famous "Lama Lodge". From the Lama Lodge to the **Ghora Tabela** military post (3,100 m) it is about a four-hour walk, and the upper section of the trail runs through an open larch forest in an increasingly widening valley floor. Passing by some interesting gompas, you arrive in another two hours at Langtang (3,500 m). From there to **Kyanjing** (3,850 m) it is still two to three hours of contemplative hiking. Altogether you should allow two and a half days for the journey from Dhunche to Kyanjiing.

The Ganja La Pass

The **Ganja La** (5,200 m) connects Kyanjing with Tarke Gyang in a line running

Everywhere in Langtang chortas and prayer flags show us that Buddhists live here.

almost exactly north-to-south. With the Gosainkund Lekh, it is the second crossing point between the Langtang Valley and Helambu. However the Ganja La is by far the more wearisome alternative, because of the high altitude and the difficult terrain.

The name means "Pass of the Great Snows", and the Ganja La is notorious for its frequent heavy snowfalls. The pass is usable from May until the beginning of November, however also during these times snow-fields must be crossed in the upper section. One must expect snowfalls here. The path is unmarked to an extent, and during fog or snow storms one can easily get confused and lost. A guide who knows the region well is recommended! Because there are no permanent settlements to be found during the three day-long stages between Kyanjing and Tarke Ghyang, tent and other necessities must be brought along.

After you leave Kyanjing going up-river – then crossing the Langtang Khola – you still have about six hours of climbing left before you reach the top of the pass. It is recommended that you spend one night underway; for example at the *goths* at about 4,400 meters. In the 400 meters of altitude before the top of the pass you must ascend through broad snowfields; the very last section before the pass requires a light scramble on a slippery base.

The descent from Ganja La in the south direction leads you over typical moraine fields. Crossing is very particularly fatiguing when a blanket of snow covers up the gaps and holes between the individual blocks of rock. A poorly placed foot can quickly result in injury. Around four hours of hiking time are necessary to get to the first *goths*. From these it is then still a one and a half day march to Tarke Ghyang. The path leads on mainly along the east side of the main range of the mountain massifs of **Dhukpu** and **Yangri Danda**.

151

Those who work in the trekking business rarely see their families during the trekking season.

A VILLAGE IN NEPAL

Today Chandra Tamang (34) is *sirdar* at a trekking agency in Kathmandu. He made his first contact with the trekking business ten years ago in Pokhara, where his father had sent him to learn the English language. His "trekking career" began first of all as a kitchen assistant, then he worked as a Sherpa before he finally advanced to his present position. At the time being Chandra is employed by his firm the whole year 'round. However, for his alloted monthly salary of 800 rupees – in his home village this is just enough for the purchase of two goats – he must actually work for only five months per year. He spends the remaining time as a farmer in his home village of **Bhalche**.

Bhalche is located more than two hours' foot-march away from Trisuli Bazar at 2,000 m above sea level on a slope high above the **Salankhu Khola**, a tributary of the Trisuli River. Chandra means *moon*, and the addition "Tamang" is an indication of his ethnic membership. In Bhalche all of the 5,000 inhabitants are Buddhists, but for all that, only half consider themselves to be Tamang, the remainder being Gurung. Marriages between the two groups, however, are thoroughly acceptable. Chandra's family has the good fortune of being among the richer in the village. They possess a stately house in Balche itself, as well as a meadow on the lekhs for pasturage during the monsoon seasons. On the farm terraces potatoes, maize, millet, wheat, barley, radishes and mustard are harvested. One hour on a path up the valley there are several fields for the cultivation of rice. Several cows, water-buffaloes, sheep, goats, chickens and a piece of forest complete the family estate. With all of this they can to a great extent provide for themselves. Only tea, sugar, soap and a few "luxury goods" are purchased from the market in Trisul Bazar. Unlike his father, Chandra can afford to send his son (16) and his daughter (8) to school for the whole year. Of course as a result he must forgo their assistance with the house and field work. During Chandra's absence in the trekking season his wife employs day-workers from the poorer families for the work on the field.

In spite of the relative affluence which Chandra's family has achieved, the way of life in Bhalche has changed only a little, partly because the village is located off the beaten path of the popular trekking routes. A transistor radio is an expression of the highest luxury, and in order to find a doctor one must go on foot to Trisuli. The population expresses their enjoyment of life and intimate contact with their religion in the traditional festivals, especially the Dasain festival in October, when the herds come down from their pasture areas and the Tamang and Gurung celebrate together.

HELAMBU / LANGTANG / GOSAINKUND

Accommodation

Those who have set off on their own with no tent will always find shelter as long as they stick to areas with human settlement. But first and foremost, keep in mind that you can simply forget about European ideas of comfort, service and the like. In the 'seventies the non-organized trekkers in Helambu and the Langtang Valley spent the night in a bhatti (tea shop) or in a private house, always in the same room as the hosting family. Today there are lodges everywhere, especially in Langtang. They are mostly a room or a house. Whereever you spend the night, the host will prepare a simple hot meal for you (lodging fees at present between 5 and 30 rupees, simple meals around 20 rupees). Attention: Beer and other bottled beverages must be carried in over long distances and are therefore expensive.

Hospital

Hospital in Trisul Bazar, pharmacy (dispensary) in Dhunche, however in case of serious illness go immediately back to Kathmandu.

Altitude Adjustment

Sufficient acclimatization of the body is essential and should be observed at the passes of Ganja La and Laurebina (Gosainkund), where in a short distance extreme altitudes are achieved.

Trekking Season

The best trekking times are autumn (Oct./Nov.) and spring (Feb.- April). While you can trek the whole year round in the lower regions of Helambu, on the higher stretches (particularly in Malemchigaon to Thare Pati) cold and snowstorms can be expected already in November. At these times in the lower-lying valleys (Helambu) it can be rather hot. The Ganja La isn't passable until at least May.

Equipment / Provisions

Crampons and rope are only recommended for the negotiation of the Ganja La and Yala Peak. There you must also take tent and provisions. This is also necessary for the excursion to Panch Pokhari, and highly recommended for the Gosainkund trek.

Guides

A locally informed and experienced local guide makes a deeper understanding of the land and the people possible. It is absolutely necessary to have a guide for crossing the Ganja La.

Various

The Kyangjin Gyang Monastery (3,000 m) is located about half a day's foot-march up the valley from the village of Langtang. Nearby it is a cheese dairy built in 1954 with developmental assistance from the Swiss. In Dhunche (Langtang region) a payment must be made at a checkpost for the entrance to the Langtang National Park. The path to Langtang through the Trisuli Gorge (later named Bhote Khosi) also marks a significant trade route which led between here and Kyirong in Tibet before the Chinese/Tibetan border was closed.

Getting There

The most important points of departure of the described treks are simple to reach from Kathmandu. The best way is to take a taxi (16 km; 1 hour) to **Sundarijal** (Helambu/Helmu trek). The trek begins west of Sundarijal at the place at the end of the road where a water pipe comes out of the mountain. To get to **Trisuli Bazar** (to the high alpine Langtang Valley and the holy mountain lakes) you can take the public bus (73 km.), which departs from the north western city-section of Paknajol (near the tourist center Thamel). A small bus brings you from there to **Dhunche**. In **Kyanjin** in the upper Langtang Valley there is a STOL landing strip; small chartered aircraft can land there – no official RNAC flights. The Ganja La Pass connects Langtang with Helambu.

Rewarding Excursions

When you have gone around the Gosainkund Lake and climbed past the four further lakes to the pass (4,600 m) you have made it to the Helambu region (ca. 7 hours from Gosainkund to Tare Pati). Located north of the Kyangjin Monastery at ca. 4,800 m altitude (see Various) is an especially beautiful vantage point, the high meadow of Yala. From here you can climb the Yala Peak (5,500 m) or the Tsergo Ri (4,950 m), which is easy to ascend. Climbing irons and pick are recommended.

From Trisuli Bazar you can undertake an excursion to the former festival town of **Nuwakot**. On the road from Trisuli Bazar to Kathmandu you drive over the Kakani Pass, where you can also stay overnight in simple accomodation. From there you can enjoy a splendid sunrise and sunset with a view of the Himalayan Range.

Festivals

Every year hundreds of believers make a pilgrimage to the Gosainkund Lake between mid-July and mid-August, in order to pay homage to Shiva and bathe in the lake during the full moon. In addition to the Tibetan New Year – called Lhosar – which occurs at the end of February / beginning of March, in May / June an interesting maskdance in Helambu is performed.

IN THE SHADOW
OF EVEREST

SOLU KHUMBU

NAMCHE BAZAR

MT. EVEREST

ROLWALING

It must be the dream of each and every visitor to Nepal to see Mt. Everest at least once. At 8,848 m it is the highest mountain in the world. This experience is much more intensive when you follow the beat of your own drummer and hike up to the area on your own instead of latching onto one of the organized excursions from Kathmandu.

Because the infrastructure of the **Khumbu** has been greatly improved in the last few years, it hardly poses much of a problem anymore either for the individual trekker or the travelers in organized groups. A network of so-called lodges – which closely resemble the traditional lodge arrangements in the Alps – has grown up over a broad section of the Khumbu. The ever-friendly Sherpas – the original residents of the Khumbu – will provide important assistance in all your undertakings.

Sherpas

The people of the Sherpas actually originate from **Kham** in eastern Tibet. The name *sahr pa* means "they who come from the East". The first Sherpas came from Tibet about 600 years ago to

*Preceding pages: Mt. Everest (and Lhotse).
Left: Chukung Ri base camp.*

settle in Khumbu. The reasons for this re-settlement are to be found as much in differences among religious conceptions in Tibet as in the violent altercations they had with the Khampas. At any rate they settled in Khumbu and lived there as half-nomadicized small farmers or as traders. The name Khumbu goes back to *Kumbila Tetsan Gelbu*, the local protector-deity, who defends the land and people from evil. The Sherpas are – as adherents of Tibetan Buddhism – a very religious people. We find examples of their religiosity everywhere; such as stupas, monasteries, gompas, mani-walls, prayer-banners or the passers-by murmuring their mantras, and prayer mills as well as the house-altars which no Sherpa household is without.

Almost all of the festivals have a religious origin. One of the most significant is called *Dumje*, which takes place in June or July. This is a celebration of the birthday of the legendary master teacher and religious founder Padmasambhava, who brought Buddhism to Tibet in the eighth century and founded the Nyingmapa Order. Along with this is celebrated the anniversary of the day when Lama Sangwa Dorche, the founder of the monastery of Pangpoche, achieved enlightenment, and also the festival for the worship of the protection-deity Khum-

157

SOLU KHUMBU TREKKING

0   5   10 km

159

bila. There are two New Year's festivals: One in January for the farmers, and one in February, when the farmers are already busy in their fields again. The Sherpas have become famous throughout the world as the tough, perserverant and enduring carriers of loads to the highest summits in the world. However, today we can also appreciate their multi-purpose services as guides, interpreters, cooks, traders, and yak and lodge owners – almost always singing and whistling, unpretentious and helpful.

Arriving

There are two possibilities to get to the Khumbu: The more comfortable, faster, but also more expensive is the flight from Kathmandu to **Lukla**. The 20-seater Twin Otter aircraft takes off as a rule only in good weather – first of all because they are flown by sight, and secondly, because the landing field in Lukla consists only of a bumpy grass strip, which gets soft in the rain.

The second possibility consists of a six-day-long march beginning in **Jiri**, which you can easily reach from Kathmandu by public bus – as long as the roads haven't been damaged as a result of the monsoons.

This tour via the **Deorali Pass – Junbesi – Tragsindo La – Nuntala** is on the one hand somewhat more fatiguing and burdensome – in that one has to climb up and down numerous chains of hills. On the other hand, however, it is also very alluring, because you have the chance to admire the rich variety of the central mountain landscape. Villages of the Tamang, Chetri and Rai are interspersed with terraced fields and rainforests. Later on you arrive to the first Sherpa settlement, and the vegetation gradually becomes scantier. There are lodges in each village, so that you can break up your journey along according to your desires and mood.

Solu-Khumbu Highway

Each of the some 9,000 trekkers who visit the Everest region annually is forced to put this section behind them twice: there and back. This is therefore the most heavily traveled path in the entirety of Khumbu and is jokingly designated the Solo-Khumbu Highway. So, it's also not surprising that here the most accommodation is offered and that it's hardly possible to lose your way on the well-trodden path.

Our detailed description of the hiking trails of Khumbu begins therefore in **Lukla**. And here we encounter the first problem: Some might think to themselves – in the face of their heaps of luggage: Who should carry all of this stuff ? The travelers with the organized group-treks can only laugh at this problem, because already upon their arrival, pack animals and Sherpas stand at the ready, so that they will have to carry only a light day-rucksack with the most essential utensils. The individual lodge-to-lodge trekker, who makes ample use of the network of accommodation in order to feed himself and have overnight quarters, will carry everything himself and shoulder his 70-liter backpack among the stifled titters of smug onlookers. However, he too – either in Lukla or other larger villages – can hire on a Sherpa or "porter" (carrier), who will carry his baggage for appropriate payment. Sherpas and "porters" are by no means the same, though.

A Sherpa functions today more in the sense of a guide. That means he knows the area very well and can make himself understood both with you and the local residents. A "porter" is frequently no Sherpa at all, rather a member of one of the central mountain clans – for example a Tamang, Magar, Gurung or Rai. These work solely as carriers, which means that you probably won't be able to communicate with him and that the organizational execution of your tour is for you to plan

Yaks can be used to carry heavy loads at high altitudes.

yourself. This usually also applies in cases where you hire a Sherpa to work as a porter.

From **Lukla** (2866 m) the path leads first of all conveniently downwards and after about two hours you reach **Phakding** (2,640 m; 3 lodges). On the way you pass numerous tea-houses and lodges, and the valley landscape of Khumbu – with its forests of rhododendron, fir and spruce, many shrubs and bamboos – invites you to dally for a while. "Down" here primarily wheat, maize, barley, millet, rape-seed and silver beets are cultivated.

On the way to the entrance of the Sagarmatha National Park – comprising a large portion of the Khumbu region – you will be confronted with the most difficult problem that exists in Nepal: the steadily progressing logging of the forest and the erosion damage resulting. If you knew what the **Dudh Kosi Valley** still looked like just four years ago you would be horrified at the numerous landslides, which, spreading ever further, threaten valuable farmland and interrupt important thorough fares. A larger part of this damage has been brought about by the recent dramatic increase in tourism; the roughly 3,000 inhabitants of Khumbu today provide more than 9,000 trekkers with accomodations (mostly constructed of wood, with interior furnishings also of wood) and food (cooking and heating is done with wood).

Save Nature!

You can very easily make your contribution to the preservation of this unique landscape by following the recommendations of the *Himalaya Trust*:

1. Make no fires yourself, and don't use any wood!

2. Don't take hot showers! This service is now offered in many lodges, however is costs a lot of wood. Abandon the idea – A little bit of dirt has never hurt anyone!

3. Don't order complicated meals in the lodges; if there are several in your party, order the same dishes – this saves wood too.

4. If you have brought cooking utensils along, cook preferably with gas or camping fuel!

5. Burn your garbage, and don't bury burnable wastes!

6. You can prevent erosion damage always keeping to the trails!

7. Try to convince other tourists and the locals to behave just as responsibly as you do yourself!

With these things in mind we arrive in Monju at the Sagarmatha National Park, and by the way, the 250 NR which each trekker has to pay as an entrance fee shouldn't bother you too much – it is not much money by our standards. In addition, this money is used by the *Himalayan Trust* – which oversees the national park – for such sensible things as the improvement of the school system, improvement of medical care, and the requirements of environmental protection.

Mani walls with carved mantras line the path in the Khumbu.

If you are traveling as a member of an organized trekking group, proof will be demanded of a sufficient amount of kerosene for cooking (per participant one liter of kerosene per day). If you don't have it, you must buy coupons for the corresponding amount (one liter 25 NR), which can be traded in at Namche Bazar.

From **Monju** to Namche Bazar takes about four hours. First you climb down to **Jorsale**, then you cross over a large suspension bridge, and afterwards you follow the river bank – always staying at the same altitude. Here you should keep in mind that the path to use after the next river-crossing (smaller wooden bridge) is the one that leads straight and relatively steeply upward into the forest. Don't turn left onto the path which leads along the river, in the way that many carriers do: of course you'll reach your goal this way too, but not until you've taken a small alpine climbing tour, and then at a later

The Sherpa settlement of Namche Bazar with its typical long houses.

point you must cover about ten meters hand-over-hand on a fixed steel cable. The valley then becomes noticibly narrower, and finally you reach another bridge. After this point the path climbs 500 meters in altitude steeply up the mountain, and by this point at the latest you should follow an important mountain-climbers' rule since you are now located at a relatively high altitude for Europeans. Go slowly! Don't try to race the Sherpas – you'll lose anyway! Once you've arrived at the tea-house – the only one between Jorsale and Namche Bazar – you have made it through the worst. Of course, the path leads still further up the mountain for about an hour, but it isn't so steep anymore. And on a clear day on the right, **Mt. Everest** makes its first appearance. The Sherpas name it **Chomolungma**, because according to their beliefs *Miyo Lungsangma*, the mother-deity of the earth, thrones on its summit.

NAMCHE BAZAR

Today **Namche Bazar** is the main village of the Sherpas and also the most populated village in Khumbu. The town has everything you need: a bank, a post office, and numerous lodges and shops in which you can purchase everything from souvenirs to mountain-climbing equipment. The handcrafted articles that are on sale everywhere – which are naturally all "old and genuine Tibetan" in reality originate for the most part from the workshops of the Kathmandu Valley, where they are frequently cheaper to get. When buying anything check both the quality and the price carefully.

Every foreign visitor must report to the police station in Namche Bazar, where his arrival is entered into a book and his trekking permit is marked with a stamp. The police station is located about 200 meters above the path on which you entered the town. Here you have the opportunity to combine simultaneously the pleasant with the necessary – climb the

163

rest of the way up the hill. Located up there is the **Headquarters of the Sagarmatha National Park** with a small **museum**, and from here you also have a fantastic panoramic view of the highest mountains in the world: to the north are **Nuptse** (7,879 m), **Everest**, and **Lhotse**, then further to the west **Ama Dablam** (6,856 m), on to **Kang Taiga** (6,685 m) and **Tramserku** (6,608 m); to the east we see the powerful massif of the **Kyajo Ri** (6,186 m), and finally further north the holy **Khumbila** (5,761 m), seat of the local deity *Tetsan Gelbu.*

Namche is the base-camp for all further undertakings, because here or shortly after the paths into the various valleys go their separate ways.

Walks around Namche

The half-day-long hikes to the surrounding villages are also suitable for acclimatizing yourself. There are two paths from Namche to the respective places. The longer – but more comfortable – is the one on the path leading out of Namche on left side of the valley, which runs on in the direction of Everest. After roughly ninety minutes you reach the **Sagnasar** "intersection", where four hiking trails meet. The path that leads up to the left takes you to **Khumjung** in only half an hour.

The shorter, faster variation leads the **Namche Gompa** to the right, steeply up and over the hill-chain and on past to the **Shyanpoche** landing field. There the path splits, and you can hike further directly to Khunde (left), Khumjang (straight) or to the **Everest View Hotel** (right). You can arrive at any of the three destinations after one to one-and-a-half hours' walking time.

Khunde has become well known because of its **hospital**, the largest in the entire Khumbu region, which was furnished by the *Himalaya Trust*. There are three permanent employees: a western doctor, who works on a two-year exchange program, and two local helpers. The hospital is financed by the Trust and by donations and income from the treatment of patients.

Looked at statistically, spread out over the year there are some 5,000 local patients, for whom the most common illnesses are infectious illnesses of the lung, dysentery, and skin and eye complaints. The preponderant majority of the foreigners who seek out the hospital annually suffer from two forms of illness: diarrhoea and altitude sickness. A hint concerning the latter: many lodges possess oxygen bottles, which can be used in emergencies to resuscitate those with altitude sickness.

The equipment of the hospital, which includes an x-ray machine, permits the treatment of all of the above-mentioned illnesses – with the exception of altitude sickness (here the only help is being transported to lower altitudes). Blood transfusions as well as more complicated operations cannot be performed here. For

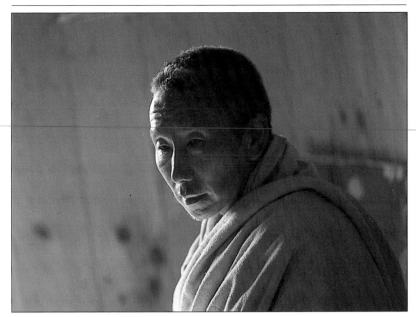

A lama at Thyangboche monastery in Khumbu. Left: A dragon on the wall of the Chiwong Gompa monastery at Solu.

these cases the patient must be flown to Kathmandu by a helicopter which must be requested from Namche Bazar. The Khunde Hospital has two external stations, which can only offer a sort of first-aid service. If you should come to Khunde, a donation of medication is always welcome. Antibiotics and drugs for gastritis are in the greatest demand.

The locality of **Khumjung** (3,790 m; two lodges) is located a bit below Khunde and, with its two-storied houses as well as its fields demarcated by a stone wall, is a typical Sherpa village. Founded roughly 500 years ago, it is the oldest Sherpa settlement and was, because of its location directly at the food of the holy Khumbila, for a long time the main village of the Khumbu.

In the houses we find granaries, stables and store-rooms on the ground floor while the upper floor is used exclusively

as living area, in which during the evenings everyone huddles around the warm stove, near which they also sleep. The gigantic, polished copper kettle is the pride of every Sherpa housewife. These often serve for the production of *chang*, the national beverage of the Sherpas, which is yielded by the fermentation process of a barley or rice mash.

Two other sights also worth seeing in Khumjung are both of the *chortas* (Tibetan for stupa – reliquary shrines), the middle section of which, called a *bumpa* (pot) shows Tibetan architectural influence. Located directly next to these one can visit one of the **Hillary Schools**, which can be attended by students free of charge.

The **Everest View Hotel** (3,850 m) which is famous for its view, was closed for a long period. After being renovated by a Japanese contractor – which also undertook the restoration of the Shyanpoche airstrip – the hotel has been in service again since autumn 1989. (Price for a double room: around US$ 150)

Namche Bazar – Thame

A well-earned rest on the Gokyo Ri (5483 m), towering above the Gokyo Tso.

This tour is a rewarding and light day's hike; the path is little-trodden, but offers a wonderful view. It is also quite suitable for getting acclimatized! The path first leads left from the gompa in Namche seemingly steeply upwards, around the mountain ridge and then continues at the same level high above the gorge of **Nangpo**. After a two-hour march through spruce and rhododendron forests – in which you might have the chance to spy a pheasant or red deer – you arrive to **Kongde** (3,500 m; one lodge). Some noteworthy things here include – apart from the begging children – several incense altars in front of the houses, as well as numerous *lhatos* – little cubic constructions bearing sticks hung with prayer-banners. These relics of the pre-Buddhist and animistic Bön beliefs are symbolic portrayals of the axis of the cosmos. Above Kongde there is a small convent of the Nyingmapa order, which one can visit – for an appropriate payment.

After Kongde the landscape becomes more meager – only some grass and a few bushes like barberries and junipers still grow here. After a further two hours and the crossing of an imposing gorge you come to **Thame Og** (3,800 m; one lodge). This spread-out farming village is located on the valley floor of the Nangpo River, and particularly in the morning sunlight you have a splendid view of the northern walls of the **Kongde Ri** (6,187 m), **Teng Kangpoche** (6,500 m), **Panayo Tuppa** (6,696 m) and strenuous task climbing up the last 200 meters of altitude to the **Thame Gompa**, a monastery which seems to be glued to a rocky wall. From the stupa at the entrance gate of the monastery grounds you can catch a glimpse, far to the right in the distance, of the **Cho Oyo** (8,153 m).

Continuing along a lengthy mani-wall with mantras chiseled into it you arrive at the residences of the monks and finally to the gompa itself. It belongs – as do almost all of the monasteries in the Khumbu – to the Nyingmapa order. A *mani rimdu* festival occurs here in May – not so very famous as that of the monastery of Thyangboche, but identical in content: It describes the legendary deeds of Padmasambhava in the form of cham-dancing (mask dancing).

Namche Bazar – Gokyo

This is a three to four-day hike along the Dudh Kosi River with beautiful views of **Cho Oyo** (8,153 m), **Gyachung Kang** (7,922 m) and the western **Khumbu Himal**. Starting from Namche you hike – as already described – to Sangnasar and in the same direction further on a steep path upward to the top of a pass (3,973 m; one hour), from where you have a wondrous view of the **Phortse** (3,840 m) opposite you. The stone walls around the fields here serve not only to demarcate the private lands, but also offer an effective protection against wind erosion and landslides.

After a one-hour descent you reach **Phortse Drangka** (lodge), a picturesque camp-site located in a forest directly on the river bank. When you cross over the bridge, you proceed upwards to **Phortse** (half hour) and on further to **Pangpoche** (four hours). From Phortse Drangka you can hike to **Gokyo** either in two heavy days of trekking – each with six or seven hours of walking-time – or, somewhat more pleasantly, take three days. There are lodges in **Dole** (4,040 m), **Luza** (4.369 m) and **Machherma** (4,410 m). At first the trail climbs steeply; after Dole it becomes flatter, but continues steadily up the mountain until you pass by summer pastures and finally reach **Gokyo** (4,750 m; three lodges) with its three crystal-clear lakes.

A well-trodden path leads in three hours to **Gokyo Ri** (5,483 m), which offers a fantastic panorama. With **Cho**

Oyo, **Everest**, **Lhotse**, and **Makalu** (8,475 m) there are four of the 14 eight-thousand-meter peaks to admire at once.

You can make it in three days to **Dughla** in the Imja Khola Valley via the **Cho La Pass** (5,420 m) and Dzongla (4,843 m). This tour is only suitable for mountain climbers. There are no lodges along the way. The path over the **Ngozumpa Glacier** is not easy to find and changes constantly. The descent from Cho La is very steep and can be icy during bad atmospheric conditions. The reward for all this fatigue is the view of the tremendous northern precipices of the **Jobo Lhaptschan** (6,440 m) and **Taboche** (6,367 m), as well as the lovely **Tshola Tso Lake**.

Namche Bazar – Everest Base Camp

This is a four-to-five day hike to the foot of the highest mountain in the world. From Namche you climb first of all via Sangnasar down to **Phunki** (3,250 m), where you cross over the Imja Khola River. After the bridge you run into a series of water-powered prayer-mills as well as two lodges.

Starting here the path leads steeply upwards to **Thyangboche**, which you reach after three hours of hard work. In 1989 the monastery burnt down completely, but work on rebuilding it has already started. However, the unique situation of Thyangboche (3,890 m; 3 lodges, 1 store) allow you to soon forget the fatigue, since the north faces of Tramserku and Kang Taiga seem almost close enough to touch, and the views of Everest, Lhotse and Ama Dablam in the light of the evening sun are unforgettable experiences. Hiking on further from Thyangboche you arrive to **Pangpoche** (3,980 m; 2 lodges), after about one-and-a-half hours' walking-time and crossing over the Imja Khola. Shortly before the village, the path divides – the lower leads past Pangpoche directly to **Periche** (two hours); the upper

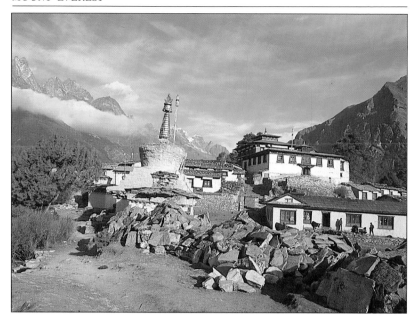

brings you to the actual village. There's a monastery here, too, which is cared for by one of the Thyangboche monks. It was founded approximately 300 years ago by Lama Sangwa Dorje and shelters the ominous **Yeti Scalp** and **Yeti Hand** in its second storey. A Sherpa legend tells how, when Sangwa Dorje had retreated to a cave in order to meditate, he was visited by a Yeti, who brought him food and water. After the Yeti died, Sangwa Dorje had his hand and his scalp preserved in the monastery. Whether or not you believe this is left to you, but at any rate if you want, you can view both relics for a small bakshish (donation). The *Dumje* festival also goes back to Sangwa Dorje, who celebrated it for the first time in this monastery.

If you want to insert a little alpine intermezzo into your tour, you can climb up to the **Taboche Meadow** (4,380 m; no lodge) in about an hour on a steep path. If the atmospheric conditions are good you can ascend a 5,305 m high sub-peak of Taboche. First you climb the crest which

High in the mountains – Thyangboche monastery which burned down in 1989.

is opposite the meadow and then it is an easy climb over the ridge (three to four hours walking time). From the summit you have an outstanding view of the surrounding ice-giants.

You can get to **Phortse** from Pangpoche by way of a little-traveled high altitude trail in around 3 1/2 hours. The trip is recommended not only for the great view of the mountains Tramserku, Kang Taiga and Thyangboche, but also because living on this side of the valley there are still a lot of pheasants and ghorals, which you might have a chance to observe.

Once you have reached **Periche** (4243 m; 2 lodges), the **hospital** of which is almost exactly as well-equipped as the one in Khunde, it's not much farther to continue on to **Lobuche** (4,930 m; 3 lodges). In the course of your four-hour hike you will notice a long series of little stupas. These were erected for the many Sherpas

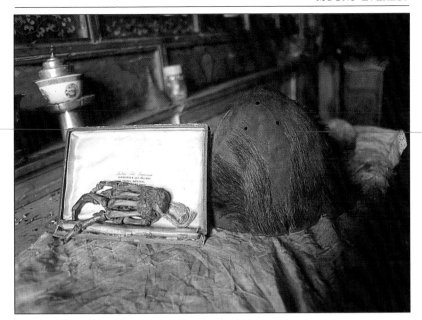

An extraordinary relic: the scalp and hand of the legendary yeti.

who lost their lives during expeditions on Mt. Everest.

In the meantime the landscape has altered considerably. Coniferous and rhododendron forests now lie far beneath us, and therefore the miniature gentian and edelweiss are a pleasant sight in this otherwise monotonous grassy desolation. On the isolated fields the only crop that can still be cultivated is potatoes, the main source of food for the Sherpas.

The final – and at over 5,000 meters the highest – lodge is located another two hours' distance from Lobuche in **Gorak Shep**. This is the starting point for two undertakings which are among the most rewarding that can be found in Khumbu: The trail to the **Everest Base Camp** leads on upward on the right side of the Khumbu Glacier, passing by ice caves and always accompanied by the continuous rolling thunder of avalanches which come echoing over from the north face of Nuptse. Ice-climbing equipment is not a necessity, because there are no steep passages to overcome and the glacier in this area is covered almost everywhere with stone rubble.

Once you have finally reached the Everest Base Camp (5,540 m) after a good three-hour hike, you are disappointed at first, because the camp turns out to consist of little more than a large accumulation and arrangement of rocks; however, the moment you shift your gaze upward you will be stunned by the gigantic masses of ice which roll downward with unending slowness from the Khumbu Icefall. You will hardly be able to imagine how mere humans have ever accomplished making their way through it. If you are lucky, you might be able to observe a few mountain climbers performing their dangerous undertaking. Please note, that the climb to the summit of Mt. Everest has virtually been booked out for several years to come.

In good weather the ascent of **Kala Pattar** (5,545 m) – staring from Gorak

Shep – is only a question of your condition. You can climb up to the summit on the well-trodden path in about three hours, from which you can get the best view of Everest and Nuptse that you could possibly wish for.

The wonderful Everest Ice Fall; seen from the Everest Base Camp.

Namche Bazar – Chhukung Meadow and Island Peak

This is a three-to-four day long hiking expedition into eastern Khumbu, with splendid views out to Lhotse, Lhotse Shar (8,383 m), Baruntse (7,220 m) and Makalu. The greater part of this trek follows a course similar to the trail to Kala Pattar, except that in Periche you don't turn to the north, but rather, in an easy half-day's hike, pass through **Dingpoche** (4,260 m; lodge) to the **Chhukung Meadow** (4,730 m; lodge).

The **Chhukung Ri** (5,546 m) rises up immediately north of the Chhukung Meadow. This roughly four-hour ascent is technically easy, because the path leads partly over moraine rubble. Looking out

from its summit you get a wonderful view of the south wall of Lhotse and Lhotse Shar as well as on over to Island Peak, Makalu and Baruntse.

Island Peak (6,189 m): This tour, which can be accomplished in two days, can only be recommended for experienced mountain climbers, who must take along ice-equipment. In order to ascend Island Peak a climbing permit (cost: 1989 US$ 300) is mandatory. From the Chhukung Meadow the way goes over **Pareshaya Gyab** (5,100 m); after which you continue left, climbing up the rib that stretches down to the south from the summit massif. At an altitude of about 5,500 meters you will find a protected campsite(walking time four to five hours).

The next day begins before sunrise; you climb through the last stretch of craggy rock and arrive to a trough at 6,000 meters' altitude after conquering a steep glacial cliff. This is crossed over by making a detour around a crevasse. After conquering one final steep section you come to the summit ridge (five hours' climb) with a tremendous view of Makalu, the south face of Lhotse and the icebergs of the Imja Basin. The later descent to the Chhukung Meadow is still possible on the same day.

A march lasting two to three days over the steep and difficult **Amphu Labtsa** Glacier and through the **Amphu Labtsa Pass** (5,780 m) brings you to the lakes of **Panch Pokhari** and down into the **Hunku Valley**. This should only be attempted by experienced mountain climbers with ice equipment.

The Hinku and Hunku Valleys

This region is reserved for those trekkers who are not dependent on the lodges. The higher-altitude areas of both of these valleys serve only as yak pasturage during the summer months; for the remainder of the year they are unoccupied. On the one hand this means that here you are completely on your own. However on the other, you enjoy the privilege of experiencing largely untouched and unadulterated nature.

You'll need six days to travel from Lukla over the snow-covered **Mera La** (5,415 m) into the Hunku Valley. First off you go in a southeasterly direction into the **Surke Drangka Valley**, and then – climbing ever more steeply – up to the 4,580 meter altitude **Zatr Pass**.

After crossing over two further ridgebacks you climb down again to a ghostly, lichen-covered rhododendron forest and proceed into the **Hinku Valley**. Going upstream, you follow the **Hinku River** almost to its source, then, however, turning east at the **Tangnang Meadow** (4,356 m) and arriving after a steep ascent behind **Khare** (5,099 m) in the glacier region of the **Mera**.

This 6,476 meter high mountain – which may still be climbed with a normal

climbing permit (1989 US$ 300) – is technically very simple, and its summit can be achieved in seven hours from **Mera La**. The descent down into the Hunku Valley takes only one more day. However those who wish to gain access to the lakes of **Panch Pokhari** from this side must pack up their belongings another three days in order to climb the thousand meters that still separate them from the 5,400 meter high lakes.

Of course if you decide to turn downriver, you can take a gigantic loop – taking seven to eight days to conquer – over the passes **Kemba La** (3,913 m) and **Surkie La** (3,085 m) proceeding on simpler trails back again into the **Dudh Kosi Valley** and so make it back to **Lukla**.

REMOTE ROLWALING VALLEY

West of the Khumbu, directly on the Tibetan frontier, there is a wild, lonely high valley – the **Rolwaling** – which is called simply "the grave" by the indigenous Sherpas on account of its location – buried down between steep ice-giants. Many mysterious stories have been passed on about this valley, through which the forefathers of the present-day Sherpas once came. It is here that the notorious and celebrated Yeti is supposed to make his home. Entire research expeditions have, so far unsuccessfully, attempted to find him.

There are three factors which have helped to preserve this splendid valley from the ravaging onslaught of tourists. First of all it is relatively arduous to get there at all, secondly there are neither lodgings nor food to buy, and third you need a special permit to be allowed to hike into Rolwaling. You must purchase – pro-forma – a climbing permit for the **Ramdung Peak** (5,925 m; cost: US$ 300) regardless of whether or not you want to climb the mountain. Those who aren't scared away by these inconveniences will be richly rewarded for

Walking through virgin snow on the journey to Rolwaling over Yalung La.

their efforts. Just the approaches to the **Rolwaling Valley** are worth your money: The path leads you through a wealth of variety – on one hand through Tamang and Chetri villages with their typical terraced fields, on the other through dense, gloomy primeval forests and over broad ridgebacks with wonderful views.

Two variations are possible: The first is a four day hike from **Jiri** (1,860 m; reachable with the bus) over the **Chordung Ridge** (3,698 m), **Suri** (1,890 m) and **Gonger** (1,040 m); the other is a six day hike starting from **Barabisi** (819 m; public bus) via **Tinsang La** (3,319 m), **Bigu Gompa** (2,519 m), **Chilangka** and **Gonger**.

You finally set foot into the Rolwaling through the village of **Simigaon** (2,000 m) located high above the Bhote Kosi. Above the **Shapka Meadow** (2,600 m) the path divides. Here the right branch is recommended, for while it is certainly

more arduous it is also decidedly the more rewarding. After a four-hour ascent you reach the **Daldung La** (3,976 m) which has a fantastic view of the 7,146 meter high **Gaurishankar** opposite. According to old Sherpa mythology, this is the seat of the goddess *Tashi Tserringma,* who is the guarantor of a long life. Gaurishankar is also holy for the Hindus: Shankar, the name of the northern peak, is a designation for Shiva in their everyday spoken language. The southern summit, Gauri (literally: "the white") is a synonym for the feminine manifestation of the god.

From Daldung La you climb down for four or five hours on a really adventurous path through the densest rainforest to the **Rolwaling River**, which you then cross. There you meet up again with the other path, which certainly also has a beautiful landscape, but doesn't snake down to Simigaon quite as spectacularly.

After about 2 1/2 hours' walking time up-river you reach the Sherpa village of **Beding** (3,693 m) – the only noteworthy settlement in Rolwaling. If it should happen that the monk belonging to the **Gompa** is in the village at the moment, you can ask him to show you round it himself. 150 meters higher a rocky hermitage is visible, where Padmasambhava is supposed to have meditated some 1,200 years ago.

The last human lodgings of the valley you can find in **Na**, which is located about three hours' distance from Beding. From here you have an overwhelming view of the mountain-giants **Chekigo** (6,735 m), **Bamongo** (6,400 m), **Kang Nachugo** (6,735 m), and above all, **Tsoboje** (6,689 m).

Over the **Yalung La** (5,310 m) you reach the Khare Kola Valley and the Bhote Kosi in 2 1/2 days.

Over the **Trashi Labtsa** (5,755 m) you come into the Khumbu in four days. This is a difficult and fatiguing tour, which requires ice-climbing equipment.

SOLU KHUMBU

This trek is among the most popular in Nepal. Therefore there are plentiful lodges and hotels along the usual routes. Costs for an overnight stay (bringing along a sleeping bag is recommended) in the dormitory: 5-10 NRs. The larger and more comfortable lodges offer two-bed rooms (very simple, thin separating walls): 50-60 NRs. Those wishing to make the trek to **Rolwaling** should bring along tenting equipment. If you use camp-sites that are located on private land, normally there is a fee of about 10 NRs for its use. Prices for meals are about the same everywhere: Soups 10-15 NRs, omelettes 18-20 NRs, cakes and muesli, 10-20 NRs. The fol-lowing applies for all bottled drinks: the further the distance from Kathmandu, the more expensive they are. Beers cost 60-80 NRs, sodas 25-40 NRs, while in contrast rakshi and chang (indigenous alcoholic beverages) cost only 3-6 NRs.

Hospitals

In **Khunde** and **Periche** there are hospitals with foreign physicians. Treatment costs: 150 NRs per treatment plus medications. For in-patient treatments: 100 NRs per night. The hospital in Khunde (3,481 m) was founded by the Himalayan Trust, which was brought into existence by Sir Edmund Hillary. In addition there are small hospitals in **Jiri** and **Paphlu**. There are first-aid stations located in **Bong**, **Chaunrikharka**, **Monjo**, **Gomila**, **Namche Bazar**, **Thame**, **Phortse**, and **Deboche**.

Radiotelephones

Since there is no telephone network here, you can only contact the outer world through radiotelephones. Installations for this purpose exist only at the tower in Likla and the police station and national park headquarters in **Namche Bazar**.

Postal Service / Bank

There are a post office and bank in **Namche Bazar**. Opening times of the bank: 10:30-14:00 hours (closed Saturdays). Post Office: 10:00-16:00 hours (closed Saturdays).

Carriers

Carriers can be hired directly on location. Two basic payment practices have developed: Either you pay your helper a lump sum and the latter takes care of his own accomodations and board, or you pay for his services separately and cover the extra for the room and board whereever you are. The fees for the service vary according to the time of year as well as what you offer and how heavy demand is. For a Sherpa-guide you can calculate approximately 70-110 NRs per day (without lodging or board). A carrier receives about 50-80 NRs per day. Those who have booked their tours through an agency in Kathmandu pay about US$ 27-30. It has been determined that in altitudes up to 6,000 meters no load above 20 kg can be carried. Over 6,000 meters only loads up to 17 kg are permitted.

Various

After the monastery **Thyangboche** burned down completely there are only two remaining monastery grounds in Khumbu that are particularly worth seeing: **Thame** and **Pangboche** (ostensibly the oldest monastery; with Yeti relics!) At this time a reconstruction of the burned-out Tengpoche Monastery is being attempted with the support of the King Mahendra Trust. In October/November there are mask dances in the Tengpoche Monastery; in May at the Thame monastery.

Each Saturday a large market takes place in **Namche Bazar**, and everything imaginable is offered for sale.

Both the National Park Museum and the Sagarmatha National Park are located here. In the park everyone must bring along his own fuels; at the entrance to the park kerosene is available. In the park grounds no wood can be cut down, gathered or purchased from the local people (this also applies to the other national parks).

Most people stop in **Khumjung** to visit the famous Sherpa artist Kappa Pasang. There are aircraft landing fields in **Jiri**, **Phaplu**, **Lukla** and **Shyangboche**.

There is an office of the RNAC located in **Lukla** (open from 10:00 to 16:00 hours daily except Saturdays). Attention: Flights depend on the weather, and frequently don't take place for days, which pushes the prices up. In Lukla you can stock up on basic food staples as well as luxury good.

Getting There

You can reach the Solo Khumbu region in a six-day march beginning in Jiri, which can be driven by public bus or rented taxi, as long as the roads aren't too damaged by the monsoons. This tour – via Deorali Pass, Bhandar, Kenja, Lamjura Pass, Junbesi, Tragsindo La, and Nuntala is certainly very tiring, but it's also very stimulating. On the drive to Jiri your trekking permits will already be checked.

You can fly in by aircraft to four landing strips: **Jiri** (1,900 m), **Phaplu** (2,700 m), roughly 10 km. south of Ringmo – from here you can get to Namche Bazar in four days; **Lukla** (2,800 m) is the only landing strip that is normally flown to daily (c. US $60 one-way), from here you can get to the Tengpoche Monastery in 2-3 days; **Shyangboche** (3,700 m).

NEPAL'S FAR EAST

KANCHENJUNGA
MAKALU

The Trail to Kanchenjunga

For some time now the remote East and the Kanchenjunga – the second-highest mountain in Nepal and the third-highest in the world – has also been opened up to group travelers, and to some extent individual tourists as well. As is also possible in the West, one can still discover a piece of the original Nepal here – without the excessive proliferation of pie shops, restaurants and lodges which transforms many a trekking experience in the heavily-traveled regions more into a trip to the coffee-shop instead of a real encounter with the country and its people.

For this hiking trip too, the traveler must bring along all the necessary provisions and articles of equipment. Particularly for larger groups, it is sensible to already have engaged the entire entourage you will need in Kathmandu, since here in East Nepal you cannot count on being able to find carriers and other assistants. There is nothing at all to be bought underway in the few pasture huts and little hamlets along the trail, and even in the larger villages the stores are for the most part not prepared for larger groups.

Preceding pages: A view of the Yalung Glacier from Kanchenjunga base camp.

The point of departure for this tour is **Taplejung**, situated in the settlement area of the Limbus. It is a small village nestled in the hill region with a landing strip located about five hundred meters higher at **Suketar**, which is flown to by the Royal Nepalese Airline, departing usually from Biratnagar. Waiting for the aircraft at the landing strip are not only local people, but also check post for the tourists. The other way to get to the region is to take a public bus to **Dhankula**, but you will be traveling in the company of many, many friendly Nepalese, chickens, goats and other domestic animals, crammed in an antique bus.

The trail leads over terraced fields onto a mountain saddle at an altitude of 2,550 meters, after which you leave the valley of the **Tamur Khola** in order to climb down to the small town of **Lal Khar** (2,200 m) and two further small hamlets. You cross over the **Phao Khola** on a suspension bridge in order finally to spend the night in **Kunjur**. Following further along the mountain chain – up for a while, down for a while – you cross the **Khaksena Khola** on a suspension bridge pass by the little villages of **Funfun** and **Anpang** and to pitch camp again in the village of **Mamakhe**.

The next day's stage leads further northeastwards in the direction of Sikkim and the Kanchenjunga, on which the small hamlet **Yamphudin** (1,670 m) presents a good opportunity to set up camp. After a steep ascent to a mountain saddle (2,440 m), the trail again leads downwards and crosses over the **Omje Khola** (2,230 m). The valley of the Omje Khola is sparsely populated and its steeply sloped flanks and its vegetation of hemlock firs, oaks and rhododendrons are impressive.

The path now climbs steeply again to the top of the **Deorali Danda** (3,300 m), which provides a wonderful view over the mountain world of the Kanchenjunga with its tremendous glaciers. After one more day's hike you set up the next camp in the little village of **Tseram** (3,770 m).

Going past the meadow of **Lapsang** you hike on to the meadows of **Ramze** and **Oktang** along the moraine of the huge **Yalung Glacier**, while the spectacular summits of the **Ratong** (6,678 m), **Kabru** (7,338 m) and the entire chain of the **Kanch** peaks – the highest of which reaches a proud 8,598 m – are always before your eyes. At **Oktang** the trail ends, and any further trek is only possible directly over the glacier – in other words, passable only for expeditions.

The Kanchenjunga was conquered for the first time on the 25th/26th of May 1955 by a British expedition under the leadership of G. Band, N. Hardie and S. Streather. The actual **Kanch Basecamp** is located further up on one of the Tso Glaciers.

For those who would like to take a further variation and enjoy beautiful views of **Makalu** (8,475 m) and the **Chamlang** (7,290 m), a return path is then recommended through the Tibetan settlement **Ghunsa**. This can be reached in two days starting from the Ramze Meadow over **Tseram** and several passes over 4,000 meters – among them the Tamo La. This trail represents an interesting change of landscape in comparison to the approach already described, and pro-

vides splendid views onto some bizarre black rock formations and giving a final glimpse of **Khumbarkarna** (7,710 m), which in mountain-climber's literature is most often referred to as **Jannu**. The first check-post along the trail awaits you beyond Taplejung in Ghunsa.

The path leads on following the Ghunsa Khola steeply up and down and soon you reach the settlement of **Phalay**, which is inhabited by Tibetans from the area of Mustang. Outward from the valley the path continues on to **Ghaia Bari**. Here you are near the source of the **Tamur**, which later joins the **Arun** to form the **Sapti Khosi**. Following the Tamur you arrive again to your departure point of **Taplejung**. For those who want to hike further, there is the path over **Dhoban** and **Nundaki** which goes further to **Chainpur**, from where **Tumlingtar** is located nearby.

The village of **Chainpur** is located at a height of 1,600 m and extends along the path over the ridgeback. It is one of those small, friendly little towns which possess their own unique charm. One is impressed by the neat houses with their beautiful wooden balconies and the often blindingly white color of their facades. This is actually a settlement area of the Rai, but in Chainpur Newar traders and craftsmen have also settled, and today making a considerable impact on the character of the village.

Chainpur is well known for its metal working and brass casting, which has been used primarily to make utility articles like lamps and vessels. Even to this day copper kettles and pots belong to the traditional dowries at weddings. The mines are gradually becoming exhausted out, however, and in particular the flood of cheap Indian mass production goods present the toughest competition to the traditional crafts.

The locality of **Tumlingtar** (3,900 m) – to which the Royal Nepalese Airline also flies – is the point of departure for two additional trekking tours. In a march lasting ten days one hikes the path already described to **Taplejung**, and then descends towards **Thapapani Danda** (1,378 m) and **Phidim** in the Mechi precinct. After passing over **Sukepokhari** (2,850 m) – the highest point in this journey – one finally arrives at the rather tropical **Ilam** (1,200 m). During many trekking tours you have to contend with some very cold and inauspicious weather, but here because of the lower altitude, it is the heat you have to tolerate. The return trip to Kathmandu can be made either by bus via Birtamod, Hetauda and Mugling – this variant requires two days'travel time – or by bus to Birathnagar and flying from there.

Starting out from Tumlingtar you reach the **Makalu Base Camp** at an altitude of 5,000 meters by making a rewarding seven-day-long tour. Since you will find yourself, from Tashigaon onwards in an uninhabited region for ten days, this tour requires elaborate preparations. From Tumlingtar the trail leads over a mountain ridge up to the district center **Khandbari** and further to Arunthan. Continuing ever further north, the path goes high along the ridgeback above the Arun and on the Munche and Num. At this point it turns in a northwesterly direction, proceeding to the last inhabited place of Tashigaon at an altitude of some 2,200 meters. From the base camp there are fantastic views of the summits of Mount Everest, Lhotse and the Makalu. The return path, which passes directly over the feet of Baruntse via Sherpani Col (6,110 m) and the passes West Col (6,135 m) and Amphu Lapbtsa (5,780 m) can only be undertaken by genuine expeditions.

The **Arun** – on the banks of which is located **Tumlingtar** – has its source in the regions of the Makalu and the Lumbusamba Himal. It is also possible to go on a three to four day long river-rafting trip, which must be organized from Kathmandu.

EASTERN NEPAL TREKKING

0   5   10 km

1 Far Western
2 Mid Western
3 Western
4 Central
5 Eastern

CHINA

Jumla
Dolpo

Annapurna
Pokhara Valley Pokhara
Langtang Helambu Solu
NEPAL Kath.Khumbu Eastern
Kathmandu Valley Nepal
Terai

Lucknow

Biratnagar

BANGL.

Patna
Allahabad Varanasi

INDIA Rajshahi

THE TERAI

LUMBINI

CHITWAN

JANAKPUR

THE TERAI

Bordered to the south by the Ganges plain and in the north by the towering foothills of the Himalayan Range, the **Terai** is the most important economic and industrial region in Nepal. This subtropical plain, in southern Nepal, is only a narrow strip stretching from west to east with a maximum width of 40 kilometers, at between 60 and 600 meters above seelevel. The Terai composes 23 percent of the total land area of Nepal, and approximately 44 percent of the Nepalese population lives here. Characteristic for this subtropical zone is its moist and warm climate with temperatures of over 40 degrees C in June/July and a precipitation level of over 2,000 mm during the monsoon season, which sets in during June. Up until that time a withering heat dominates, with temperatures of over 50 degrees C, which begins in April.

Just about half of the Nepalese population here is linguistically and ethnically influenced by neighboring India in particular. Among the oldest ethnic groups who live here are the Tharu, numbering roughly half a million. They live predominantly in villages which are strewn

Left: A dangerous meeting with a rhinoceros in the tall elephant grass.

around western and central Terai, today making their living from agriculture. Up until now their cultural origins have remained unclear. One of the remarkable cultural features are their roomy houses, built of clay and decorated with fish patterns and other frequently abstract animal motifs. The Tharu still worship their own gods and spirits for the most part, however here and there a few Hinduist deities can also be found in their villages.

The Tharu are the only ethnic group who had probably already been settled here in Chitwan during the twelfth century. Up until a short while ago they still lived from hunting, gathering and fishing in small groups. With the exception of the wild-growing grains which they harvested they were hardly familiar with genuine agriculture. Scarcely anyone else ventured into this region because there were no roads; in addition almost the whole valley consisted only of swampy primeval forest full of malaria-carrying mosquitos and wild animals.

In the search for new farmland and better living conditions, about 10,000 families annually have been moving out of the mountainous regions into the Terai for some time now, where land shortages are becoming a constantly growing problem. In comparison to the high mountain regions – where around 25 people per

181

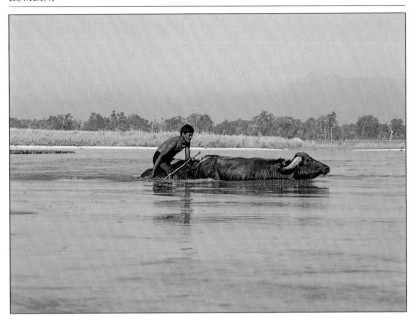

square kilometer live – in Terai there is now an average of 200 people per square kilometer. The numbers are increasing because the border with India is open for the Nepalese and Indians. It is assumed that the uncontrolled immigration wave has given three to five million Indians the opportunity to settle in the whole of Nepal as vegetable sellers, factory workers and especially as wily businessmen. Especially notorious are the Indian *Marwari*, a trader group which, it is said, participates in two-thirds of the important trading businesses and has enormous influence over Nepalese economic policies. Together with roughly 10 percent of the larger Nepalese landowners they are supposed to own some 50 percent of the usable land.

The population increase leads more and more to tension, especially in the important industrial and trade centers in the Terai. However, in the country too, overpopulation is putting pressures on the availability of the highly fertile land. Roughly two thirds of the country's agri-

A Taru crosses the Narayani river on the back of a water buffalo.

cultural production comes from the region of Terai. Rice, maize, wheat, beans, lentils, jute, sugar cane, and more recently even coffee are being cultivated here. In several areas the farmers even produce up to three harvests annually, because sediments important for the soil are deposited onto the flat plains, dissolved and carried by the torrential rivers plummeting from the Himalayas. But the swollen rivers also create flooding – harvests are destroyed, huts are washed away and entire villages inundated.

BUDDHA'S BIRTHPLACE

Those travelers who enter Nepal from India through the small city of **Bhairawa** in the southwest should not fail to visit **Lumbini**, 20 kilometers' distance from there. Buses make the trip regularly, and you can also make an agreement to take a taxi there. As the birthplace of Siddharta

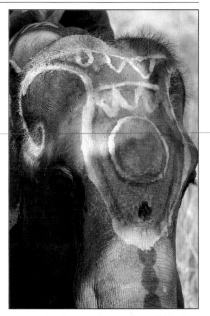

A fisherman at work. Right: A ceremonially decorated elephant.

Gautama – also named Buddha Shakyamuni, the enlightened, the historical Buddha – Lumbini has become a famous place of pilgrimage for Buddhists around the entire world.

Like so many of the royal sons of his time, Siddharta also lived surrounded in luxury at his father's court. At the age of 29, during four trips to the city, he was confronted for the first time with human misery. The sight of an old man, of a sick person and a dead body taught him the perishability of all material. His encounter with a monk kindled in him the desire to work toward eliminating misery from then on. He secretly left his home, wife and child. After years of asceticism in Bodh Gaya near Benares, and with the help of various meditation exercises, he achieved the enlightenment that made him Buddha, the Awoken One. He answered the question about the reason for the entanglement of living beings in the cycle of existence in the first of his Sarnath sermons, known as "The Four Noble Truths". They form the very heart of his teachings. Some of the most important postulates that have been handed down to this day are the ideas that, 1) Everything in the world is transitory and filled with pain, 2) The misery of existence is caused by lust and ignorance, 3) Freedom from this cycle is only possible through quenching the "thirst", that is the will to live, for which Buddha suggested an eight part road to salvation involving schooling in morals, meditation, wisdom and judiciousness. Release – i.e. enlightenment – is synonymous with the extinguishing of existence, with the complete freeing from this world, with the achieving of Nirvana. Before reaching this point, man the person must go through an endless cycle of different existences, including some painful states.

Hinayana, or Buddhism of the "small vehicle", grew from this original Buddhism around the 4th and 5th centuries B.C., and later split further into Ther-

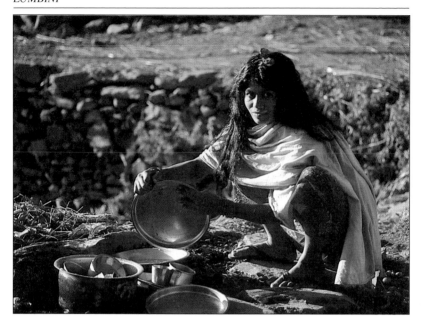

avada Buddhism among others. By the end of the first century A.D., however, conflicting views of the teachings led to separation climaxing in Mahayana Buddhism, the Buddhism of the "great vehicle". The idol of this tendency is the figure of the Bodhisattva ("whose being is enlightenment"), who had already earned the necessary requirements to become Buddha and achieve Nirvana, but who deliberately avoided the final step in order to help other beings on their way to enlightenment. The special manifestation of Mahayana Buddhism known as Vajrayna Buddhism, with its exercise of magic and secret teachings is still alive and well in Nepal today.

In 1895 a German archeologist first discovered the now famous stone columns of the Indian Emperor Ashoka, who had them erected around 250 B.C. in honor of Buddha and as a memorial of his visit here. The inscription on the columns describes the place of Buddha's birth in the **Kapilavastu Plain**, the capital of which – during Buddha's lifetime – was

A Magar girl adorned with red flowers washes the dishes.

probably **Tilaurkot**, 27 km away. King Suddhodhana, ruler of Kapilavastu, was the father of Siddharta Gautama. Descriptions of this place were made by Chinese monks from the 5th and 7th centuries A.D.; in the 13th century Malla rulers from West Nepal made journeys to this place of pilgrimage. Since the 13th century the increasing influence of the islamic Moguls caused this once so sought-out pilgrimage destination to be forgotten.

Lumbini stepped again into the limelight in 1967, as the then General Secretary of the United Nations, U Thant – himself a pious Buddhist –, visited this village. At his initiative a design was put forward for a program of international support for the re-building and expansion of this pilgrimage destination. With Mecca and Jerusalem as the centers of Islam and Christianity as examples, Lumbini should – according to Thant's plan –

A Buddhist monastery in Lumbini, the birth-place of Buddha.

receive a similar position of value for the Buddhists of the entire world. The original plan was impressive: it included representative monasteries for all of the Buddhist teaching-orientations and countries, an archeological museum with finds from excavations, a library and an information center as well as a large garden crossed with canals, in which it was envisaged that monasteries and pilgrim lodgings would be erected so that an appropriately quiet and contemplative atmosphere could be provided.

But those who look for these things in Lumbini will be disappointed. Besides the **Ashoka Columns** and several votive stupas and the stone foundation of the ruins of a monastery, today there is also a lamaist monastery in Lumbini with a larger-than-life sized portrait of Buddha Shakyamuni in its interior, and a monastery with a marble statue of the enlightened one donated by Burma.

The **Maya Devi Shrine** located nearby was named after Siddhartha Buddha's mother, in which there is to be found a stone relief with a represenation of the birth of the enlightened one – which according to the legends is supposed to have occurred here.

According to another legend, on the way from Kapilavastu to the house of his parents Queen Maya Devi is supposed to have settled under a shorea tree in the palace gardens of Lumbini in order to give birth to a son. Located south of the shrine is the **Pushkarni Pond**, where Buddha took his first purifying bath.

STALKING IN CHITWAN

The **Chitwan** region demonstrates just how different the regions of Terai can be. Towering to the north is the 3,000 m high Mahabharata Range, in the south the Siwalik Hills (150-500 meters high), also called the Churia Range, separate the valley from the flat plain of exterior Terai. Here the subtropical jungle is broken up by broad grasslands and impenetrable swamp land.

In earlier times, when the logging of the forests had not yet begun, this region in the interior of Terai was an impenetrable jungle populated by wild animals and contaminated with malaria, where only the Thurus could live, for they are supposed to be resistant to this illness.

On the other hand the Chitwan Valley was a splendid hunting grounds for the Nepalese and Indian Rajas, who enjoyed organizing for their European guests large hunting expeditions for tigers and other wild animals. Hundreds of elephants were employed for such safaris. However, today the existence of many species of animals is endangered.

Since the Nepalese Government started carrying out its large campaign against malaria contamination, in cooperation with the World Health Organization, roads have been constructed and the attempt has been made to gain more farmland for the increasing population; this has brought with it the logging of the shorea forests. With this, however, the living area of wild animals has been pushed back. For example, today in Chitwan there are no longer any wild elephants. For this reason in 1973 it was decided to found the **Chitwan National Park**. The success is encouraging. The number of animals is increasing – as is the number of visitors, which now has become almost a matter of concern. The park is considered one of the most interesting and beautiful in all of Asia.

As a result of the extension of the road network (Kathmandu-Muglin-Narayangadh) and its connection with the East-West Highway, Chitwan is becoming an important intersection for Nepalese transportation. Within the shortest time new schools and hospitals were built in the neighboring cities of **Narayangadh** and **Bharatpur**, and in the meantime in **Hetauda**, 50 km away, a considerable small industry has even been developed.

JANAKPUR – SITA'S BIRTHPLACE

Not far away from **Biratnagar**, the largest city in the Terai with around 120,000 inhabitants and 128 km distance from Kathmandu, **Janakpur** is in the southeast section of the plain. To experience some local color, you can take a chance with the bus that shuttles day and night from Kathmandu.

In mythical times this is supposed to have been the location of the capital of the old Mithila Kingdom, the king of which was the holy Janak, the father of Sita. The place played a significant role in one of the two great Indian epics, the *Ramayana*, as the birthplace of Sita, later the wife of Ram, the hero of the epic named after him. Ram as well as Sita are worshipped as incarnations of the god Vishnu and his spouse Lakshmi.

Each year on his birthday in April, Ram is worshipped as rescuer, emancipator and protector by the hundreds of pilgrims who stream into Janakpur to **Ram Mandir**, the temple dedicated to him. In 1927 the building was renovated by the Rana-Premier Chandra Shumsher. The golden roof also originates from that time. Sita's birthday – *Janaki Nawami* – is celebrated in May – just as elaborately – at the **Janaki Temple** dedicated to her. It is a destination for Hindu pilgrims from throughout the Asian subcontinent.

The the enormous grounds were constructed by the Maharani of Tikamagadh (India) and completed in 1907 after 12 years of building time, in the style of the Mogul-Rajasthani architecture. The temple is the main attraction in Janakpur.

The most significant festival in Janakpur is the *Vivaha Panchami* in November/December – commemorating the anniversary of the marriage of Sita and Rama. Thousands of pilgrims from Nepal and India come here then. A traditional marriage procession and ceremony then takes place. The festival is still celebrated every year with great enthusiasm.

NARAYANGHAD

MODERATE: **Narayani Safari** with swimming pool and tennis court in the neighborhood of the landing strip; reservations available through Hotel Narayani in Patan, Tel: 521711.

INEXPENSIVE: **Chitwan.**

There are various hotels and safari camps located in **SAURAHA** and within the park area.

BHAIRAHAWA

INEXPENSIVE: **Shambala Guest House, Pashupati Lodge, Lumbini, Himalaya Inn, Kailash.**

LUMBINI

INEXPENSIVE: **Wellcome, Janakpur** and **Rainbow.**

BIRGANJ

INEXPENSIVE: **Diyalo, Sagar Lodge** and **Koseli.**

HETAUDA

INEXPENSIVE: **Avocado.**

Hospital / Post Office / Bank

There are hospitals, a post office and banks in all of the above- mentioned cities (however in cases of serious illness return immediately to Kathmandu). The cities are connected to Kathmandu by a telephone network. You can also make radio connection from the respective control towers at the airports of Bharatpur, Meghauli, Bhairahawa and Simra/Birganj.

Miscellaneous

Elephant Polo: In the first half of December each year in Chitwan a "World Championship" elephant race is carried out. The venue is in Meghauli.

Bhairawa / Sonauli is located on the Nepalese/Indian border and is one of the most popular points of travel both in and out. Starting from here you can drive over Tansen to Pokhara or get to Kathmandu through Chitwan/Narayanghad (either over Muglin or over the old road in Hetauda). There is also a tourist office located on the Nepalese border.

The city of **Birganj** is another popular point of travel into and out of Nepal. At the Nepalese customs there is an affiliate of the Nepal Rastrya Bank. Attention: those leaving from India must set their watches ahead ten minutes. There is also a tourist office in Birganj located across from the bus station.

Traffic Connections
NARAYANGHAD / CHITWAN PARK:

Bus and Automobile: Narayanghad can also be reached from Kathmandu with bus lines and taxi – both start out from the central bus station. The

trip takes about five hours by bus. If you want to take the bus to Chitwan, then take the one in the direction of Hetauda / Birganj and get out at Tadi Bazar behind Narayanghad. From there on foot or by ox-cart you go about 8 km in an hour or so to Sauraha. On the way – on foot – you must wade through the Buri Rapti River if no jeep, ox-cart or boat is crossing over. From Kathmandu you can also take an organized excursion including hotel reservations in Chitwan for a lump sum. **Boat:** You can book a three-day-long river trip in a rubber raft from Muglin to the Chitwan Park or Narayanghad during which you will be received at some safari camps. Such tours are booked in Kathmandu.

Flight: There is a landing strip located in Narayanghad / Bharatpur, which, however, is not always in service. In addition, in the area of Narayanghad there is also the Meghauli landing field – from there you can get to the Tiger Tops Jungle Lodge, 8 kilometers away.

BHAIRAHAWA / LUMBINI: Bus: From the central bus station in Bhairahawa you can ride to Pokhara by public bus via Tansen (184 km.); the fastest connection to Kathmandu from Bhairahawa goes through Narayanghad and Muglin (ca. 10-12 hours, 292 km.). Those wanting to go to Chitwan Park can get out in Tadi Bazar before Narayanghad. Night buses also travel this route. **Flight:** There is also a landing strip for domestic flights in Bhairahawa. There is a daily direct flight to Kathmandu; flights once a week to Pokhara (for exact times ask the RNAC). From Bhairahawa to Lumbini with **automobile** and **bus**: There are regular bus connections from Bhairahawa to Lumbini, 22 kilometers away. The bus ride takes about one hour. Its faster by taxi. You have to haggle about the price.

BIRGANJ: Bus: Buses to Birganj start out from the central bus station in Kathmandu. There are also night buses. From Birganj busses drive through Muglin to Kathmandu (272 km). In addition you can also use the old road behind Hetauda through Daman – it is 100 km shorter, but time consuming because it is full of curves. **Flight:** There is a landing strip with direct flights to Kathmandu in Birganj/Simra. Attention: In the monsoon season the strip is often under water and therefore unusable.

JANAKPUR: Bus: Daily bus connections to and from Kathmandu – nights also. The journey lasts about 12 hours. The buses drive over Birganj part of the time. **Flight:** The RNAC offers regular flights from Kathmandu to Janakpur.

NATIONAL PARKS

If the measure of economic well-being was a country's natural endowment, then Nepal would certainly be one of the richest lands in the world. Within scarcely 200 kilometers this kingdom of interior Central Asia presents a truly unique ecological spectrum, beginning with an altitude of less than 100 meters above sealevel and rising up to the highest point on earth at 8,848 m.

Inside the 147,000 square kilometers of the country there are four distinct biotic provinces. Almost 23% of the area of Nepal consists of the hot and humid Terai lowland, a continuation of the fertile subtropical Ganges Plain of India. The "Midlands", a central region of rugged mountains and terraced farmland, takes up almost 44% of the country. The remainder is dominated by the Himalayan Mountains with their extensive uninhabitable zone of eternal snow and ice, and with the Trans-Himalaya Region, which, with its treeless steppes, has the character of Tibet.

These extremes are endowed with a wealth of fauna and flora which is beyond comparison in the entire region. Geography has made of Nepal a crossover zone between both of the most extreme ecological spheres in the world – between the paleoarctic region in the north and the oriental provinces of South Nepal. These regions offer a natural laboratory for zoo-geographical and ecological investigation.

In the steaming, hot and wet jungles and the grasslands of Terai alone there are over 100 kinds of mammal – from prehistoric pachyderms such as the Indian rhinoceros and elephant, to large predatory cats like leopards and tigers. The cold temperate zones of the highland and the mountains of the north shelter one of the rarest types of wildcats in the world – the snow leopard – and various kinds of wild sheep and mountain goats.

Nepal is a paradise for bird lovers. Over 800 bird species have been observed here – more than half of all the recognized species in South Asia. While South Nepal offers refuge to a series of coastal birds like herons, seagulls, terns, ducks and moor hens, the oak and rhododendron forests of the Mahabharata Mountains, the advance ranks of the Himalayas, are the home of at least a dozen kinds of pheasants with iridescent plumage. In addition to the birds, Nepal can also offer a broad array of butterfly varieties. Up to this time over 600 varieties have already been registered; and among them are several of the rarest species on the planet.

Unfortunately, only little is known about the country's plant kingdom. One analysis of Nepal's flora shows that so far 5,000 kinds of flowering plants and 540 types of ferns have been isolated, of which 250 are indigenous varieties of angiosperms. The combined number of varieties is two-and-a-half times larger than the known count for Great Britain, a country which is three times as large as Nepal. Among the flowering plants of Nepal there are thirty types of rhododendron alone, one of which is the national plant. The country has a wealth of rare and endangered varieties of orchid, many kinds of medical herbs and wild ornamental plants – the ancestors of a number of garden flowers that decorate many a western living-room today.

As opposed to many of its fellow developing nations, Nepal has at its disposal an excess of water resources: meltwater fed rivers, lakes, streams and other bodies of water with a great wealth of lifeforms; for example, the *tomahseer*

Preceding pages: An early-morning elephant ride in Chitwan National Park.

NATIONAL PARKS

– one of the most coveted freshwater fish among Asian anglers. Other types of aquatic animal include the rare, now threatened with extinction Ganges dolphin and two kinds of crocodile – the swamp crocodile and the Ganges gavial. Besides this "megafauna" there are also smaller kinds of animals in great numbers to be found in Nepal, among them various snakes – some poisonous or dangerous, others perfectly harmless –, lizards, turtles and other reptiles.

Nature Conservation in Nepal

The animal world of Nepal has in fact always attracted the attention of adventurers and explorers. At one time Nepal was also popular as the Shah and Rana rulers' hunting grounds for the great beasts. With the collapse of the Rana regime in 1951 and the political instability of the 'fifties there followed a heavy destruction of the forests and wildlife, with significant losses. Thanks to the far-sightedness and intervention of the then-

King Mahendra, only in the middle of the 'sixties, was protection guaranteed against the encroaching clear-cut deforestation and the pressures for agricultural land. Mahendra's son, the present King Birendra Bir Bikram Shah Dev, has lead this initiative. Since then, natural protection has become an integral part of the socio-economic development planning of Nepal. At present there are thirteen national protected areas, which comprise more than 9% of the total land area – one of the highest percentages in all of Asia. The National Park and Nature Protection Decree of 1973 placed 26 mammals, nine species of bird and three reptiles under comprehensive protection, so that their hunting and commercial exploitation are responsibly prohibited.

You can get the best insight into the fauna and flora of Nepal through a description of the national parks and wildlife reservations, which have been purposely distributed about the country so that they provide an exemplary representation of the kingdom's eco-system.

191

CHITWAN NATIONAL PARK

The Royal Chitwan National Park (RCNP), the first in Nepal, was established in 1973 – 100 years after the dedication of Yellowstone National Park in the USA, which was the first national park in the world. The RCNP is located in inner Terai, covering an area of 93,200 hectares, and extends through a river valley which includes the flood plains of the **Rapti**, **Reu** and **Narayani Rivers**. Its altitude reaches from 150 up to 815 m at the **Churia**, a chain of hills that divides the park into two major watershed regions.

The climate is subtropical with maximum temperatures up to 38 degrees C in May and June, with the lowest values (5 degrees C) in December and January. The average annual precipitation stands at about 2400 mm; the wettest months are from June until November, during which some 90% of the monsoon rains fall.

The flora and fauna of the Chitwan are among the most abundant and richest in Asia. In addition this is the territory of the last surviving examples of the Asiatic rhinoceros in Nepal which has been almost completely eradicated because of the alleged aphrodisiacal properties of its horn.

The vegetation is dominated by shorea forests, which cover 70% of its surface. The remainder is a mosaic of bottomland forests, tall grasslands, lakes, swamps, and other bodies of water. There are pure shorea woodlands in the lowlands by **Kasra** – the headquarters of the park. In the remaining area these are mixed with other types of trees and bushes. Fir trees appear in the Churia Chain and often stand mixed with shorea trees. The grassland and the lowland forests are in a constant state of change as a result of frequent overflooding and fires. Khair acacias and the sissoo dalbergia predominate in the flood plains of the lower rivers and on the islands of the Narayani River. Otherwise in the lowland forests, the kapok tree and the vehellar dominate the tree species. More than ten kinds of tall,

CHITWAN NATIONAL PARK

0   5   10 km

dense grass cover over the forest clearings and glades; these are collectively designated as elephant grass.

In addition to the approximately 300-350 rhinoceroses, the Chitwan National Park is rich in other types of large animals. Among the predators there are also some 60-70 tigers, the biggest hunters of the park, which have been the subject of intensive study over the last fifteen years. This reseach project, which is collectively supported by the Royal Government of Nepal, the King Mahendra Trust for Natural Conservation, the Smithsonian Institution and the World Wildlife Fund, is the only one of its kind in Asia. The methods of investigation are a combination of traditional hunting techniques of the indigenous peoples and modern scientific research techniques with a western stamp on them. Large mammals such as tigers and rhinoceros are anaesthetized with chemical drugs. The sleeping animal is then fitted with a specially designed neck-band carrying a radio transmitter before he reawakens

and is set free again. These free-running animals are then followed with radio apparatus from the backs of tame elephants.

Other common predators from the cat family are the leopard, the swamp lynx, and the bengali cat. In the scattered territory of the park – alongside jackals, foxes and wild dogs (dholes) – there are also smaller predatory animals represented such as civet cats, martens, mongooses and otters. One can also observe the sloth bear from the omnivore family here as he seeks through the forest floor after termites, while two types of apes – the rhesus monkey and the langur – swing from limb to limb in the tree-tops. Wild boars and deer including the sambar, chital or axis deer and the muntjac are the most frequently seen hoofed animals in the park. Visitors who come to Chitwan during the dry season (between the end of February and May) are often rewarded for this by getting a chance to see a gaur – the largest asiatic species of wild cow – as they move from the Churia Hills to the floodplain lowlands and grasslands.

193

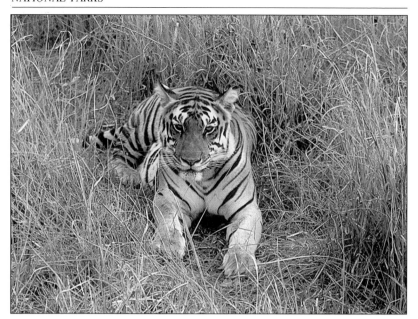

With the recorded number of over 450 species, the park is famous for its profusion of birds; several types like the bankiva hen and the peacock are to be found here all year-round. Others, such as the demoiselle crane, change their locations inside the park, still others, like the Indian goose and the rust duck spend only their winters in the park.

Visitor Information: In 1984 the Royal Chitwan National Park was declared a World Heritage Site by UNESCO – an agency of the United Nations – because of the abundant variety of its animal world. Located only 90 km southwest of Kathmandu as the crow flies, it is the most popular tourist destination in the Terai. There are flight connections to **Meghauli** and **Bharatpur**. You can reach the park by automobile on the Tribhuvan Rajpath Highway – by turning west from **Hetauda**, or by turning south in the direction of Narayangadh from the road between Pokhara and Kathmandu at **Mugling**. From **Narayangadh** you drive eastward to **Tadi Bazar,** from where it is

Unfortunately there are now only 60 - 70 tigers left in the Chitwan National Park.

still 6 kilometers to **Saura,** one of the entrances to the park.

There is a well-developed network of overnight lodgings, from unassuming "low-budget" accomodation up to the super-deluxe category, which vary in price between less than US $15 per day for an accomodation outside the park, to more than US $190 for a resort hotel within the park limits. The most popular way to see the park's wildlife – and a unique experience – is with a safari through the jungle riding on the back of an elephant. Round trips and bookings for a visit into Chitwan can be arranged in Kathmandu. Tiger Top's Jungle Lodge, Gaida Wildlife Camp, Chitwan Jungle Lodge, Machan Wildlife Resort, Narayan Safari, Temple Tiger and Island Resort have received concessions from the government enabling them to maintain tourist establishments inside the park. These companies have their own ele-

Unluckily the Ganges gavial is rarely seen in the wilderness nowadays.

phants and are recommended because they work under the supervision of the state. Other accomodation is outside of the park dependent on the state-owned elephants in Saura – which are only available to tourists when they are not required for state purposes. They are given out only in the mornings and evening hours according to the "first come, first served" principle. Altogether, they are not available very frequently – as a rule only between January and March. Several private hotels in Saura have their own elephants, which are not allowed to enter the park, bringing their guests instead to the **Tikoli Forest**, a forest that has already suffered heavy destruction. The visitor centers in Saura and the Ghavial Conservation Center offer opportunities to learn about the flora and fauna inside the park boundaries.

Seeing the park on foot cannot be recommended, since several people are gored or killed by rhinoceroses every year. The best opportunity to observe wildlife close up – in safety – is by taking a ride on an elephant with the professional guidance of one of the parks personnel.

One further available form of observation is a river cruise on the **Rapti** with a dugout boat, which costs 25 rupees for a 45 minute group trip. Dugouts are, however, known for their tendency to capsize occasionally, therefore you should take precautionary measures for your cameras and binoculars.

SAGARMATHA NATIONAL PARK

"As the highest point on the surface of the earth, Sagarmatha and its surroundings are of the greatest significance not only for Nepal, but for the whole world." With these words Nepal's Prince Gyanendra announced the establishment of the highest national park of the world, as he spoke before the Third International Congress of the World Wildlife Fund.

195

The park encompasses an area of 1,243 sq.km in the upper watershed region of the Dudh-Kosi River and is located northeast of Kathmandu in the Solu Khumbu District. The territory is characterized by a dramatic landscape, since the park includes many of the highest mountains in the world. Seven of its summits are higher than 7,000 meters, among them that of Sagarmatha or Mount Everest (8,848 m), and geologists contend that their altitude is increasing, as their folding continues further. The climate is cool and moist in summer, in winter cold and dry. 80% of the rain falls during the monsoon months (June-September), receiving on average less than 1,000 mm annually.

The park is extended over six zones of vegetation. The lower sub-alpine area between 3,000 and 3,600 meters altitude has forest consisting of spruce, Scot's pine and juniper. The upper sub-alpine zone above 3,600 meters consists of birch and rhododendron forests. Scrub brush with dwarf rhododendron are found in the lower alpine zone above the tree-line (3,800-4,000 m) together with several flowering herbs such as the lily and the primrose. The density of the brush decreases with the temperature. Above 5,000 meters the snow-rhododendron is the only representative of its species, together with alpine plants such as the buckthorn, horse-tail or shave grass, and the blue Himalayan poppy. Above this zone the vegetation is confined to species of lichen, moss, and dwarf and reed grasses and finally discontinues altogether at the permanent snowline, which is around 5,750 meters.

As a result of a combination of geological and geohistorical factors there are only a few types of mammals in the Sagarmatha National Park in comparison to the Terai region. In spite of this, from the goat-antelope family there are the serau, the goral and the Himalayan thar; from the deer family there are the musk-deer or moschus and the muntjak. The smaller mammals which appear in the park include the calling hare or pika, the Tibetan mountain-shrew, the Tibetan woolly hare, the Siberian fire-weasel, the masked palm civet-cat, and the marmot.

The bird community is estimated to include about 120 species. Among the more remarkable are the Himalayan pheasant and the blood pheasant. The Himalayan griffon-vulture and the bearded vulture have been seen at altitudes of 7,600 meters, and mountain-climbing expeditions have reported that they have encountered mountain crows at up to 8,200 meters. Among the 30 types of butterfly which occur in the park is also the silver mountain butterfly.

The Sagarmatha National Park has great cultural significance. Here is also the home of the famous Sherpas. It was therefore one of the first locations placed on the list of World Heritage Sites by the United Nations. The existence of the legendary creature of the snows, the Yeti – a kind of Nepalese Big Foot – probably did not play a major role in the decision.

Visitor Information: The best time to pay a visit to Sagarmatha is between October and May, excepting the months of December and February, during which the daytime temperatures usually stay well below the freezing point and the region also records heavy snowfall, which naturally make hiking difficult if not impossible. The park has over 6,000 visitors per year, so that along the main trekking route a number of lodgings have been established, among them the Everest View Hotel in Shyangboche. Carriers can be hired in Lukla for a fee to be bargained, and meals are served in many of the little tea-houses along the whole path up to the Everest Base Camp.

LANGTANG NATIONAL PARK

The Langtang National Park, which has existed since 1973, is located in the

Rapacious vultures in upper Langtang feast on scraps.

central Himalaya region of Nepal, 32 km north of Kathmandu. It encompasses a land area of 171,000 hectares, representing the main watershed areas of the Trisuli and Bhote Kosi Rivers. The altitude reaches from 790 meters at the Bhote Kosi up to 7,245 m on the summit of the Langtang Lirung. The northern limits of the park are defined by the international Nepal-China (Tibet) border; the Gosainkund Lake and the Dorje Lakpe range divide the park into eastern and western flanks. One of the most outstanding characteristics of the park is the great variety of its vegetation types. Located in the altitudes below 1,000 meters there are tropical species like the shorea tree. The Indian castanopsis and the Scots pine are to be found in the sub-tropical sector between 1,000 and 2,000 meters. The vegetation in the montana zone between 2,000 and 3,000 meters consists of oak and Himalayan hemlock, especially in the wetter areas. In the sub-alpine zone coniferous trees predominate; in the more arid areas are the larch and the Scots pine, while rhododendrons are to be found everywhere. The occurence of larches is of particular interest because of the unusual distribution of its species in the Langtang.

The vegetation in the Langtang is especially varied because of the immense differences in altitude as well as microclimatic conditions. Found among the smaller mammals in the park are the small panda bear, the calling-hare or pika, the showy marmot, and several varieties of shrew and wolf. One of the hoofed animals that can be seen on the slopes of the Langtang Valley is the Himalayan thar, which has a population of about 200 animals. Other larger mammals which are distributed through the park are the goral, the serau, wild boars, muntjaks and the musk-deer. The ape species are represented by the rhesus monkey and the langur, while the Himalayan black bear is the only representative of his species.

The Trisuli and Bhote Kosi Valley system is an important route for migratory birds, which fly back and forth between the Indian Plain and Tibet in autumn and springtime. More than 180 types of birds have already been registered in this region, among which are found such rare species as the long-billed ibis, the white-crowned redtail, the scaly woodpecker, and the golden-tailed honey guide. The pheasant, partridge, eagle, vulture and hawk species are the same as have already been described for the Sagarmatha National Park.

The park also has things of cultural interest to offer, for example Helambu or the holy lakes of Panch Pokhari and Gosainkund. The latter attracts tens of thousands of Buddhist and Hindu pilgrims annually, especially during the *Janai Purne* festivals in summer.

Visitor Information: Traveling to this park is very much easier than getting to the other national parks in the Himalayas. From Kathmandu you can ride either by taxi or by bus to **Dhunche**, where the

A lively stream in the Annapurna Conservation Area.

park's headquarters are located. As an alternative you can also take the public bus to **Sundarijal** and hike in through Helambu. To get to the remote areas in the eastern sector you start out on foot from **Chautara** or **Tatopani**, both of which can be reached from Kathmandu with the bus.

SHEY-PHOKSUMDO NATIONAL PARK

Shey-Phoksumdo is the largest national park in Nepal (355,500 ha) and was established in 1984. The greater part of it is located to the north of the Himalayan Main Range on the Trans-Himalayan Plateau in the Dolpo district. Of particular interest in this park are the **Kanjiroba Himal** and the **Phoksumdo Lake**, Nepal's second-largest lake, which lies at an altitude of 3,660 meters. The landscape in the heart of the park resembles

At high altitudes lichen thrives on the few scramny trees.

the cold arctic desert such as one also finds in the Tibetan Highland, where annual precipitation is under 500 mm.

The vegetation of the trans-Himalayan region consists of sparse bush with juniper, caragana, lonicera and others which are adapted to the cold northern conditions of the semi-arid climate. On the river terraces there are also isolated occurences of poplar and walnut.

Several of the Himalayan mammals which have already been described for Langtang and Sagarmatha are also to be found here. This notwithstanding, the park is also famous for the rare snow-leopard and the pamir sheep – also called the *nayan*. Additionally, several of the endangered animal species of Tibet, such as the wild yak, are found here. According to unsubstantiated local assertions, the chiru and the Tibetan wild ass occasionally cross over the border from Tibet. The 55 varieties of bird which are to be found

in the park include particular trans-Himalayan species such as the Tibetan lark, the mountain linnet, and the Adams snow-finch.

Shey Gompa is a monastery from the eleventh century which has great religious significance for the Buddhist pilgrims of the surrounding area. A herd of half-tame blue sheep are kept there, which are carefully taken care of by the monks and can be observed close up.

Visitor Information: Large sections of the park may not be entered by non-Nepalese, however one can obtain a trekking permit for the ascent of **Ringmo**, which is on the south west side of the lake. If you don't want to travel on foot from Jumla, then the best way to arrive to the park is by aircraft. There is a regular flight from the Royal Nepalese Airline between Nepalganj and Juphal, which is two hours' distance from the seat of the Dunai district administration. Leaving from there you reach **Sundawa** – where the park headquarters are – in a two-day-long hike. From there it is still one-and-a-half days further to Ringmo. The best visiting time is between April and June – the months with the mildest climate. There are, however, no services for tourists, so that visitors unluckily are completely on their own.

RARA NATIONAL PARK

The Rara National Park, established in 1976, is in the **Mugu District** in West Nepal, 24 kilometers north of **Jumla** in the region of the Karnali River. It encompasses an area of 10,600 hectares, of which 1,020 are lake surface.

The Rara Lake is the most beautiful in landscape as well as the largest lake in Nepal, and lies at an altitude of 2,990 meters. The lake basin forms the northern half of the park area; the **Chuchamara Dara** stands – in the shape of a horseshoe – at the lake's edge and rises up to the highest point in the park with 4,038 m. The lake is 167 m deep, and is thus the deepest in the whole region. Rainfall during the monsoon season (May-August) amounts to some 400 mm, while in winter (November-March) you may easily have to contend with a blanket of snow more than a meter thick.

The lake is surrounded primarily by spruces, which are mixed in several places with oak, rhododendron, juniper and also Scots pine. The northern slopes of the Chuchumara Mountain have spruce and birch above 3,350 m

Almost all of the Himalayan animals which have already been described are also found in this park, such as the small panda, the Himalayan black bear, the wild boar, the musk-deer and other hoofed animals.

There are more than 60 species of birds; permanently settled game birds, most of the pheasant and partridge varieties as well as migratory waterfowl are important representatives of the park's bird world. To name a few among the former: the stone hen, the Himalayan

royal hen and pheasant types such as the red-back pheasant, the valaisian pheasant and koklas pheasant; among the latter the mallard duck, teal or greenwing duck, the great crested grebe and the coot. Otters are frequently seen in the water, and the marinka is a common fish in the lake.

Visitor Information: There are two ways to get to Rara. The first is by air from Kathmandu to Jumla, followed by a two-and-a-half day hike. The other requires a week-long foot march after arriving at **Surketh** by aircraft or by bus. The best times for a visit are from October to December or between March and May.

Along the narrow hiking path to **Bhulbhule** in the neighborhood of the park border there are several tea-shops which also offer some food. By the park headquarters in Rara there is also a guesthouse which visitors with the permission of the park administration may use – they must, however, bring along their own sleeping bag and food.

ANNAPURNA CONSERVATION AREA

The Annapurna Conservation Area (ACA) is in the central Himalayas north of Pokhara. It covers an area of 2,600 square kilometers, which is extended over five districts of the Gandaki and Dhaulagiri zones. The area is famous for its high mountains – just within its bounds there are seven peaks measuring over 7,000 meters. It is also known for its deep valleys, which contrast with the immense mountains.

The landscape of the region changes with the altitude, which ranges from 1,311 meters in Tatopani to 8,091 m on the summit of Annapurna I. Accordingly, the climatic conditions here are also enormously differentiated. The southern slopes of Annapurna receive among the highest annual amounts of precipitation, with over 3,000 mm, whereas the northern area in the rain-shadow of the Trans-

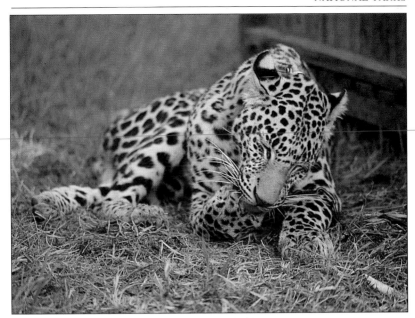

A snow leopard in the Chitwan National Park has his daily wash.

Himalaya sector registers the lowest precipitation levels in the country (under 300 mm).

As a result of the huge differences in climatic conditions and altitude, the breadth of biological variation in the animal and plant world is particularly high. During the trek lasting a few days you cross bamboo forests from the subtropical world of Pokhara before entering the magical glacial paradise of the Annapurna Base Camp. In the lowest places one finds subtropical communities; schimas, the indian castanopsis, alders, and Scots pines stand on the dry slopes. In the temperate forest zones at the higher altitudes oaks and rhododendrons are distributed, while bamboos are growing in the wettest regions – for example in the Modi Khola Valley.

Higher up on the drier mountain slopes the bamboos are replaced by coniferous trees – Scots or pitch pines, spruces and

hemlock firs. Above these regions are located sub-alpine communities including birches and junipers, while yet further up in the alpine zone species of rhododendron bushes are to be found.

In the conservation area there are more than 400 species of birds, among them the only endemic (indigenous) or exclusively Nepalese variety – the harrow thrush. The Kali-Gandaki Valley also represents an important stretch for more than 40 migratory birds, among them also the demoiselle crane. Almost all the species of pheasant, predatory bird and small animal species that are found in other sections of the Himalayas also occur here. The snow leopard, the small panda, the Himalayan musk deer, the muntjak and four varieties of sheep and goat-antelope species are found in this region as well.

The Annapurna Conservation Area Project (ACAP) is Nepal's most recent initiative for the protection of this unique region. With a less restrictive and more flexible style of management than is

Unpious Rhesus monkeys at Svayambhunath. Right: Rhododendrons in Nepal flower in March-April.

usual in the national parks and reservations, the indigenous populations in the conservation area are permitted to continue their traditional life-styles and subsistence agriculture. These ways of life are integrated into the greater framework of a plan for a healthy management of resources and economic development.

The ecological and cultural disposition of this region is influenced by a series of factors: too rapid population growth, badly advised agricultural development, and the immediate effects resulting from trekking tourism. As a response to these negative influences the **King Mahendra Trust for Nature Conservation (KMTNC)** has developed a new approach in which nature conservation is combined with consideration of human requirements and local development.

These conservation measures began in 1986, and the ACA is the most recent of

Nepal's protected regions. The program is multi-dimensional and attemps to find a middle way between the requirements of the indigenous peoples and those of nature.

Nature conservation on a small scale and the application of alternative energy sources ought to keep the environmental consequences of the visiting tourists as slight as possible, while simultaneously guaranteeing a sustaining future for both the land and people.

With 30,000 visitors annually, the ACA is far and away the most popular trekking destination in Nepal, partly because it is at only a few days' walk.

Visitor Information: The Annapurna Conservation Area is best reached by taking a bus or aircraft to Pokhara. There, continuing from the end of the road, you arrive after a two-day-long hike to **Gandruk**, the ACA headquarters. In addition to the information posts in **Chomrong** and **Gorepani,** the ACA maintains a small museum and visitor center on the Prithvi Narayan Campus in Pokhara.

Except during the monsoon season (June to September) one can visit the ACA almost the whole year round. Tourists must pay 200 rupees per visit for an ACAP user's-fee, which is charged in addition to the trekking fees. The user's fee serves to support various ACAP projects. Establishing kerosene depots is considered as important here as educating the owners of the lodges in various modern methods of nature conservation. The problems caused by excess refuse is particularly accute in those areas visited by mass tourism.

THE KING MAHENDRA TRUST FOR NATURE CONSERVATION

The King Mahendra Trust was called into existence in 1982. The Trust is an autonomous, non-governmental organization for the common good, which is established under the general leadership of

King Birendra Bir Birkam Shah Dev. It is directed by a committee, the members of which consist of prominent Nepalese from both the public and private sectors, as well as foreign members of international repute.

The committee chairman is His Royal Highness Prince Gyanendra Bir Bikram Shah Dev – Nepal's foremost defender of nature. The Trust has branch offices in the whole world – Canada, France, Germany, Japan, England and the United States. These well-known international establishments support the Trust in their respective countries and deliver essential financial and technical resources to the Foundation.

Considered superficially, the combination of the goals of conservation and economic development could be seen as self-contradictory. The Trust, however, does not share this viewpoint. In consideration of the constantly recurring flooding and landslides, and in the face of the fact that the country is almost completely dependent on its own resources, the Trust emphasizes that effective conservation of nature brings with it an appropriate approach to development and building of the economy. Therefore the Trust pursues the goal of "natural conservation for development toward self-preservation" and plans its measures accordingly.

The Trust is engaged in two main working areas: The first as coordinator and mediator, the other as the executive judge of model projects which should put together a reasonable utilization of natural resources with the economic and social development of the population of Nepal.

A great portion of the time of the employees of the Trust in Kathmandu is applied to their tasks as coordinators and mediators. For example, interested parties must be brought together to promote projects and development activities which they wish to have supported by the

Trust. The Royal Government of Nepal also receives technical advice and suggestions concerning environmental and development policies. The Trust also lends its support to the Department of National Parks and Wildlife Conservation. Close connections are also maintained with foreign assistance organizations which are active in the area of environmental protection in Nepal, among others, the World Wildlife Fund.

Over the last five years, the Trust has been responsible for the management of over 20 different projects. For some of these the main concern was the improvement of basic data, in other cases environmental management, nature conservation research or development.

The Trust is an institution for the common good and receives no regular governmental budget appropriations. Therefore it must devote a great deal of time to procuring necessary means. For this purpose the Trust has an ambitious program with which it mobilizes support both domestically and in foreign countries.

SYMBOLS

When you will have landed at Kathmandu's Tribhuvan Airport, the Nepalese will greet you with a *namaste or namaskar*, which is a demonstration of respect and deference. With this he places his hands together at chest height, while bowing slightly forward. The deeper this bow is, the more respect, love, honor and reverence is being demonstrated towards one's counterpart. The **national hymn** of Nepal is a song in praise of the king, who is also considered to be a reincarnation of the god Vishnu. All three branches of authority – legislative, executive and judiciary – rest in his hands.

Nepal's **national coat of arms** consists of a variety of symbols: under the crown of the king are two red national banners with the obligatory crossed *khukris*, the Himalayan mountains flanked by the sun and moon, a facsimile of the Pashupatinath temple, the holy Bagmati River with the holy cow – highly worshipped by the Hindus – and a danphey pheasant, the

Preceding pages: Artistic carvings of Hindu gods. An umbrella is repaired for a procession. Left: Preparations for the Indrajatra festival.

country's **national bird**. Also on the coat of arms is Nepal's national flower, the red rhododendron, flanked by two soldiers – one Gurkha marksman armed with a *khukri*, and one warrior equipped with a *khukri*, bow and arrows. Finally on the coat of arms is written in Sanskrit that "mother and motherland (are) greater than the heavens".

In **Nepal's flag** there are illustrations of the sun and the moon, which are seen by the Hindus as being symbols of the Hindu deities Surya and Chandra. The origin of this symbolism is to be found in the India's Vedic period, since the Aryans principally worshipped nature-deities.

The red rhododendron which is called *laliguras* in Nepal was chosen as Nepal's **national flower**. It grows in the Himalayas at altitudes above 2,000 meters in real rhododendron forests.

Simrik is the Nepalese name for carmine red – their **national color**. In one example, the statues of the ape-god Hanuman is generally painted with a mixture of red pigment mixed with mustard-seed oil, and then covered with a red cloth.

Red is also the color of the point-shaped *tika* that one sees on the foreheads of the Nepalese. This consists of a mixture of powdered cinnobar, rice flower and yoghurt. The *tika* is applied by a brahman or elder as a blessing of the gods; it is received after a visit to a temple or after a *puja*. On certain high festival days women wear red saris, especially the Tij-festival and on the day of their marriage. Also, Nepal's living goddess Kumari – an incarnation of the goddess Taleju – wears red.

The word *Om* and the *svastika* – or sun-cross – are among the symbols of religious belief in everyday life. OM has its origin in Sanskrit, and is considered a holy syllable, and as such is frequently used at the opening of religious ceremonies and at the beginning of works of literature. In the private realm this symbol is frequently found on visiting cards and letter-heads. One also finds OM applied to the doors of houses, and various equipment and machines. The svastika was originally a symbol for fire. They are thought of as lucky symbols, and are to be seen on temples, stupas, pagodas, and house-doors. This sign is supposed to bring prosperity and success, since it is a symbolic representation of the concept of life as a constant process of coming into being.

On the house-doors in Kathmandu and on the stupas of Svayambunath and Bodnath one will notice the all-seeing **Eyes of the original Buddha**, which look upon the people with compassion and sympathy. Between the eyes there appears – as a sign of enlightenment – the mystical third eye, as it is erroneously characterized. This is really a tuft of Buddha's hair, the so-called *urna*. Appearing where the nose would be is the number 1, a symbol for unity.

The streets of the Kathmandu Valley are full of holy cows – notorious for their calmness and nonchalance. The Hindus believe that the five products of the cow – milk, sour milk, butter, urine and dung – have purifying properties. Besides this, the cow is Nepal's **national animal**, called *Gaitrimata* (mother-cow). Once a year in the Kathmandu Valley, the Gaijatra festival – which extends over days – takes place in honor of the holy cow and to commemorate the dead.

The **national weapon** of Nepal and, respectively, the Gurkha soldiers is the *khukri*, a curved knife. No household in Nepal lacks one, where it is used to chop wood, meat and vegetables. The good luck of the Gurkha batallions is thought to depend on the aptitude of the Gurkha in the employment of his *khukri*. As the symbol of the Gurkha army, crossed *khukris* are illustrated in the Nepalese national coat of arms. The knife's sheath is made of simple wood which has been embellished with leather or ornamented with silver and turquoise stones. There are also two smaller knives kept in the sheath of the *khukri*; these are called the *kardo* and the *chamak*. The kardo is sharpened and is used for cutting; in contrast the chamak is blunt and is used to sharpen the *khukri* and – together with a flint-stone – to kindle fires.

The Himalayan pheasant *(lapophorus impejanus)*, which the Nepalese call the danphey-chari, is Nepal's **national bird**. The male danphey is particularly conspicuous with its strikingly beautiful plumage and its long tail.

Yeti, the snow-man, has also become a national symbol of Nepal. In the face of numerous yeti-quests – or even hunting expeditions – the Nepalese government was forced to set down laws forbidding its killing and declaring this creature to be the property of the people.

GURKHAS

Gunfire flashed through the darkness. As soldier Lal Bahadur Thapa tried to make his way through the lane he jumped a watch-post equipped with machine guns and slit the throats of two enemy soldiers with his *khukri*. Creeping stealthily he climbed the hill; on the way two more men fell victim to his fluted knife. A short time later Gurkha Lal Bahadur was awarded the Victoria Cross, England's highest decoration, for his bravery in North Africa during the Second World War in a battle where the British attacked fortified German and Italian positions roughly 200 miles south of Tunis.

In 1982 the British Gurkhas again did justice to their reputation; the BBC reported: "As the Gurkhas advanced on Argentinian positions, the enemy troops dropped their guns and abondoned their mortars and machine guns." The only Gurkha killed in the Falklands War was Buddha Prasad Limbu, who lost his life as he searched for Argentinian mines. Many Falkland civilians paid him their last respects.

"Ayo Gurkhali" goes the fear-inspiring battle cry of the agile Gurkhas, who enjoy an almost legendary reputation because of the skill they demonstrate in the jungle. This shrill cry has frequently created fear and panic in the enemy lines. The Japanese as well as Rommel's Africa Corps were beset by fear and horror in this manner. When the Gurkhas pull their *kukhris*, Mahakal's nectar (that means blood) must flow.

Who are the Gurkhas? For the history of Nepal and the Gurkha troops, the Gurkha principality located west of the Kathmandu Valley – founded by the Shah Dynasty – is of particular significance. In the 15th century the Rajputs from the Indian Rajasthan retreated from the Islamic Mogul rulers to West Nepal and, in addition, constructed a strong fortress there,

from which sprang the present-day town of Gurkha. Around the middle of the 18th century, the ruler of the Gurkhas, Prithvi Narayan Shah, felt himself to be powerful enough to attack the Kathmandu Valley and respectively the Malla Kings which governed there. The Valley was conquered in 1768. The conqueror named himself the King of Nepal and introduced a period of Nepalese expansion. This was first put to a halt by the British General Ochterlony in 1816. The British-Nepalese Treaty of Sugauli was signed on March 4th, 1816, and Nepal had to surrender the provinces of Kumaon and Gharwal to England. Also in the treaty, the right of the English to conscript Nepalese for the British colonial wars was introduced.

Today the holy Castle of Gorakhnath watches over the city of Gurkha, to which the Gurkhas owe their name. The expression Gurkha or Gorkha has its origins in the Sanskrit words "go" which in translation means "cow"; and "rakh" (raksha) which means "protector". An allusion is thus made to Hindu tradition as "protector of the cows". However, not all of the Gurkha soldiers are Hindus. The majority belongs much more to the various ethnic groups of the central Hill Region and the high valleys of the Himalayas. The Gurkhas are not, as is frequently incorrectly assumed, an ethnic group of the same origins; they come primarily from the Gurung and Magar in West Nepal as well as from the Kirati groups – the Rai and the Limbu in the East of the country. Today, Tamang and Thakali are also counted among them.

Presently in the Royal Nepalese Army, the largest group among the Gurkha troops is formed by the members of the Hindu caste of Chetris. The first two Gurkha battalions were formed in 1763. In 1768 they fought against the British. One of these two battalions was put into action against the Tibetans, the other in the British- Nepalese War of 1814.

Relief on the Sahid Dheka in Kathmandu showing a Gurkha parade.

Nepal earns in 30 million dollars a year through the Gurkhas. Besides tourism they represent one of the most important sources of foreign exchange.

After India became independent of the rule of the British, the Gurkha regiments were divided between the two nations. They still take their oaths to the British monarch and, furthermore, march in procession before Buckingham Palace as honor guards for the Queen. British Gurkhas have served in Malaysia, Indonesia (Borneo), Hong Kong, Brunei and Cyprus.

The Gurkhas have better chances than other Nepalese on the marriage market, especially the British Gurkhas, since their wives and children have the opportunity to travel abroad (London, Brunei, Singapore and Hong Kong) which is a real dream for the majority of the 17 million Nepalese. The Gurkhas live very spartanly and bring the money or gold they have earned home with them. Many young boys among the Gurkhas are called Bir or Bahadur, which means "the courageous"; courageousness is highly regarded in the world of Nepalese men. Better to die with courage than to live as a coward, it is said.

Since India took over the role of the policeman of South Asia, the Indian Gurkhas have been put into action against enemies of India, which is clear to see in the examples of Sri Lanka and the Maldives.

Although the Gurkhaland movement in the Darjeeling district (India) was crushed in 1988 after 28 months of militant agitation, the problem of the Gurkhas – from Nepal and India – is still not solved; there are many Gurkhalis of Nepalese origin who live in India or work in the Indian armed forces.

In harmony with King Birendra's idea of declaring Nepal as a peace-zone, Gurkhas have been sent into action in the Sinai Desert and Lebanon on behalf of the United Nations.

DANCING AND FESTIVALS

At the New Year's festival in Thimi. Right: Newar classical dancer.

The Nepalese both love and dread the festivals, which fill their calendar. Of course they cost money, and one often develops a bit of an upset stomach after the inevitable – and unavoidable – festival banquets and accompanying revelries, which require mountains of meat and rivers of rice-beer and spirits. The Newar in the Kathmandu Valley have carried both celebration and festival banquetry to the greatest of extremes. According to one saying: Mountain-dwellers ruin themselves with their display of status symbols, and the Newar in the valley ruin themselves with their feasts. However, the health and financial ruin is compensated for by the happiness gained by celebrating with all one's friends and relatives, as well as having been closer to the gods. For part of every festival is a worshipping of the gods – called a *puja* – in the process of which the god or goddess is venerated and receives offerings – sacred water, flowers, coins, grains

of rice, burning wicks and incense, red paint powder, fruits or vegetables; frequently liquor and animal sacrifices as well. In return, the believer receives *prasad* (blessing in material form); a blossom, a paint- mark on his forehead, or a little bit of the food that was offered to the gods. Included in some festivals is the so-called *jatra*, a procession in which a god is either carried about in a chest or pushed in a festival chariot. The procession follows a pre-determined route through the city or village as the god receives offerings and gives blessings. The numerous private festivals – with their protracted preparations and seemingly uneventful conclusions – require of the occidental guest exceptional patience and the ability to remain seated, as well as a robust digestive system. If you do not possess these prerequisites, then acceptance of an invitation to a Nepalese wedding celebration – by all means with expression of polite regret – should be avoided. In contrast, the action-packed and exciting town rituals are among the most colorful and impressive experiences of a trip to Nepal.

New Year Festival

The most spectacular of all Newar festivals is the New Year festival in Bhaktapur. It begins two days before the Newari New Year on the ninth of April and ends ten days later. In the weeks beforehand, carpenters assemble both of the festival carts for the gods Bhairava and Bhadrakali on the Taumadi Place. On the afternoon of the ninth of April Bhairava takes his place in his wagon, and as soon as the priests give the sign, the chariot procession begins. At this time old rivalries break out between the upper and lower sections of the city, often leading to dangerous brick-throwing fights. The wagons, which weigh tons, are pulled by hundreds of strong men with heavy ropes, about 20 meters in length, fastened to either side. Because of the aggression which suddenly flares up, it is advisable to observe this contest from a safe distance – for example, the stone platform on the southern edge of the square. In any case, one should not join in the rope-pull. Each year there are serious accidents in which people are run over or hit with bricks.

Three days later, on the evening before the New Year, the activities of the multitude are concentrated on the Yoshimkhel Place, which is on the Hanumante River. A huge tree-trunk is erected as a symbol of creation and reproduction. With this act the New Year begins. During this night Bhakapur is filled with music. In the early morning of New Years Day the entire population, festively dressed, sets off to the river, takes a ritual bath, and worships the gods Bhairava and Bhadrakali, who have in the meantime been bethroned in open buildings in the area of

the tree. The vigor and liveliness of this New Year's morning, peopled with the freshly-bathed festival throng, is an unforgettable experience. Each family carries a sacrificial rooster to the wagon of Bhairava, on a pole of which is bound Betal, a spirit of chaos, who receives the roosters' blood. In the evening, after the family feasts, the throngs assemble again at the Yoshimkhel Place in order to bring the tree-trunk crashing down; a rather dusty event – and not without its dangers. Four years ago the trunk broke off four meters above the ground and crashed down on the crowd of people who were fortunately able to be rescued. The erection of the pole signals the beginning of numerous processions in different parts of the city, in which the local gods, accompanied by groups of musicians, are carried in chests through their area of influence and receive sacrificial offerings.

On the morning of the second day of the New Year, a visit to the neighboring village of Thimi is very rewarding. Early, around 6:30, all of the local gods are gathered at the Bal Kumari pagoda, and the shrine is encircled with hundreds of torch- carriers and drummers. The air is full of orange paint powder, with which everybody dusts each other. This festival is already over at around half-past eight. You have to get up very early and bring along a dust-brush for your camera. The powder comes out of clothing easily, without requiring more than a beating and washing. However, you can save yourself the bother if you are going to participate in the impressive procession of the Tantric mother-goddesses Mahakali and Mahalakshmi, which happens in the afternoon of the same day. In this, another paint powder, this time blood-red, is thrown about. After separately circling the Bhoulachan quarter in the north-east section of Bhaktapur, the chariots – with both of the goddesses in them – are thrashed against each other many times with great force, making a symbolic show of the reproductive act. The chariot carriers take about 50 meters of running space, and then rush towards each other, crashing together and falling on top of one-another under the weight of the bucking and rearing chariots. Almost all of them are drunk on rice-beer and liquor. Here the ecstasy of the drummers and dancers reaches its climax.

On the fourth day of the New Year all of the music groups drum their way along the procession route through Bhaktapur, seeking the gods. Following behind the musicians are the women in festive, dark red saris carrying the sacrificial offerings. All the gods are on display to receive the offerings and dispense their blessings for the New Year. This is the day of the never- ending Newar feastings and revelries. Comparable chariot- festivals also occur in Kathmandu and Patan.

A Merry Death Festival

Particularly in Bhaktapur, the *gaijatra* – or dance festival for the dead – is very

impressive. It happens as the rainy season fades away, namely on the day after the full moon. Families which have suffered a death in the previous year build a symbolic cow out of bamboo sticks and cloth, with horns of straw. On this is hung a photograph of the deceased. The holy animal is supposed to direct his soul on the right path. The desire for life of those left behind forges ahead with music, dancing and masquerade.

On this day hundreds of cows are paraded through Bhaktapur's procession route. One typical dance shows Newar farm women, firing their men with home-distilled liquor. Others mask themselves as gods and goddesses. However, it is always the young men who take the female roles. Newar women never make public appearances with music and dance. They also very rarely sing in groups during the rice-planting season. If a man turns up, the song is immediately broken off with embarrassed giggling. In contrast, among the Nepalese mountain-folk the women sing very confidently, in rivalry with the men.

In the week following the *gaijatra*, the numerous dance and theater groups move around from one place to another, where an appreciative audience then immediately gathers. Here one might have the good luck to experience one of the great Bhaila-pyaka or Devi-pyaka mask dances, which are often presented in a badly garbled and distorted form in the larger hotels. The Radha- Krishna dance with flute accompaniment is enchantingly lovely, in which farm-boys personify the legendary Indian lovers.

On the day after the *gaijatra*, the population of Patan celebrates the monumental *matyapuja*, in the course of which light-offerings are placed at some 300 locations in the buddhist areas. One can experience the ancient music of Buddhism at its best either here or on the Hill of Svayambhunath. During the Buddhist procession-month Gumla (August/Sep-

The bars in front of the White Bhairava are removed during the Indrajatra festival.

tember), musical groups from Kathmandu proceed every morning before sunrise to Svayambhunath, where they play – as a signal to the gods that they wish to gather merit for their favorable reincarnation. In the Tibetan cloister on the Svayambhu Mountain one can eavesdrop on Tibetan ritual music during the entire year. Guests are allowed to enter and go through the temple up to the door of the monks' prayer-room and, from there, be present at the services.

Further festivals include the *indrajatra* in Kathmandu and the autumn-festival *dasain* in all three Newar cities, during which the virgin goddesses appear, and the tantric Mother-goddess is worshipped. Particularly, Durga's victory over the demon Mahishasura is celebrated over the entire country, with countless animal sacrifices. The highpoint of Dasain occurs on the ninth day, on which all work tools and equipment,

including cars are sprayed with sacrificial blood.

The musical traditions in Nepal are as manifold as the different ethnic groups in the country. By far the most complex musical culture in the whole Himalaya region is that of the Newar in the Kathmandu Valley, which over the past 2,000 years has been influenced again and again by Indian traditions – but without having lost its own individual character. Music and dance are always drawn from ritual and, of course, vary according to the locality. The people of the hills particularly enjoy group-singing in pentatonic structures and the playing of the *madal* drum. The Gaine minstrels with their *sarangi* fiddles originally served the function now occupied by the media. Today they entertain tourists. The media broadcasts almost exclusively modern pop- songs with the single theme "love, love, love", and, for the highbrow classical music from the Indian tradition, which has also been practiced in Nepal for about 250 years.

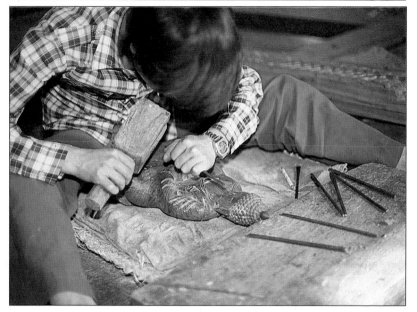

ART THEFT

Newar wood carving has earned a world wide reputation.

No one has ever counted all of the temples, shrines, and statues of the Kathmandu Valley. That would be a futile exercise. In nearly every courtyard and in many squares one finds an idol, an inscription, or the sculpture of some ruler or rich donator. Many of these art objects are centuries old, and some are of incalculable value.

For years now, the organized theft – particularly of statues – has been increasing. Sometimes a small, supposedly inconspicuous statuette is missing, and sometimes you even hear about the (unsuccessful) attempt to steal the large golden statue of King Bhupatindra Malla on the palace square of Bhaktapur with a mobile crane. Occasionally the statue is "beheaded" or valuable pieces are broken off. Old manuscripts are also painted over – mostly with erotic pictures – in order to ease their transport and later sale.

The stolen objects are purchased by tourists and collectors, but also – through middlemen – by western museums. It is rarely discovered who the culprits are. There has been talk of drug dealers or influential politicians who have statues be sawn up, in order to get them out of the country by diplomatic post.

It has also been said that western art historians and other scientists are participating in this unparalleled and outrageous theft of the treasures of Nepal (and Tibet). Photographing, measuring and drawing bronzes or temples appears suspicious to many Nepalese. The scientists' situation is paradoxical even without such an accusation: The more widely they make the history and the value of a statue known, the more likely it becomes that a theft will occur, and the more lucrative the business becomes.

How can the Kathmandu Valley – this living museum – be protected? By having watchmen patrol through the cities? By cementing all of the figures in or chaining

New copies of old pictures – take care when buying a thangka.

them tight? By having the statues put in the museums and damning them to business hours? These proposals are all being seriously considered by politicians and developmental assistance volunteers. The law of the Nepalese government which requires sealed export authorizations from the Department of Archeology for older works of art has hardly brought any significant change. The customs officials are too corruptible and the civil servants are too inexperienced to be able to judge whether a statue is more than one hundred years old, and therefore excluded from export. As long as the statues are still gods, the best protection is undoubtedly contact with, and respectful fear of them. Wherever they are worshipped day after day, they are looked after much better than paid museum attendants are capable of doing. The power of the god (statues) – which can bring about disaster, sickness, and even death –

certainly still prevents the majority of the population from daring to make the quick and relatively easy deal.

On the streets one hears time and time again the story of a man who attempted to steal a statue, but who was found dead the very next day, whereas the god was recovered safe and sound. If only the buyers could hear (and believe) this!

Nevertheless, you need not worry too terribly much when buying a "genuine antique" *thangka* on Durbar Square, even if it is covered with a corresponding film of filth and grimy smoke. The real thing usually travels out of the country through other channels. Even with this in mind you should not consider the "new" art objects as being inferior, for there stands behind them a great and ancient tradition of craftsmanship. The purchase of such souvenirs is also a contribution to a sort of "developmental assistance" for the crafts. An artist often needs months for a really beautiful and finely-painted *thangka*, and in comparison to the price asked for it is usually ridiculously low.

NEPALESE CUISINE

Only after a better acquaintance with the country does the foreign visitor realize that Nepalese cooking does not consist solely of *daal bhat* – lentil soup with boiled rice – which is often portrayed as the national dish of Nepal.

Normally a Nepali eats *daal bhat* twice a day – in the morning after the first fieldwork, or before he goes to the office around 10:00, as well as in the evening after sunset.

Nepalis still usually eat with the right hand; the left is considered unclean. Included in the basic foods eaten daily, besides a large portion of lentils, are the steamed seasonal vegetables – called *tarkaari*. These can also include potato, which is classified as a vegetable in Nepal. An especially delicious accent is lent to the dish by a bit of *achar* – a sort of chutney or paste made of pickled, sharply spiced fruit or vegetables. Instead of rice flat breads – *chapati* or *puri* – made of various kinds of flour are often used.

Normally meat is offered only on special occasions. No main meal can be served without a glass of water. Very spicy dishes are often complemented with yoghurt. The spices – called *masala* in Nepal – which no vegetable or meat dish lack – include cumin, coriander, turmeric, fenugreek, chillis and pepper.

The choice of ingredients in a meal depends on location. In flat Terai in the South, with its warm, humid climate, some of the foods eaten before work are: *chana churia* – chickpeas in curry sauce with mashed rice; or for instance the delicious freshly-prepared *puri julebi*. Puri is a flat bread which is fried in oil, which is eaten with fresh-fried, sweetened julebi pastry and curried vegetables. In addition there is the obligatory milk-tea, sometimes refined with the addition of spices like cardamom, cloves and cinnamon. So as not to go to work on a completely empty stomach, *halawa* and *swari* are eaten. Halawa is a sweetened pastry made of rice flour or semolina with melted butter, sometimes enriched with nuts, while swari is a thin flat-bread which is fried in butter.

In Terai the first main meal of the day is served, at the ear liest, around twelve o'clock noon. This consists mostly of daal bhat, sometimes served with vegetables and achar, but rarely with meat or fish. In fact, the Hindus, who live primarily in India-influenced Terai, rarely eat meat; the especially strict believers among them, none at all. They live as vegetarians. But the situation is quite different in Terai and the central highlands, in contrast to the population of the high valleys, who eat animal products as a result of the limited land for farming.

Generally a light snack is taken in the afternoons, for example some *gundruk bhatmas,* which are roasted soybeans with vegetables which have been pickled and later dried in the sun; or *pakoras,* which are fried balls of cheese and vegetables. Equally tasty are fried potatoes, fried egg, roasted bits of meat, or peanuts and roasted corn.

In the high mountains, where no rice and wheat grow, the locals love *dhedo,* which is barley or buckwheat flour boiled together with liquid and fat; this is eaten with sauce or vegetables – similar to polenta. Another commonly served and well-liked dish is daal bhat, however here the rice is often substituted by corn, barley or millet, while for the daal the widest variety of lentils and types of beans are employed.

The Tibetan-influenced ethnic groups – for example the Sherpas or Manangis – especially enjoy *tsampas*, roasted barley flour mixed with liquid and fat, which can also be eaten blended with the notoriously well-known "salty butter-tea". Because most of the people in the high mountains are Buddhists, they are also allowed to eat yak meat. The milk of the

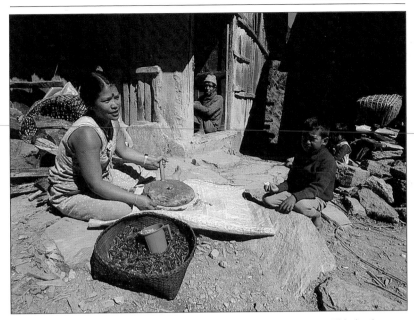

No Nepalese meal is complete without ground chilli.

yak-cow, fresh yoghurt snd dried yak-cheese are considered to be particular delicacies. Steamed *momos*, which resemble ravioli, can be filled with meat or vegetables. They are especially well-liked among the Bhotyas – a Tibetan- influenced group – but the Newar enjoy them too. When fried they are called *kothay*.

The highly distilled fruit brandies, produced either from apples, apricots, or even pears, also came from the high mountain valleys. Here the brandy from Marpha in north-western Nepal attained considerable renown, and now fetches high prices in Kathmandu. Of course, Terai has its own specialties to offer in this regard. Here there are anise liqueurs and *todi* – a milky beverage with about 5% alcohol content, which is produced from a type of palm-tree. *Chang*, a drink resembling beer, is produced from rice, corn or wheat; it has become popular throughout the country. This is also true of *rakshi*, a spirit made from the same grains. The Newar are particularly expert at the brewing of these beverages. The Tibetans have made *tongwa* well-known; it consists of fermented millet over which hot water is poured.

Brahmans and – for the most part – the Chetris do not eat what is cooked by other castes. Alcohol, chicken, garlic, onions, tomatoes and chillis are considered by orthodox Hindus to be stimulants to the body and the senses; these are therefore avoided. They also refer to the alcohol-drinking population groups disparagingly as Matwali, who stand far beneath them in the caste hierarchy.

And finally, here is a vital piece of advice: Should you be invited into a private home in Nepal or to some party, please keep in mind that the main course is traditionally served toward the end of the visit. Before the host offers tasty little morsels such as fried liver, Sel Roti, a deep-fried rice-meal pastry, roasted chick peas and of course alcohol.

219

THE NEPALESE AND TIBETAN CALENDARS

Small butter lamps burn in front of the gods in Buddhist monasteries.

If you want to become conversant with the Nepalese and Tibetan calendars, you must be able to keep straight the differing counting methods of the calendars as well as the different epochs. The calendar divides the year into months either within the lunar or the solar system. The epochs count the years of a chronology from a fixed point in the past. At present in Nepal various calendars are in use. The most important of these are the *Vikram Samvat* (reference year 56/57 B.C.) which is the official calendar, *Nepal Samvat* (reference year 870/880 A.D.), which is used by the Newar population, and the Christian calendar. Of these only the Nepal Samvat calendar is of local origin; the Vikram Samvat and the less frequently used *Shaka Samvat* (reference year 78/79 A.D.) have been taken over from Indian tradition. In none of the three calendars, however, has the historical significance of the reference year been un-

equivocally clarified. The Tibetans count in 60-year cycles. According to this system we find ourselves in the 17th cycle at the moment. The exact determination of the year can be done in two ways: either within a cycle *(Rabjung)* or outside of it, based then on the year during which the *Kalacakra* system was introduced (1027 A.D.). This system has its origins in Tantric philosophy; its name translates as the "Wheel of Time".

The Elements

Furthermore, the Tibetan years are designated by the five elements iron, water, wood, fire and earth, which apply respectively for two years in a row – a feminine and a masculine year; these elements are linked with twelve animals: monkey, rooster, dog, pig, mouse, bull, tiger, hare, dragon, snake, horse and sheep. The Tibetan calendar is coordinated with moon cycles, whereas the Vikram Samvat can use counting methods based on the moon and the sun as well. The lunar calendar is based on a year consisting of twelve 30-day months, in which each month is divided into two periods – those of the increasing and decreasing moon or the decreasing and increasing moon; this is determined according to whether the moon phase of the corresponding year cycle ends with the full moon or the new moon. At any rate, twelve genuine lunar months result, whereby at the end there are about six days missing from the expected 360, so that those who know their way around this whole production must be prepared to undertake a few adjustments. As a result a lunar-day (named *Tithi* from Hindu tradition) rarely lasts simply from the time of one sunrise to the next, and a few days are entirely obliterated – or even, if necessary, repeated.

Moreover, it is necessary to insert six additional months into the year every nineteen years in order to bring the lunar year back into agreement with the solar year. There are various traditional systems for getting around these difficulties. In Nepal there is an official committee which is entrusted with the task of producing a new Vikram Samvat lunar calendar each year, which is named *Pancanga* or *Patro*.

Among the Tibetans there are from time to time differing versions of the same calendar (from Dharamsala, Bhutan etc.) which are produced by various personalities. These people take various factors into consideration in their determination of the calendar and the decision of which days should be repeated or eliminated, in particular the combination of certain lucky or unlucky elements with individual days.

Days of Sun

The solar year here also has twelve months of differing length. In the Vikram Samvat calendar they vary between 29 and 32 solar days. According to this system the new months begin around the middle of the months in western calendars. According to the Vikram Samvat system, which is used in Nepal, the year begins with the month *Baishakh* (mid-April to mid-May). The following months are named *Jesth, Ashadh, Shravan, Bhadra, Ashvin, Kartik, Mangsir, Push, Magh, Phalgun* and *Caitra*. These designations are also applied in colloquial speech to the lunar months.

Nepal Samvat is purely lunar calendar, which has its own Newari names for the months. It begins with the day of the new moon in the month *Kartik* (October-November).

The Tibetans count their months without giving them special names, unless they are associated with a particular festival. The first month of the year, during which the new year festivities are held, begins with a full moon which as a rule is in February – however sometimes also in March.

Among the Hindus as well as the Tibetans the days of the week – as also found in western tradition – are named after the sun, moon and five planets. In Nepalese these are: *Aitabar* (Sunday), *Sombar, Mangalbar, Budhabar, Bihibar, Sukrabar,* and *Sanibar.*

Calendar comparison table

Chr. Reck.	Nepal Samvat	Tibetan Year
1990	2047/48	Iron-Horse
1991	2048/49	Iron-Sheep
1992	2049/50	Water-Monkey
1993	2050/51	Water-Hen
1994	2051/52	Wood-Dog
1995	2052/53	Wood-Pig
1996	2053/54	Fire-Mouse
1997	2054/55	Fire-Ox
1998	2055/56	Earth-Tiger
1999	2056/57	Earth-Hare

WOMEN IN NEPAL

The laughter-lines around the almond eyes of an elderly Tibetan woman; the closely- cropped scalp of a Brahman widow; the tatooed thigh of a married Tharu woman; the black skirt with unmistakable red stripes of a Jhapu farm woman; the holes in the ears of the unmarried girls, which at their weddings are to be filled with the most ostentatious jewelry possible – considering the ethnic diversity of the Nepalese population there is neither a typical face of "the" Nepalese woman, nor a typical silhouette, nor a typical style. There are considerable differences between north and south: The women of the Terai are scarcely distinguishable from their Indian neighbors, thus the characteristic mongoloid traits of the womens' faces increase the closer they live to Tibet. Differences in the appearance of the women depending on where they live can be perceived when one knows about the cultural peculiarities; thus for example the Newar women as a rule wear no nose-ring. Even the Nepalese have to ask strangers about their ethnic membership.

The familial relationships – which have long term impacts upon the life of a woman – vary to a considerable degree from ethnic group to ethnic group; accordingly, the relationship of the woman to the members of the family with whom she forms a household after her marriage takes different forms. Roughly the half of the women in Nepal, especially Hindu women, enter into marriages arranged by their relatives. Among the entire population of Nepal monogamous marriages predominate – the more so since this is also legally prescribed – and which for the Hindu woman, at least in theory, is indissoluble. Among many ethnic groups and also among the Indo-Nepalese population polygamy is practiced: primarily then when a couple has no offspring, the husband enters into a second and oc-

casionally even a third marriage, frequently marrying the younger sister of his wife. Among several groups of Tibetan origin, in contrast, fraternal polyandry is possible: brothers may marry one woman in common – a form of marriage that is closely connected to economic necessities. Marriage is a great dividing line in the life of a woman, because almost all women move from the household of their parents to the house of the husband, and live there with his blood relatives. Among many ethnic groups there is a popular custom that a daughter marries the son of her father's sister, so that after the wedding the bride comes into the household of the paternal sister, where she is already comfortable and knows her way around. The Hindu women of higher castes, on the other hand, most of the time marry into households where they have no relatives. Correspondingly, they have a great fear of moving from the house of their parents – where they are treated with love – to that of the husband, where they are mostly unknown, and their parents-in-law, who usually are very strict and mistrustful towards them, at least during the beginning period – and frequently up to the birth of the first child. The contact with their parents continues during this time. Particularly on ritual occasions the daughters seek out their parents, and are then confronted by the situation of how very much their roles have changed from daughters and sisters to wives and daughters-in-law.

The Man's Role

With the exception of a very narrow class of the well-to-do, the Nepalese women have a very significant economic contribution to perform in the household. On the average the working hours are estimated to be eleven per day (3.5 working hours more than those of the men), and the demands vary with the season. The women of all groups are primarily

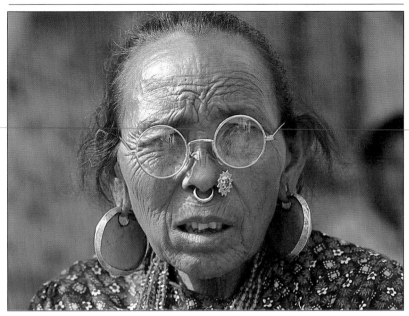

Ear- and nose-rings – Tamang women love to show off their gold jewelry.

occupied with the household (this includes the provision of water, food and fuels). However in addition, their labor is needed in other economic realms; the majority of them must also work in the fields. The members of the ethnic groups find supplementary income selling their own products in the local markets, and hire themselves out as seasonal workers far outside their villages, in order to manage a small reataurant or tea shop, for example. They are often affectionately addressed by the population as "Didi" (older sister) or "Bahini" (youger sister).

Married Life

Naturally, the cultural norms vary here in relation to women – between the much freer and more tolerant Tibetans and the far more restricted freedom of movement for women in Hindu customs. The gender-specific division can be observed not only in the area of work, but also in everyday social intercourse with relatives and acquaintances. The majority of Hindu women only converse with male members of their group behind closed doors, and in the process must observe a series of rules: They may not touch the older brother of their husband or pronounce the name of their husband and must cover their face vis à vis their fathers-in-law. The social behavior of women in the Tibetan areas of influence is much freer in relation to men, demonstrated in the first place by the fact that they can sometimes leave their villages. Nevertheless, there are also limits set on their freedoms, and their economic independence is relative. Although they have their own income at their disposal, they are at any rate clearly disadvantaged compared to the men – as are Hindu women, when it comes to the rules of inheritance. And, even as free as some Nepalese women may appear in daily life, they are still practically excluded from political positions and influence.

SHAMANISM

In a darkened, gloomy room in a Gurung house the family sits together at night watching the gesticulations of Lal Bahadur, the local shaman, who has come to a decision. Beforehand there had been a detailed questioning concerning the circumstances surrounding the illness of the eldest daughter in the house, as well as an examination of her by means of eye and pulse diagnosis. The procedure also includes a repeated questioning of the rice oracle, which isn't always definitive in cases concerning the effects of spirit beings or witches. But he could also find nothing in the gleam of the oil-lamp's flame, which was consulted. Lal Bahadur discloses his diagnosis to the family: No indication of the existence of evil spirits or a witch in the house. It must be something else – perhaps the Medi-cine Lama or the hospital can help.

Change of scene: In the emergency room of the Kanti Childrens' Hospital in Kathmandu a flurry of activity dominates

– like any morning there. The waiting times are considerable. Ram Prasad has been traveling on foot from the moun-tains for three days with his little daughter, who he has carried in uncon-scious. The little one has had fever and a heavy case of diarrhoea for days. Her skin is wrinkled, her face is sunken, and her feverish eyes seem lost in their sock-ets. It was possible to help her at the last minute, though, with antibiotics and a salt infusion.

In Nepal both types of medicine exist side by side – western trained allopathic doctors, Ayurvedic doctors, Lama healers and shamans, known here as Ihakris.

The traditional healers frequently orig-inate from the lower strata of society – i.e. castes, and increase their social status through their occupation as a shaman. A thorough knowledge of the physiology of the worlds of gods and spirits is essential, since illness is seen mainly as an impair-ment of the harmony between the human world and the world of gods and spirits, and there are enough evil powers like human witches *(bokshi)*, black magici-ans, spirit witches and evil ghosts around to disturb this sensitive balance. After de-termining the diagnosis, the "healing" then takes place in the form of sacrificial offerings, among them rice, animals, fab-ric etc. This is supposed to appease the aggressor and strengthen the protective powers. If the sacrificial offerings are in-sufficient, the members of the household gather together with friends and acquain-tances and get thoroughly merry on beer and rakshi. In the presence of previously prepared dough figures of the possible causers of the illness (witches, gods, spir-its of the dead) the shaman goes into a trance and speaks, stuttering and trem-bling as a tool of the god who has entered him. The words indicate the diagnosis and the description of the therapy.

By nature, there are limits set on the success of the spirit and natural healers' therapies, which most recognize very

Figures made of dough to drive away evil spirits. Left: A shaman ceremony.

well, then recommending other treatment approaches. However, the insufficiency of the public health system is clear.

At this point at the latest all of the obvious wants of public welfare will become apparent. Average medical care for the population at large is poor at best, especially out in the province and in the mountains. Child mortality rates during the first 5 years is close to 50 percent, and the overall life expectancy is below 50 years, with women even worse off than men. Infant mortality is the highest of all Asian nations. The extent of epidemics and malnutrition is among the highest in all the developing nations. There are far too few hospitals – a total of 96 – , and these are usually in regions that are difficult to reach and are by and large poorly equipped. During the past few years about 800 health posts have been set up to give nurses and hastily trained health workers the opportunity to give the most

basic form of health care. These people not only heal, but also occupy themselves with the hygienic conditions, nutritional problems and birth control.

In spite of progress in the last few years there are still considerable problems with the public health system, which gave rise to the development of her strategies. One approach which isn't to be underestimated is the effort from the public sector to draw the religious and ritual healers into preventative medicine and health maintenance, since they still enjoy the confidence of the population and are distributed in large numbers especially through the rural areas. Workshops are held with the traditional healers in which problems of overpopulation, hygiene and basic medical care are discussed. The healers then take this information back to the regions. The involvement of the healers in the public health system represents a sensible integration of traditional healing measures, and thus helps in the dissemination of preventative health maintenance and therapy.

225

NEPAL'S HIGHEST PEAKS

A view of Everest from the Kala Patar. Right: The eastern flank of Dhaulagiri.

The 2,400 kilometer long Himalaya Range with its tectonic giants is the geo-historical result of a collision of the Indian land mass with the Asiatic. The Indian subcontinent is thought to be moving to the north five centimeters annually, in the direction of Central Asia. Because of the tectonic circumstances of the young region, earthquakes recur constantly – most recently at the end of August 1988. Kathmandu was totally devastated by an earthquake in 1934.

The highest summits of the Himalayas are to be found on the northern border of Nepal, dominated by Mount Everest, with some ten icy peaks, each of which exceeds 8,000 meters in altitude. In addition, 40 seven-thousand-meter peaks tower above the world here. Of the 14 mountains over eight thousand meters in height in the world, eight are located either entirely or partly in Nepal.

The Nepalese see the seats of the gods as being in the Himalayan summits; and thus in their point of view one shouldn't desecrate these divine thrones with mountain climbing, but instead offer worship and love to them. This feeling is also expressed in the names of the individual mountain giants. For example, the "Gaurishankar" is the personification of the goddess Parvati and her consort Shiva, while the "Ganesh Himal" carries the name of the son of these two deities; "Annapurna" is the goddess of abundance. Especially ascetic monks and yogis retreat to the mountainous isolation of the Himalayas in order to meditate under the protection of the gods.

Starting out from Tibet, the English undertook the first attempt to ascend Mount Everest already in 1922. In the process, seven Sherpas lost their lives in avalanches. Summit XV of these mountain giants was named by the British in 1865 after the then-leader of the "Geological Survey of India", Sir George

Everest. It was only later discovered that the Tibetans and Nepalese had their own names for the highest mountain in the world: The Nepalese call it "King of the Heavens", *Sagarmatha*, and the Tibetans see in it *Chomolungma*, who rides on a snow lion over the sea of clouds.

The first successful ascent of Mt. Everest, on May 29th, 1953 by the New Zealander Edmund Hillary and the Nepalese Sherpa Tenzing Norgay, was a world wide sensation. But, from the Nepalese side alone ten expeditions up Mount Everest have been abortive – not to mention the many frozen, fallen and injured people which such undertakings have claimed. The most modern means of assistance offer little protection from avalanches, falling rocks and ice, sudden changes in the weather and altitude sickness. Since then more than a hundred mountain climbers have ascended Mt. Everest. According to the statistics for every two successful climbers of Everest there is one death. Despite considerable currency revenues for the Nepalese government from trekking and climbing expeditions, there is still no social security for the Sherpas and carriers.

Unfortunately the expeditions and agencies frequently fail to equip their Nepalese guides and especially the carriers appropriately; thus, success doesn't depend on their persistance, knowledge and willingness alone.

Although all of the eight-thousanders in Nepal and Pakistan (Karakorum Range) had already been climbed between 1950 and 1960, there are still some 250 unclimbed peaks over 6,000 meters with varying degrees of difficulty. Among the most beautiful summits in Nepal are the **Pumori** (7,145 m) in the northeastern part of the country closely neighboring Mt. Everest, and the much-described **Ama Dablam** (6,856 m), on the foot of which lays the famous Buddhist Tengboche Monastery – which unfortunately burned down in 1989. In

northwestern Nepal **Macchapuchare** rises up over the Phewa Lake near Pokhara. A British expedition team gave up shortly before arriving on the top, apparently because they didn't want to offend the religious feelings of the local population. There are also still a few mountain summits, which – as seats of highly worshipped gods – are taboo for mountain climbers: Until today the Nepalese government hasn't opened them for ascent.

Eight-thousanders from West to East

Dhaulagiri, 8,167 m, May 13th, 1960.
Annapurna I, 8,091 m, June 3rd, 1950.
Manaslu, 8,156 m, 9th/10th/11th May, 1956.
Cho Oyu, 8,153 m, 19th Oct., 1954.
Mt. Everest, 8,848 m, May 29th, 1953.
Lhotse, 8,051 m, May 18th, 1956.
Makalu, 8,475 m, May 15th/16th/17th, 1955.
Kanchenjunga, 8,598 m, May 26th, 1955.

NEPALESE LIVING CONDITIONS

The Nepal of today, which was united by Prithvi Narayan Shah in 1768, has gone through a long process of development. The character of the many-peopled state of Nepal has been formed by numerous immigrants from neighboring lands – a process which had already begun in prehistorical times. As a result of the many different origins of the Nepalese, up to the present a cultural diversity has developed which bears the stamp of more than 20 different larger racial groups alongside a broad variety of smaller ethnic groups, which altogether speak more than 36 different languages and dialects. It is interesting to note that there is no other country on the face of the Earth where contrasting religious communities have managed to live so peacefully next to each other as here in Nepal.

The way of life of the Nepalese is very broad-ranging, influenced equally by both physical and socio-economic conditions. The extremes of the topography and limitations on the availability of agriculturally useful land, as well as the increasing population, all wield an influence on the everyday life of the Nepalese. The hierarchical caste system – which was of course legally abolished in 1962 – in reality, still exerts a dominating influence on the culture. Education, choice of profession and thus a deciding factor between a life of poverty of wealth is closely bound with caste membership. The Newaris who have settled in the Kathmandu Valley are traditionally profiled as being successful traders, in contrast, the Tamang as load carriers scrape their livings on the very edge of the minimum needed for existence. To be sure, however, tourism has improved the living conditions of several ethnic groups, such as the Sherpas.

The population explosion is making life more difficult. Today – in spite of international assistance – the situation is already such that the basic requirements of roughly 40% of the population can not be met – a problem, furthermore, that results from the fact that a portion of the foreign assistance trickles away into the wrong channels. The unequal distribution of what is – at any rate – minimal income serves to harden the barriers between the poor and the rich. 9% of the households have over 55% of the income at their disposal, for example.

The mounting population pressure is, alongside tourism, also a reason for the increasing deforestation of woodlands. Traditionally, wood is the only burnable fuel used by the majority of Nepalese. As a result of the insufficient expansion of the electricity supply network, no other alternative exists than using wood for fuel among the inhabitants of places far removed from the larger cities.

In addition, the government has discovered the forests as an additional source of revenue and has proceeded to market its products commercially – without simultaneously carrying out a carefully planned logging program. This has brought about serious ecological damage – for example the devastation of essential agricultural lands which serve 89.9% of the population as their source of livelihood. While there is still no solution in sight for the problem of population growth, the possibility of improving the ecological balance through the application of solar and hydroelectric energy provides some ray of light on the horizon.

From Traditional Trade to Modern Enterprise

The Nepalese economy experienced its golden age with the beginning of the British colonial dominion of India, as Nepal profited from the through-traffic of goods between Tibet and India. During this period a brisk trade with Tibet dominated; this represented a source of revenue not only for the Nepalese business-

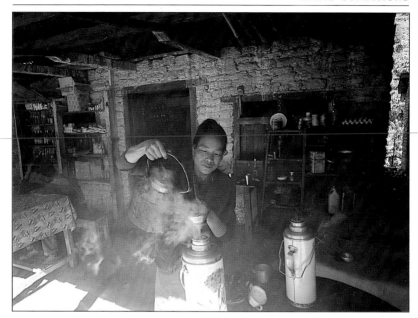

A traditional Nepalese institution – the didi or older sister.

men, but also for the craftsmen who settled along the trade routes. However, India's economic interest in Nepal and the opening of the domestic market to British textiles brought about a decline in the Nepalese textile business. The remaining population was primarily occupied with agriculture. Thus many of the individual villages were in a situation where they were largely able to provide for themselves. After 1951 the industrialization of the agricultural states was begun, but the success of this undertaking remains only moderate.

On the basis of their very highly developed abilities as craftspeople – one might here think of the stonecutters, bronze casters, woodcarvers and textile and carpet weavers – the Nepalese have managed in this area to participate in international trade, thanks, not least, to the existence of tourism. For many, this has been a reason to attempt a re-orientation from their position as indigenous traders and craftspeople to involvement in import-export enterprises. Since the domestic industries do not produce many commodities and consumer products, the largest portion of these must be imported from India. However, the insecure constellation of trade agreements with India – which is especially affected by the political situation – has motivated the Nepalese to produce essential goods to the extent they are able. Nepal strives for international and bilateral support, and is attempting to encourage foreign investment – which is not an easy matter with their limited domestic market. While the development process is lagging in production industries such mining, energy and water systems and the processing (industrial) sectors, the area of service industries is relatively successful. The tourism industry has not only brought change to the lives of traditional families in the Himalayan region, but it has also produced employment for many people in the capital city. The government wants to

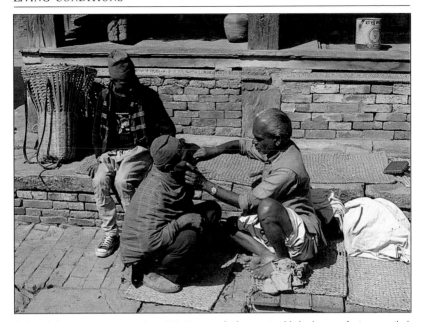

industrialize at any cost – but failed to take the environment into consideration.

In the countryside barbers prefer to serve their customers outside.

Political Awakenening and the Monarchy

A degree of participation in Nepalese politics first became possible for a broad section of the population at the beginning of 1950, after the 104-year-old Rana familial oligarchy was brought to an end by the efforts of King Tribhuvan and the Nepalese people.

In the time which followed, Nepal attempted to introduce a political system following western examples, and decided on a multi-party system. A lively political scenario thus came into existence. On February 18th 1959 the first parliamentary elections in Nepal were held. After only 18 months, King Mahendra deposed the parliamentary government of the Nepalese congress by convocation of the articles of emergency in the constitution. The parties were officially forbidden – for the stated reason that Nepal was still

not be "mature" enough for such a political system.

In 1962, as an alternative, the so-called Panchayat Constitution was put in force and the partyless Panchayat system, organized in pyramid form – at the first glance having the appearance of a soviet system – order was established. At the lowest level in this system the village/town Panchayat representatives responsible for altogether 4053 villages were elected; on the next highest level there are the emmissaries of the 75 district Panchayats, and at the national level the so-called Rastriya Panchayat (the legislative branch) with 112 members has been directly elected by the people since 1981.

All ministers must be members of the Rastriya Panchayat; the prime minister must unconditionally come from the ranks of the elected members, since besides the elected representatives, an addi-

An ex-Gurkha soldier gives his new possession a good shearing.

tional 28 members of the Rastriya Panchayat are nominated by the King. In addition the prime minister requires the approval of the King for his appointment.

The multiple reforms of the Panchayat system and the constitution were brought about by the agitation and demands of the Nepalese people. The system is controversial both at home and abroad because it doesn't permit the organization of parties. As the present King Birendra ascended to the throne on January 1st 1972, many had expectations that he would introduce a multi-party system. It wasn't until the middle of 1980 – as a result of mass protests – that a national referendum was carried out to put the Panchayat System to the vote. However the majority (54.7%) of the voters decided in favor of retaining the existing system; the opposition claimed manipulation.

The Panchayat system is oriented towards the traditions of Hinduism. Ac-

cordingly, the King exercises the highest governmental authority, also deciding the constitution. His right of rulership is founded on the notion that he is considered the "defender" of traditional values of Hindu culture, simultaneously embodying both tradition and progress.

The monarchy is recognized even by the officially forbidden parties of Nepal – which continue to exist illegally. The monarchy is felt to be a necessary institution for the preservation of this stability and independence of the state. The criticism of the people and the parties is directed in particular against the gigantic apparatus of the palace secretariat – which appears to be more powerful than the governmental apparatus.

As a member of the non-aligned nations, Nepal is trying to achieve the status of "peace zone", for which it needs the acquiescence of India – its huge neighbor. However, the goal of being able to satisfy the provision of basic needs for its population by the year 2000 is still remote for Nepal.

231

EDUCATION SYSTEM

Those who stay for only a few days in Kathmandu might well meet numerous outstandingly well-educated Nepalese, who frequently have studied in foreign countries. The reality, however, is quite different: over 70% of the Nepalese population is illiterate. In the majority of villages you will meet only a handful of people who are capable of reading and writing. In spite of this, the Nepalese are proud of what they have accomplished to date: a modern educational and training system only came into existence in the beginning of the 1950's.

From a historical point-of-view, the educational and training system certainly has an old tradition, which extends back to the Vedic scriptures – however here we are also concerned with Brahman and Hindu as well as Buddhist educational concepts which were closely bound together with religious rules of behavior.

In the 104 year long period of the Rana dynasty from 1846 to 1950 only a small amount was done for the education of the nation's people. Prime Minister Jung Bahadur Rana was so impressed by the English system of education when he traveled to England for the first time, that in 1853 he had a school established in his palace for his own children based on the example of the English. The teachers were brought in from Europe and India. Later this school was also made accessible to other members of the Rana family. Besides this, as ever, the traditional Sanskrit schools for Brahmans were promoted. For the normal population there wasn't anything else left to do than to extend their education privately – as far as this was possible.

The rapid development of education took place after the establishment of an education ministry in 1951 following the fall of the Rana regime. In this process Nepal received the support of the government of the United States in particular. Today over the entire country there are almost 12,500 primary schools – attended by roughly 79% of the children –, nearly 5,500 secondary schools, attended by only 50% of the potential students, and 63 colleges which are directly connected to the University, as well as 78 privately organized colleges. Today there are 83,000 students in higher education. In all of the levels of education the proportion of women is considerably smaller than that of men. The present-day educational system corresponds to the Anglo-Saxon western pattern. In 1959 the Tribhuvan University was founded, which today has numerous faculties and institutions under its wing.

The education system as it stands today begins with a five year period of primary school, which is only free of charge up to the second year, after that one must make a tuition payment for each additional year of education. Following the primary school is a five-year long stay – until graduation from school – in a middle and higher school (secondary

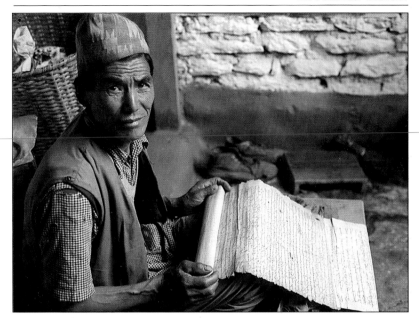

A Thakali with a scroll. Left: Buddhist monks with ancient writings.

level). After that a choice can be made between university studies or a vocational training. The course of studies at the only university in the country – Tribhuvan University in Kathmandu – lasts in general about six years.

But Nepal's educational system still has serious deficiencies – particularly in the rural areas. Parents send their children to the capital city since they know that there are better educational opportunities there. As ever, there is a great shortage of technical and natural science subjects. Only in the last few years have subject areas been established for engineering and medicine. Nepal is also making efforts to preserve its cultural identity; thus in 1987 a Sanskrit University in Dang (West Nepal) was opened in the only Hindu kingdom of the world.

In the 1970s Nepalese government attempted to guarantee the provision of a unified education to the population,

which was to have culminated in the elimination of all of the private schools. Government-paid teachers were hired. However this step proved to be both financially and politically unfeasible, so that private schools were again permitted to exist.

At present, the primary point of emphasis is the rapid bringing of literacy to adults. It is questionable if the global goal of eliminating illiteracy by the year 2000 will also be reached in Nepal. By that time in the future the government also intends to make primary schools tuition-free. The shortage of professional manpower is difficult for many to understand since many academics complain about the lack of corresponding positions. A frequent result of this is the so-called "brain drain" problem, and many well educated Nepalese are leaving their country in order to continue their training in a foreign country and settle there. The Nepalese thirst for knowledge is unquenched. Foreign studies remain a dream goal for many.

233

NEPAL – A DEVELOPING COUNTRY

At the beginning of the fifties, Nepal was not only self-sufficient in food production – the central region (the population of which then comprised three-quarters of the entire population) even produced a small surplus of basic food staples as well as certain goods intended only for the market (for example milk products, livestock, spices and vegetable oil). These surplus products were brought by the farmers by foot and on their own backs to buyers on the Indian border to the South and the Tibetans in the North. Since that time the economic situation of the rural population has deteriorated drastically: On average the farmers are now only producing basic staple foods for around eight months a year. In order not to starve during the remaining four months they are forced to seek employment as menial laborers in the cities, in the Terai or in India, to earn the necessary cash to procure the food they need. Many farmers in the central regions see no other alternative than to migrate to the Terai (a fertile flatland) or to leave the country altogether. By the beginning of the next century, the Terai will be completely overpopulated. Considered as a whole Nepal has become a grain deficit-land, and the deficit will increase further by the year 2000 – to almost 2 million tons annually.

Ecological Causes

This unhappy development has its origins in inappropriate developmental assistance and in ecological conditions: The population explosion with the corresponding increase in livestock has led to the cultivation of marginal soils at great altitudes, on slopes that were once forested, and in places which are too steep. Too-intensive cultivation in unsuitable locations – without taking simultaneous measures for the preservation of the soil fertility – have the effect of leaching out the soil. The usable land per capita has decreased from 1/3 hectare in 1970 to only 1/5 hectare in 1986. The yield per hectare for maize decreased from 1,970 kg to 1,330 kg between 1970 and 1980; for millet from 1,210 kg to 990 kg. The per capita grain production sank from 177 kg to 161 kg in the central region between 1967 and 1979 and even in the Terai from 504 kg to 433 kg (according to the FAO the gross per capita grain production must reach 230 kg in order to insure a minimal level of nourishment).

The reduction of the forests to less than the half of what they were in 1950 is a result of livestock foraging and increased cutting of the forests by the more than doubled population – it has increased from 8 million in 1950 to 17 million (and growing) now. Thus in the year 1982/83, 160,000 hectares of forest were cut down, while during the same period only about 3,000 hectares were reforested. The annual wood consumption amounted to around 10 million tons in the year 1982 (primarily used as fuel wood for cooking), while the natural forest regrowth is estimated at only about 2.5 million tons. The regrowth deficit of 7.5 million tons in 1980 has considerably increased since then.

Further ecological consequences include the increasing erosion of soils, the exhaustion of numerous wells as a result of the more rapid water run-off, and the increased threat of flooding in the lower courses of the rivers. As a result of the general deterioration of the economic situation in the central regions, the migration out of the rural areas (seasonal and long-term) had increased from 3.6% to 12% of the population in the year 1981.

Questionable Development Policies

In all of the government's previous five-year-plans, neglect has been shown

A walk along the Bagmati River reveals many environmental problems.

toward the development of appropriate environmental measures for agriculture and forestry, preferring instead to focus their attention on road construction. Thus until 1974 the budget for road construction laid claim to over 40% of the entire budget for development. During the same time agriculture and forestry were treated in a perfunctory manner, and up to 1980 received no more than 20-25% of the budget allocations. The developmental assistance from international organizations also demonstrated the same disproportion up to 1980.

For the farmer, the implementation of ecological measures is very time consuming. His efforts are not rewarded and he won't invest if he can't expect to get a fair price for the products of his land, relative to the amount of work he has put in. No large development project financed by foreign contribution is known to the author which has consciously com-

bined increases in productivity at attractive prices for the farmers with comprehensive ecological measures. Instead the large aid organizations have been flooding the country with their grain surpluses – which are being used in Food-for-Work programs. In such projects the farmers are paid for their rural work with imported foodstuffs. The long-term effects of such projects are questionable – frequently even destructive. The impoverishment of the farmers is not reduced, since no income is made; no development process is advanced in the sense of self-reliance.

Instead of this, the farmers neglect their agricultural work and become dependent on outside help. Added to this, they must take a portion of the food they receive to sell at the local market, in order to get cash to buy urgent necessities – resulting in a depression of the local market prices. It becomes less and less worthwhile for the farmers to secure their sustainance through work in the fields – a real vicious circle.

Nelles Maps ...the maps, that get you going.

Nelles Map Series:

- Afghanistan
- Australia
- Burma
- Caribbean Islands 1 / Bermuda, Bahamas, Greater Antilles
- Caribbean Islands 2 / Lesser Antilles
- China 1 / North-Eastern China
- China 2 / Northern China
- Crete
- Hawaiian Islands
- Hawaiian Islands 1 / Kauai
- Hawaiian Islands 2 / Honolulu, Oahu
- Hawaiian Islands 3 / Maui, Molokai, Lanai
- Hawaiian Islands 4 / Hawaii
- Himalaya
- Hong Kong
- Indian Subcontinent
- India 1 / Northern India
- India 2 / Western India
- India 3 / Eastern India
- India 4 / Southern India
- India 5 / North-Eastern India
- Indonesia
- Indonesia 1 / Sumatra
- Indonesia 2 / Java + Nusa Tenggara
- Indonesia 3 / Bali
- Indonesia 4 / Kalimantan
- Indonesia 5 / Java + Bali
- Indonesia 6 / Sulawesi
- Indonesia 7 / Irian Jaya + Maluku
- Jakarta
- Japan
- Kenya
- Korea
- Malaysia
- West Malaysia
- Nepal
- New Zealand
- Pakistan
- Philippines
- Singapore
- South East Asia
- Sri Lanka
- Taiwan
- Thailand
- Vietnam, Laos Kampuchea

NEPAL
©Nelles Verlag GmbH, München 45
All rights reserved
ISBN 3-88618-362-9

First Edition 1990
Co-Publisher for U.K.:
Robertson McCarta, London
ISBN 1-85365-188-5 (for U.K.)

Publisher:	Günter Nelles	**DTP-Exposure:**	Printshop Schimann, Pfaffenhofen
Chief Editor:	Dr. Heinz Vestner		
Project Editor:	Dr. Susanne von der Heide	**Color Separation:**	Priegnitz, München
Translation:	Roger Rosko		
Cartography:	Nelles Verlag GmbH / C.Heydeck, P. Waider	**Printed by:**	Gorenjski Tisk, Kranj, Yugoslavia

- 01 -

236

TABLE OF CONTENTS

PREPARATIONS

Climate / Travel Times

The best time to travel in Nepal starts at the beginning of October and lasts until the end of April. May is relatively hazy and very hot. The monsoon season lasts from the beginning of June to the end of September. In this season it is very warm, however the climate is comfortably tempered by the corresponding pouring rain. However, you should remember that in the area surrounding Pokhara the rainstorms can sometimes last for days on end. Less pleasant during this period is the proliferation of leeches, that tend to squeeze their way through the finest tears and loop-holes of shoes and clothing. During the autumn – from September to the end of November – in the central hill regions it is delightfully warm and also very comfortable in the evenings, but in winter this region can be perceptibly cool. In the high-altitude tourist destinations weather conditions are often raw. Terai is therefore very suitable for a stay, whereas in summer it is the other way around – almost intolerably hot. You get the clearest views from October to December, after which this period of beautiful weather is interrupted by a few days of persistent rainfalls. During the monsoon the peaks are frequently shrouded in thick volutes of mist for days an end. The best time to go trekking is during the months of October, November, March and April. From March on, you can see the natural environment in its full splendor. In the Kathmandu Valley in summer it can heat up to 37 degrees C; at times in Terai to over 40 degrees. The winter in Kathmandu brings night temperatures of below freezing, while during the days the temperature can jump to 10 degrees in the shortest time. The humidity in Kathmandu during the monsoon season is very high, and in Terai the preceeding months of May and April seem all the more dry.

Clothing

Your route and the time of your travel are decisive in the question of clothing. You should alway be prepared for a sudden change in the weather, even in summer. Therefore, you should take a sweater in summer as well. In winter a light and warm sweater/jacket is recommended. In the mountains, at any rate, you need warm wool or down clothing. You are better off forgetting about clothes made out of synthetics. In the mountains hiking shoes are always recommended. By the way, cotton clothing and sweaters as well as down jackets can be obtained in Nepal, or you can hire them in special shops. The best places with the greatest selection of new and used expedition and mountaneering equipment you can find in the Tibetan shops of Thamel in Kathmandu.

Currency / Money Exchange / Bills

The Nepalese national currency is the rupee (NR), at this time the dollar stands (end 1989) at 28.60 NR, while you receive 16 Indian rupees for the dollar in India. Of course, these figures depend on the swings of the market. The NR is subdivided into 100 paisas. Coins of 5, 10, 25, 50 paisas and one rupee as well as bills in values of 1, 2, 5, 10, 20, 50, 200, 500, and 1,000 rupees are in circulation. Nepalese money can be taken neither in nor out of the country.

Money Exchange: Money should only be exchanged at banks or authorized agencies. Officially, only these places are permitted to handle foreign currency. Generally recognized credit cards and travelers' checks are accepted at many hotels, restaurants and shops. The use of Eurochecks can be problematic. The procedure is very costly and time consuming. Travelers checks in rupees do not exist.

Currency Regulations: Foreign currencies – with the exception of the Indian rupee – are under government control. The introduction of foreign currencies is not forbidden, however inquiries will be made on your entry concerning how much you are bringing with you. Indian and Nepalese rupees can not be brought into Nepal. If you want to exchange back in the currency that you have already exchanged you must present the corresponding bank statement, but you still get only 15% of the value of your money back. You should definitely hold onto your bank statements, because these are important, for example, for extending of your visa. Until recently, foreigners have basically had to pay for their accomodation in foreign currency. However, simple, smaller lodges accept – as ever – Nepalese money, even in the trekking areas.

Departure

It is recommended that you re-confirm any flight reservations one or two days before departure. This is especially necessary with the domestic Royal Nepalese Airlines because short-notice changes are frequently undertaken and, in general, the flights are overbooked. Also inquire repeatedly about the exact departure times! The passenger clearances at the Tribhuvan International Airport take a long time. For this reason one should be at the airport at least two hours before departure. At the time of clearance at the Tribhuvan Airport you must also pay an airport fee of 200 rupees.

Entry Regulations / Visas

Foreign tourists can stay in Nepal altogether for 3 months per year. Those with special reasons can under certain circumstances have their visas extended for another month. The Ministry of the Interior, to which the Immigration Office belongs, makes these decisions. Tourists who haven't already applied for a one month visa at home receive a 15-day visa at the airport or border stations (up to recently only 7 days). There is an important new rule which requires that foreigners who want to re-enter Nepal may do so

only at least one month after their exit. Foreigners who have entered with a tourist visa are not permitted to work (paid or unpaid) either for organizations or as individuals. Those who get their visas on entering Nepal at the border crossings (maximum validity 15 days) must pay US $10. The fee for a double-entry visa is US $40, while the multiple-entry visa costs US $80. Those who propose to get their visas prolonged for another month must present a bank statement which indicates that for each day of the month applied for, US $10 has been exchanged. The same applies for extentions of a third month. In addition, to prolong your visa for the second month there is a fee of NR 75 per week – and for the third month you must pay NR 175 per week. The Immigration Office has been located lately in the tourist quarter of Thamel in Kathmandu, opposite the SAARC secretariat in the Tridevi Marg (Street). The office is open from Sunday to Thursday from 10:00 in the morning to 5:00 p.m. (middle of November to the middle of February only until 4:00). Visa applications and extentions as well as trekking permits can only be applied for from 10:00 to 1:00 daily (Fridays only until 12:00).

You can also apply for or have your visa extended in Pokhara. Here the Immigration Office is located between the airport and the Phewa (Fewa) Lake. The opening and application processing hours correspond to those in Kathmandu. In contrast to Kathmandu, a visa can only be prolonged for up to 15 days.

The visa regulations are frequently changed. Find out about the most recent rules on your arrival in Nepal.

Health Precautions

There are no longer obligatory vaccinations for Nepal. However, it it advisable to get immunized aginst cholera, typhus, tetanus, and hepatitis. In any case, seek the advice of your doctor/health service. Travelers in Terai should under certain circumstances take a prophylaxis against malaria. In your travel apothecary you should definitely pack the following medications: malaria tablets if required, drugs against nausea and diarrhoea, antibiotics, insect repellents (lotions), sun protectants (especially in the high-altitude areas), antiseptics, bandages and mineral tablets. Please note that many medications in Nepal are quite inexpensive but be careful: the expiration date is often some time in the distant past. Also medications requiring prescriptions in the west are frequently available over the counter. Micropure or chlorine tablets suitable for the disinfection of water should be brought; they need at least an hour to be effective. If you don't take these tablets with you, make sure that you boil any water for food or drinking for at least 20 minutes. It is now common that the water offered in most hotels, restaurants and families has already been boiled and filtered. If you're not sure, you should either buy mineral water or tea as a substitute. Fresh salads can only be enjoyed without problems in the better restaurants and hotels. Always avoid consuming salad, peeled fruits and ice-cream in smaller restaurants and cities. Foods which are prepared freshly over flames are, in comparison, relatively safe.

Nepal in Statistics

Total area: 147,000 sq.km; population (1987): 17.6 million, (population growth: 2.7% annually); 5 regions, 14 zones, 75 districts; capital: Kathmandu (ca. 300,000 inhabitants).

Religion: Hindus 89.5%, Buddhists 8%, Moslems ca. 2%, Christians under 1%. Many Hindus are also simultaneously adherents to Buddhist conceptions.

TRAVEL ROUTES TO NEPAL

By aircraft: Eight international airlines fly to the capital Kathmandu, with over 65 flights arriving weekly. Kathmandu can be flown to: via Bangkok with Royal Nepal and Thai Airways; via Calcutta with Royal Nepal, Indian and Singapore Airlines, via Dacca with Royal Nepal, Bangladesh Biman and Singapore Airlines; via Delhi with Royal Nepal and Indian Airlines; via Frankfurt with Lufthansa and Royal Nepal Airlines; via London, Dubai and Rangoon with Royal Nepal; via Hong Kong with Royal Nepal and Dragon Air/Hong Kong; via Karachi with Royal Nepal, Pakistan Airlines and Lufthansa; via Lhasa with Royal Nepal and CAA of China; via Paro with Druk Air/Bhutan; via Patna with Indian airlines; via Singapore with Royal Nepal and Singapore Airlines; and via Varanasi with Indian Airlines. Royal Nepal also offers foreign charter flights at request. Choose your destination airport in Nepal according to your further travel plans.

By automobile: Those arriving by automobile can come into Nepal over the Indian-Nepalese border crossings of Gorakhpur/Sunauli (West), Raxaul/Birgunj (Central), Siliguri/Kakarbhita (East), and over the Tibetan border crossing Kodari. An international *carnet de passage* is mandatory for all vehicles. You can travel by train or by bus / automobile from almost all of the large cities of India to the border of Nepal. Entering over Kodari (Tibetan border) is often not possible during the monsoon season because of damage caused to the mountain road from landslides.

TRAVELING WITHIN NEPAL

Railroad

The only short connection for public transport exists in Janakpur in South Nepal. The old locomotive might be of interest to railway buffs.

Airlines

The domestic service of the Royal Nepal Airlines has regular flights to all of the important population centers in all 0f Nepal. Moreover, there are additional flights to several famous tourist spots, for example to Lumbini (after Bhairahawa) – Buddha's place of birth; to the Chitwan National Park (after Bharatpur and Meghauli) as well as various further national parks in Nepal.

The schedules of domestic flights are frequently changed without notice. Find out at the Domestic Service of the Royal Nepal Airlines in Thapathali (Tel: 2144532/214862). Information about domestic flights is announced every evening at 9:15 over Radio Nepal.

This information should also be available in the near future over an automatic telephone announcement service. Foreigners must pay the price of their flights in dollars. The prices are set somewhat higher than for the native population. All year round there is a daily (twice from September to May) Mountain Flight with

Royal Nepal Airlines over the Himalayan Range, including Sagarmatha (Mount Everest). The flight depends on the weather and can be cancelled at short notice. The flight costs US $80 plus an airport fee of 30 rupees. Booking is possible at any travel office or flight agency.

Local Transportation

Buses and cars are the most important means of transportation. They are not the safest vehicles on the road and should be selected with care.

Buses: The majority of buses within Kathmandu are completely overflowing with passengers and are therefore scarcely suitable for tourists. Small buses to Kirtipur (university), Patan, Bhaktapur and Dakshinkali start from around the Ratna Park and at the Bagh Basar. Larger overland buses start out from the Central Bus Station, opposite the Tundikhel Plaza next to the Exhibition Road. In addition there is an overland bus station at the Central Post Office; primarily tourist buses to Pokhara depart from here. A trip to Pokhara costs somewhere between 50 and 100 rupees.

Taxis: Besides taxis and group taxis, there are also *tempos*. Prices are a matter of negotiation. Normal taxis have a meter. However often an extra fee is charged because of the changing prices for gasoline. Private automobiles and taxis can be rented through travel agencies and hotels; mostly with driver (per day in the Kathmandu Valley ca. 600 rupees; outside the valley ca. 1,200). At night you pay double – or at least 50% on top of the basic price on the meter. The same is often true in bad weather! There is a night taxi service, Tel: 224374.

Bicycle rickshas: These are used for private city sight seeing and shorter distances. They are almost exactly as expensive as taxis; the price should be negotiated before the beginning of the trip.

National Parks / Reservations

For Chitwan, Sagarmatha, Langtang, Shey Phoksundo and Rara National Parks, please see the chapter on National Parks.

Royal Bardia National Park: in western Nepal in outer Terai. Commercial flights from Kathmandu to Nepalganj, then further by car or bus. By bus to Motipur, then the remaining 8 km on foot. The park will be better accessible when the Mahendra Highway is finished. For tourist accomodations in the park there is a campsite on the banks of the Karnali River and a 24 bed rangers' house in Chitkaiye in the area of the park headquarters. Booking only through the West Nepal Adventure Company, a subsidiary of Tiger Tops, the office of which is in the Durbar Marg in Kathmandu. Otherwise one has to completely fend for himself – this means bringing along camping equipment and food.

Suklapantha Wildlife Reserve: in Terai in the southwest of the country. Weekly commercial flights to Mahendranagar, whose airport directly adjoins the reservation. Except for the Silent Safari Camp, which is only open during the season, there are no further tourist arrangements.

Koshi Tappu Wildlife Reserve: located in southeast Nepal in Terai. Daily commercial flights to Simra, from there on further by bus to the headquarters in Adhabar. Here there is, however, no sort of board or overnight accomodation possibilities, so that you must undertake your sight-seeing either from Hetauda or Birganj, arranged through the simple hotels.

Shivapuri Reservation: located in Kathmandu above Budhanilkantha. Can be reached by bus, taxi, bicycle or on foot, no overnight accommodations.

Khaptada National Park: in western Nepal in the central mountain country. One can fly into the following places from Kathmandu, Nepalganj or Dangarhi: a) Bajhang – from there a two day hike. b) Doti (Dipayal) – from there a three day hike. c) Bajura (Kolti) – from there a four day foot-march. d) Acham (Saphebagar) – from there a two day foot-march. No facilities for tourists. For sleeping and other needs you have to provide for yourself. More detailed information: King Mahendra Trust for Nature Conservation, Kathmandu, Babar Mahal, POB: 3172, Tel: 223229/220109.

Travel Restrictions / Closed Zones

Not all areas of Nepal are open to tourists without restriction – in particular the regions in the inner Himalayas are closed sectors for tourists. Certain precincts such as North Mustang are not accessible to tourists for diverse political, ecological and military reasons. A list which gives further information can be viewed at the Immigration Office. Information in foreign counties is also given by Nepalese diplomatic representatives. Their information, however, can occasionally be out-dated due to short-notice changes. For several years the Jumla region in the west has been opened to trekking. The Dolpo precinct located nearby is to date only partially opened. Trekking permits for these are only available through trekking agencies for group travelers. Several groups have had conflicts with local authorities at their destinations and have sometimes had to turn back or take another route than the one declared. In the eastern Himalayas a trekking route has been open since 1988 along the third-highest summit in the world, the Kanchenjunga (from Taplejung – reachable by aircraft – to the base camp). Here too, only trekking agencies are permitted to issue permits for group treks. The government allows only a limited number of visitors per year into the region in order to keep damage to the environment as slight as possible. In the near future, further openings of routes in western Nepal are planned. If your travel program includes new routes you should be ready for some surprises, as it often takes a few years before an infrastructure is built up. Please stick exactly to the restrictions which the immigration gives out in order to avoid unnecessary inconveniences.

Trekking Permits

The trekking permits are issued in the immigration offices. They can only be applied for in Nepal. The process is executed in the same manner as with visas. If you plan to undertake two different trekking tours, you must also apply for two separate permits. In the first month a fee of NR 90 per week must be paid, in the second and third months the fee is NR 112.50 per week. Because of the fact that various trekking destinations are located within Conservation Areas/National Parks, here, in addition to the permits, an entrance fee is charged. However, if you have a trekking permit, a visa is not required. Procuring a trekking permit through one of the trekking agencies is usually timesaving and frequently even somewhat cheaper. Don't forget to bring

enough passport-sized photos with you! The permit must be taken with you during your hike and presented at checkposts along the trails. The trekking areas are determined by the Tourism Ministry. Those who enter into the closed zones, such as Mustang, for example, without permission must also reckon on being banned from the country.

Round Trips

The Kathmandu Valley and Pokhara are the traditional sightseeing areas for tourists. Almost all travel agencies organize sightseeing tours in the three royal cities of the Valley. In addition there are organized excursions to the surrounding villages, such as Dakshinkali, Budhanilkantha/Nagi Gompa-Shivapuri, Phulchowski, Kakani, and Kodari. The prices vary considerably. You can either join one of these group tours or hire a guide by yourself. There are freelance guides for foreigners who can be ordered through hotels. Find out information about the usual local prices beforehand. Several travel agencies are specialized in particular regions and offer matching tour packages. There are round trips offered between three and fourteen days in length; these vary in their degree of comfort. At best, rely on the following travel agencies:

President Travel & Tours, Durbar Marg, Tel: 220245/226744. GSS Travel & Tours, Bisal Nagar, Tel: 226639. Sagarmatha Trekking, Kantipath, Tel: 414991. Marco Polo Travels, Kamal Pokhari, Tel: 414192/416432. Tibet Travel & Tours, Keshar Mahal, Tel: 410303/415126. Lama Excursions, Durbar Marg, Tel: 220186/226706. Himalayan Explorers, Jyatha, Tel: 226142. Gaida Wildlife Camp, Durbar Marg, Tel: 220940/220186. Silent Safari, Thamel, Tel: 2277236. Machan Wildlife Resort, Durbar Marg, Tel: 225001/227001. Temple Tiger, Kantipath, Tel: 221585/225780.

PRACTICAL TIPS

Accomodation

Nepal offers overnight accomodation to correspond to any budget and every taste. A list of hotels published by the Hotel Association of Nepal is made available by the Tourism Ministry. It is urgently recommended that you make prior reservations at your desired hotel during the tourist season from October to April. Because Nepal maintains no tourist offices in foreign countries, hotel reservations can only be arranged either through a travel agency which specializes in Nepal or directly with the hotel itself. Besides the renowned large hotels in Kathmandu, there are many smaller hotels and lodges with the most exceptionally reasonable prices. Since it is frequently difficult to find means of tranportation in the time at hand, it is recommended to seek your lodging – if at all possible – in the city center. For those who want to stay in Kathmandu for an extended period, very reasonable flat rates are available at lodges.

Accomodation during a trek is organized by the responsible trekking organizers. Single travelers who have a trek in mind can also have their tour arranged through a trekking office. There are only a few hotels along many of the trekking routes. Houses of the local residents or the tent one has brought along serve for overnight stays.

Alcohol

The buying and selling of alcohol in Nepal requires no special permission. There are good domestic spirits, which are produced at three distilleries. Some spirits which have become especially famous are the red Khukri rum and vodka from distilleries in Kathmandu as well as the fruit brandies from Marpha and Tukche (on the Jomosom/Muktinath trek). The Nepalese are not familiar with wine, however attempts have lately been made at producing fruit wines with similar methods. Foreign alcoholic beverages are comparatively expensive due to the high import duties on them.

Banks

The teller windows are open from 10 to 2 p. m. Sunday through Friday. Only the exchange windows in the airports are open longer and on Saturdays. With few exceptions the banks stay closed on official holidays. Domestic and foreign banks have their representative offices all around the Durbar Marg. Money transfers can take – in our experience – a very long time; therefore you would be better off to take sufficient checks with you.

Bookshops

There is an enormous selection of English-language and other foreign literature in the bookstores of Kathmandu – books as well as magazines, etc. The leading book dealer and simultaneously the largest publishing house in Kathmandu is Ratna Book Distributors in Baghbazar (Tel: 220501/223026) in front of the French cultural house) with further sales locations distributed around the city. Ratna Books publishes a catalogue with an outstanding index of the literature of Nepal. Some further interesting booksellers include for example: Educational Enterprises (Mahankal, diagonally opposite the Bir Hospital); Himalayan Book Sellers (at the Clock Tower), and Pilgrims Book House (Thamel, in front of the Tukche Peak Hotel).

Cinema

Primarily, Hindi films are presented in the numerous cinemas of Kathmandu. The majority of foreign cultural institutes or embassies also have film programs.

Customs

The international customs regulations apply here: Don't bring in or out any illegal drugs, weapons and radio equipment;

cigarettes and alcohol in the usual amounts; articles for personal use, for example film and photography equipment in appropriate amounts. Sometimes value assessments are entered into passports upon entry; upon exiting these must be presented again. Keep in mind that antiques which are more than 100 years old can not be taken out. If you are not sure of something in connection with this, have the Archaeology Department give you a certification: Ram Shah Path, Kathmandu, open from Sunday through Thursday from 10:00 to 16:00, Friday 10:00 to 15:00.

Electricity

The electrical current carries 220 volts (alternating current). The variations are very large however, and frequently the current stops completely! Schuko plugs rarely fit, because the majority of sockets in Nepal are three-pronged.

Festivals / Calendar / Vacation

The dates of Nepalese festivals are set according to the Moon Calendar (the official calendar of Nepal is called Vikram-Sambat and originated in 57 B.C.) and are thus newly calculated by astrologers year for year. Most of the travel agencies in Kathmandu have lists of the dates. Besides this, there are the Newar calendars: The Nepal-Sambat, which began ca. 790 A.D. and the Shakya Sambat (it originated 77/78 A.D.). The official holidays, such as the King's Birthday (end of December), the Day of Democracy (beginning of February), and Constitution Day (end of December) are also set according to the Moon Calendar. On the other hand, international holidays are based on the western Gregorian Calendar. Famous festivals in the whole of Nepal are:

Dasain (festival in honor of the goddess Durga, beginning of October, starts on the day after the new moon, high-point ninth and tenth days).

Lakshmi-Puja/Tihar (Festival of Lights New Year for the Nepal Era, end of October, new moon).

Bhai-Tika (brothers are honored by their sisters, end of October, second day after new moon).

Holi (several-day-long festival in worship of the god Krishna, paint fight; March, full moon).

For further festivals see Guidepost Kathmandu Valley.

Food

In the first few days you should avoid consuming the local food, which are cooked with a lot of oil and are heavily spiced. Most of the restaurants in the Kathmandu Valley and Pokhara offer a variety of culinary delights. Besides Nepalese cuisine, you can find everything from Italian to Russian food. In some of the restaurants in the larger hotels you can eat in the evenings until midnight, in other places until around 10:00 or 11:00.

Guides

There are numerous tourist guides in Kathmandu who have mastered English or another foreign language. You can get guides or organized tours through any travel agency, in Kathmandu sometimes also through hotels. Fees per day are set according to the guide's degree of knowledge and the goodwill of the travel agency and the guide. On average you should count on a price of between 500 to 1000 rupees for a tour through Kathmandu, for example. The guides must have completed an examination and have a license.

Hospitals

There are public and private hospitals: **Kalimati clinic**: Tel: 270923. **Bhaktapur Hospital**: Tel: 610798. **Bir Hospital** (Kanti Path): Tel: 221988. **CIWEC Clinic** (Baluwatar): Tel: 410983. **Kanti Hospital** (Maharajganj): Tel: 411550. **Maternity Hospital** (Thapathali): Tel:

213216. **Teaching Hospital** (Maharajganj): Tel: 412303. **Teku Hospital**: Tel: 211344. **Patan Hospital** (Lagankhel): Tel: 522278. **Nepal International Clinic** (Hitti Durbar): Tel: 412842.

At the Red Cross on the Exhibition Road (Tel: 228094). **AIDS tests** can be performed. There are already several cases of AIDS in Nepal. Each embassy has its own confidential doctor – please inquire.

Pharmacies
Medications can be purchased here without prescriptions. They are less expensive than in the West.

Photography
In most places in Nepal photography is allowed, except at military installations and certain holy places. If you want to take individual photographs of the inhabitants, please first ask them in a friendly way if this is possible. For religious reasons some Nepalese will refuse. Film is available everywhere in Kathmandu and Pokhara. Development is also possible and is good. However, you should always have slides developed at home.

Postal Service
The postal service works very unreliably. You would be better off not using mail boxes. Mail should be handed in directly at the post offices, and you should also have the stamps cancelled. You can also send your mail from the large hotels. Letters can be sent to the main post offices of cities, where it will be stored until it is picked up: Name (underline family name), G.P.O. poste restante. Parcels and packets are handled in Kathmandu next to the General Post Office in the Foreign Post Office – it is however very time-consuming , and the customs formalities are nerve-wracking. G.P.O. business hours: 10:00 to 4:00 p.m. Sundays through Fridays; 10:00 to 3:00 p.m. Saturdays.

Press
Newspapers are published in English and the native languages. "The Rising Nepal" is the only daily newspaper appearing in English. On the New Road in Kathmandu there is the so-called "newspaper tree" where the majority of newspapers are sold.

Radio and Television
Radio Nepal is the only Nepalese radio station. Mornings, noons and evenings news in English is broadcast; the evenings include a one-half-hour English program. For a couple of years a television station has existed, but the programming can only be received in the Kathmandu Valley, Pokhara and a few villages in Terai. Indian television has wider range in Nepal.

Rescue Helicopter
If you become seriously ill during a trek, a rescue helicopter can be ordered from the next radio, telegraph or telephone station through your trekking agency or embassy. It is important that you have a surety voucher in Kathmandu which guarantees the assumption of the costs. The flight costs between US $600 and $1700 per hour, depending on the type of helicopter. A rescue flight to Everest or Annapurna takes about 2.5 hours. For further information: Himalayan Rescue Association, Thamel, Tel: 222906/418755.

Rules of Conduct
The codes of conduct of the Nepalese bears the impressions of various religious concepts and particularly the system of castes. Especially the rules which determine what is "pure" and "impure" are impenetrable and confusing for most of the foreigners.

Therefore, in general you should observe the usual international forms of politeness. Most Nepalese will overlook unfamiliarity with the usual rules of the country. Shaking hands for greetings and saying good-bye is not common. Instead of this, one puts the palms of ones' hands together and greets with the word "*namaste*", especially when addressing women. The Newar in the Kathmandu Valley greet each other with a slight shaking of the head, which in general in Nepal is also as a gesture of affirmation. Bodily contact such as embracing or kissing is still very uncommon between men and women in Nepal and often generates animosity toward foreigners.

If you should be invited into a Nepalese household, please pay heed to the fact that it is seen as impurifying to the household not to remove one's shoes before entering the dining room. Entering the kitchen is subject to strict taboo in the majority of Hindu households. It is considered the extremity of impoliteness to show someone the soles of your feet. This can very easily happen when you are eating on the floor, as is common to a degree. As soon as you have eaten only a tiny morsel from a plate, it becomes impure, just as do the eating utensils you have used. Therefore observe this when passing food around, and drink out of a canteen. Don't sample something out of a cook-pot twice with the same spoon. In Hindu households it is uncommon for women to eat together with the men. This also applies to guests. To insist otherwise would be impolite. Don't be surprised when you are not immediately thanked if you bring a hospitable gift with you. Mostly these are immediately put aside and also not unpacked. In no case does this represent an insult.

Nepalese behave very spontaneously in temples and other religious establishments. Leather articles are not admissible in such places, therefore one usually takes off ones' shoes.

Shopping

With a lot of time and leisure, you can make a wonderful shopping trip in Nepal. Haggling is a prerequisite! Finished handicrafts are on sale everywhere, for example statues of deities made of brass and bronze, beautiful wood carvings, religious pictures called thangkas – painted following old traditions, and fine works of stonecutting (for example in the old quarter of Kathmandu, Bhaktapur, Patan Industrial Estate, Thimi, Thamel). The jewelry of the Nepalese gold and silversmiths is especially beautiful (in Kathmandu and Patan). Hand-woven textiles like linen and cotton material as well as silk from Nepal, China and India; printed or painted in the most beautiful colors available (in the tourists centers in Thamel, Durbar Marg, Asan Tole, Indra Chowk Balaju in Kathmandu and the old quarter in Bhaktapur). Batiks, cloth handbags, clothing, wool blankets (particularly of the light, fleecy Pashmina fabrics of fine sheep and goats' wool) and hand-knitted sweaters can be bought in all sorts of variations. Meanwhile in Thamel and Durbar Marg there now exists a variety of fashion boutiques with some noteworthy designer pieces – but these are also correspondingly expensive. Hand-woven Tibetan wool carpets (which have meanwhile also been being produced in Nepalese weaveries) are available in all sizes and colors (carpet centers are Bodnath and Patan/Jawalakel). Calendars, art prints, gift wrapping paper, memo books and postcards from hand made tussore silk are popular mementos (everywhere, especially in Thamel). Music cassettes with classical pieces and Nepalese folk music have become sought-after souvenirs (in the New Road).

Telecommunication

You can call foreign countries or send a telegram in Kathmandu from the Central Telegraph Office, which is near the National Stadium. In most hotels you can also call foreign countries directly. Ask first about the price per minute – it changes from time to time. From Germany you can telephone Nepal directly if you dial as a prefix: 00977-1 for Kathmandu, 00977-61 for Pokhara and 00977-5620 for Chitwan.

Time

Nepalese Standard Time is 5.45 hours ahead of Greenwich Mean Time (in central Europe, add 4,45 hours in the winter time and 3.45 hours in summer time.

Tipping

Luggage porters receive about 2 rupees per piece of luggage. Room service waiters receive between 2 to 5 rupees, errand runners get 5 to 15 rupees and hotel pages about 5 rupees. Carriers on trekking tours receive, besides the previously-agreed daily pay, an extra 5% to 10% (according to length) of their total earnings.

Normally, waiters receive 10%. Granted, in hotel prices the tips are inclusive, however it is usual to give somewhat more for good service. Luggage carriers, maids, waiters and errand runners then receive between 5 and 15 rupees. With group trips or private rides with chauffeur the driver usually receives an additional gratuity.

Tourist Information

The Department of Tourism maintains information offices at the following locations. Kathmandu: New Road in the area of Durbar Square, Tel: 220818. Kathmandu Tribhuvan International Airport, Tel: 410537. Pokhara, Tel: 20028. Birganj, Tel: 2083. Bhairawa, Tel: 304. Janakpur, Tel: 20755.

The offices are open daily from 9:00 to 18:00 (in winter until 17:00) except for Saturdays and holidays. On Fridays the offices are only open until 16:00.

The Ministry of Tourism is located behind the National Stadium.

To date there are no Nepalese tourist information offices in foreign countries.

Weights and Measurements

The metric system has been introduced in Nepal, however in the country and the mountains calulations are made, as ever, in the traditional units of measurements. Silver and gold jewelry are sold by weight, expressed in *tolas*, which correspond to about 11.5 grams. The value of gems depends on their carat weight – a carat corresponds to 0.2 grams.

ADDRESSES

Embassies

Australia: Bhatbhateni, Tel: 411578/411304.
China: Baluwatar, Tel:411740.
Federal Republic of Germany: Kantipath, Tel:221763/222902.
France: Lazimpat, Tel: 412332.
Great Britain: Lainchaur, Tel:411789/414588.
India: Lainchaur, Tel: 410900/414913.
Israel: Lazimpat, Tel: 411811/413419.
Italy: Baluwatar, Tel:412280/412743.
Japan: Pani Pokhari, Tel: 414083/410397.
Korea (South): Tahachal, Tel:270172/270584.
Pakistan: Pani Pokhari, Tel: 410565.
Thailand: Thapathali, Tel: 213910/213912.
USA: Pani Pokhari, Tel: 411179/412718.
USSR: Baluwater, Tel:412155/411063.

Consulates

Belgium: Lazimpat, Tel: 414760.
Denmark: Kantipath, Tel: 227044.
Finland: Khichpokhari, Tel: 220939
Netherlands: Kumaripati, Tel: 522915/524597.
Austria: Kupondole, Tel: 410891.
Sweden: Khichpokhari, Tel: 220939
Switzerland : Jawalakhel, Tel: 523468.

Airlines

Aeroflot Soviet Airlines - Kantipath, Tel: 212397. **Air Canada** - Durbar Marg, Tel: 222838/224854. **Air France** - Durbar Marg, Tel: 223339/223871. **Air India** - Kantipath, Tel: 212335/211730. **Air Lanka** - Kantipath, Tel: 212831. **Alitalia** - Durbar Marg, Tel: 220215. **American West Airlines** - Durbar Marg, Tel: 220155. **British Airways** - Durbar Marg, Tel: 222266. **Cathay Pacific** - Kanti Path, Tel: 226704. **China Airlines** - New Road, Tel: 227219. **Dragon Air** - Hong Kong Durbar Marg, Tel: 227064/223162. **Indian Airlines** - Durbar Marg, Tel: 223053. **Japan Airlines** - Durbar Marg, Tel: 222838/224854. **KLM** - Durbar Marg, Tel: 224895. **Korean Air** - Kantipath, Tel: 212080. **Kuwait Airways** - Kantipath, Tel: 222884. **Lauda Air** - New Road, Tel. 227315. **Lufthansa** - Durbar Marg, Tel: 224341. **Pakistan International Airlines** - Durbar Marg, Tel: 223102. **Pan Am** - Durbar Marg, Tel: 411824. **Royal Nepal Airlines** - Kantipath, Tel: 220757. **Singapore Airlines** - Durbar Marg, Tel: 220759. **Swissair** - Durbar Marg, Tel: 222452. **Thai Airways** - Durbar Marg, Tel: 223565/224917. **TWA** - Kantipath, Tel: 226704.

EXPRESSIONS IN NEPALI

Nepali is the official language of the country and is understood by over 90% of the population. English is understood primarily in the Kathmandu Valley and only in isolated instances on trekking routes.

Hello / Goodbye . . . . *Namaste*
What is your name? . . . .
Tapaaiko naam ke ho?
My name is... . . . . . *Mero naam ... ho*
I live in... . . . .
Mero ghar ... ma ho
Where is the...? . . . . *Io ... kaha chha?*
How far away is...? . . . .

Kati tadha chha/parchha?
How do I get to...? . . . .
Ma ... makassari pugna sakchhu?
How much does that cost? . . . .
Esko kati parchha lagchha?
That is expensive! . . *Io mahango chha*
Could I have the menu? . . . .
Malai menu dinus
I would like something to drink . . . .
Malai piune kura dinus
The bill please! . . . . *Bill dinus*
I am staying here for ... days. . . . . .
Ma iaha ... din baschhu
What is that? . . . . *Io ke ho?*
What is he doing? . . . .
Whaha ke garnuhunchha?
I don't feel well . . . .
Malaai sancho chhaina
How late is it? . . . . *Ahile kati bajyo?*
I . . . .*ma*
you . . . . *tapaai/timi*
we . . . . *haamiharu*
okay . . . . *thik cha*
yes . . . . *ho*
no . . . . *hoina*
large . . . .*thulo*
small . . . . *saano*
today . . . . *aaja*
afternoon . . . . *diuso*
evening . . . . *saanjh/beluka*
night . . . . *raati*
week . . . . *hapta*
month . . . . *mahina*
year . . . . *Saal/barssa*
clean . . . . *saafa*
dirty . . . . *phohar*
hot . . . . *tato*
cold . . . . *chiso*
please . . . . *kripaya*
thank you . . . . *dhanyebaad*
less . . . . *thorai/alikati*
more . . . . *dherai*
come . . . . *aaune*
go . . . . *jaane*
price . . . . *mool/mullye*
shop . . . . *pasal/dokan*
medicine . . . . *aussadhi*
market . . . . *basar*
room . . . . *kotha*

vegetables	. . . . *tarakari/sabji*
water	. . . . *paani*
tea	. . . . *chiya*
milk	. . . . *dudh*
yoghurt	. . . . *dahi*
rice	. . . . *bhat/bhuja*
sugar	. . . . *.chini*
salt	. . . . *nun*
butter	. . . . *nauni*
food	. . . . *khaana*
breakfast	. . . . *nashtaa*
1	. . . . *ek*
2	. . . . *dui*
3	. . . . *tin*
4	. . . . *.char*
5	. . . . *paanch*
6	. . . . *.chha*
7	. . . . *saat*
8	. . . . *aath*
9	. . . . *nau*
10	. . . . *dos*
20	. . . . *.bis*
25	. . . . *pachhis*
30	. . . . *. tis*
35	. . . . *paitis*
40	. . . . *chaalis*
45	. . . . *paitaalis*
50	. . . . *pachhaas*
60	. . . . *saathi*
70	. . . . *.sattari*
80	. . . . *assi*
90	. . . . *nabbe*
100	. . . . *saai/eksaai*
1,000	. . . . *hazaar*
10,000	. . . . *dos hazaar*

AUTHORS

Susanne von der Heide graduated in ethnology/art history and is employed at the Museum for East-Asian Art and the Rautenstrauch-Joest-Museum in Cologne, West Germany. Her special relationship with Nepal developed after her first trip to Nepal in 1978. Since then her knowledge of Nepal has deepened through long years of residence there. She is active in the German section of the King Mahendra Trust for Nature Conservation in Nepal.

Hansjörg Brey studied ethnology, sociology and geography. Since 1978 he has traveled to Nepal regularly. He has spent several years as a scientific geographer, which has given him an insight into the problems of Nepal. His special interests are questions of rural development and environmental protection.

Wolf Donner has studied political economy, sociology, and economic geography and was for twelve years an advisor for agricultural development in service to the United Nations (FAO). From 1966-1969 he worked in this function in Nepal. He is the author of numerous books and articles, among them *Nepal: Raum, Mensch und Wirtschaft.*

Toni Hagen, engineer and natural scientist, was employed in 1952 as a government geologist in Nepal and performed geological exploratory surveys under contract from the United Nations, for which he worked out plans for rural development from 1959-1960. He is the author of handbooks on developmental and catastrophic assistance; since 1989 he has advised for the King Mahendra Trust for Nature Conservation.

Jürgen Huber was for many years a trekking leader in Nepal.

Wolfgang Koch is a qualified chemist, however his greatest interest today is the study of the Chinese and Tibetan languages as well as ethnology. He has achieved international renown as a travel guide and mountain climber.

Axel Michaels studied indology, law, and philosophy and was the director of the Nepal Research Center in Kathmandu from 1981- 1983. Today he is an academic counsellor at the University of Kiel, West Germany. His research work in Nepal is concentrated primarily on the temple area of Pashupatinath.

Hemanta Raj Mishra, one of Asia's most pre-eminent zoologists, was born in Nepal. Today he is responsible for the leadership and conception of the King Mahendra Trust for Nature Conservation. In 1987 he was awarded the J. Paul Getty Prize for Natural Protection. Dr. Mishra has become internationally famous as the author of numerous books and films on wildlife research.

Joanna Pfaff-Czarnecka has been concerned with Nepal since 1979, where she collaborated in research projects as an ethnologist. Since 1989 she has worked as a scientific assistant at the University of Zurich. She is primarily known for her scientific publications on the Nepalese caste system.

Philip Pierce studied indology, linguistics and Greek at the University of Kiel, West Germany. He has lived in Nepal since 1984, where he works as a scientific assistant at the Nepal Research Center. He has collaborated as author in numerous publications about Nepal.

Ludwig von Savigny, internist and cardiologist, has visited Nepal regularly since 1980. In 1980/81 he worked in the Kanti Childrens' Hospital as well as the Bir Hospital. Later he resided predominantly in the North of the country, there developing an understanding of the natural healing methods and shamanism.

Ganesh Lal Shakya, born in Patan, has studied economic geography in Munich, West Germany, since 1987. As a Newar he has developed above all an understanding of his own culture in Nepal. In Nepal he was already looking after various travel groups; since 1987 he has been employed at a leading German travel enterprise.

Satis Shroff, a Nepalese journalist living in Germany, studied biology and geology in Nepal before he received a stipend for medicine in Germany. He has written for years for various international newspapers.

Ram Pratap Thapa studied economic science in Kathmandu, Nuremberg and Bamberg. Today he works at the Asia Pacific Center in Cologne, West Germany. As a founding member of the German Committee of the King Mahendra Trust for Nature Conservation, his engagement concerns the economic and ecological development of his country

Gert-Matthias Wegner studied musical ethnology. Since 1982 he has researched the musical life of the Newar in the Kathmandu Valley. He is famous for his concerts and films, which provide insight to the cultural background of Newar musicians.

PHOTOGRAPHERS

Bondzio, Bodo 1,2,22,37,38,42,46,52,64 70,82,98,204/205,206/207,220,223, 232
Brey, Hansjörg 152
Chwaszcza, Joachim 10/11,20,28,31,34, 40,51,54l,59,80,87,95,107,112,118, 119,124,198,215,219,227,229,231
Frommelt, Ursula 130/131,137
Grosse, Heinz 55,91,139
v. d. Heide, Susanne 26,60/61,123,140, 184,185,201,213,224,233
Hinze, Peter 23,32,36,62/63,71, 74,92,102/103,109,217
Huber, Jürgen 174/175
Kaempf, Bernhard 27,75,94,230
Koch, Wolfgang 136,226
Kubitzer, Tim 161,166,168,
Maeritz, Kai 8,14,43,79,116,117,120, 121,142/143,151,235
Müller, Ernst 108,199
Müller, Kai Ulrich 72,73,202
Nelles, Günter 148,162,169
Poncar, Jaroslav 56
Proksch, Oliver 156,165,170,172
Savigny, Ludwig v. 39,47,50,54r, 97,122,128,180,182,195,225,Titelfoto
Schwarz, Berthold 149,183 l/r,188/189
Shakya, Bishwa 29,45,197,203
Shroff, Satis 211
Spiess, Jürgen 194
Thapa, Ram Pratap 208,216
Tomlinson, Ian 12/13,25,48,57,83, 89,125,126,127,154/155,164
Wegner, Gert-Matthias 212
Wolf, Edda 163